THE MILITARY
CAMPAIGNS

OF THE WARS OF THE ROSES

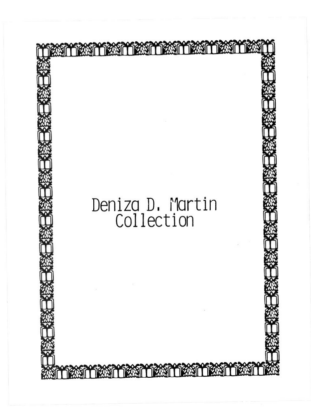

Detail from R. Caton Woodville's engraving of the *Battle of Towton*

THE MILITARY
CAMPAIGNS
OF THE WARS OF THE ROSES

Philip A. Haigh

SUTTON PUBLISHING

First published in 1995 by
Alan Sutton Publishing Limited, an imprint of Sutton Publishing Limited
Phoenix Mill · Thrupp · Stroud · Gloucestershire · GL5 2BU

First published in the United States of America in 1997 by
Combined Books Inc. · 151 East 10th Avenue · Conshohocken · PA 19428

Paperback edition first published 1997

British Library Cataloguing in Publication Data

Haigh, Philip
  Military Campaigns of the Wars of the Roses
  I. Title
  942.04

ISBN 0 7509 1430 0 (paper)
ISBN 0 7509 0904 8 (case)

Cover picture: detail from a manuscript illustration of the Battle of Barnet (Ghent
University Library, MS 236, photograph reproduced by courtesy of Geoffrey Wheeler)

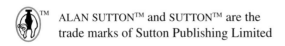 ALAN SUTTON™ and SUTTON™ are the
trade marks of Sutton Publishing Limited

Typeset in 11/12 Times.
Typesetting and origination by
Sutton Publishing Limited.
Printed in Great Britain by
WBC Limited, Bridgend.

DEDICATION

This work is dedicated to Lewis and Charlotte, my children, and my wife Sarah, without whose support, encouragement and input it would never have been completed. (It must be a unique experience to be a fifteenth-century war widow in the twentieth century.) Also to the memory of Richard Brooke and Alfred Burne, two historians to whom we should all be grateful.

CONTENTS

LIST OF
ILLUSTRATIONS

The author and publishers would like to thank Geoffrey Wheeler for his invaluable advice and help in the sourcing of illustrations for this book, many of which are from his own collection. Thanks are also due to the following for kind permission to reproduce material in their care: Peter Newark's Historical Pictures (frontispiece); Society of Antiquaries of London (2, 11); The British Library (4, 5, 9, 20, 21); the Board of Trustees of the Victoria & Albert Museum (6); Queen's College Cambridge (19); Her Majesty the Queen (27); the National Portrait Gallery (30, 32).

FOREWORD

The preservation and interpretation of battlefields is fast becoming a deep and meaningful interest to many people in all walks of life. The battlefields of the Wars of the Roses are no exception to this new-found fervour, although many of these sites have already been sadly eroded, or have in fact almost completely disappeared, chiefly due to twentieth-century developments. Thankfully, however, these fields, and in some cases streets, which saw the forming of English battlelines have not been forgotten, and much work has been done to map out and pin-point the main killing fields where the Houses of York and Lancaster, and their later divisions, settled their differences by the sword.

As this interest has grown these areas have become the subject of much heated debate over the years. There is plenty of scope for argument, especially since there is very little contemporary evidence in the chronicles about these battles and what occurred during them. The fifteenth-century chronicler William Gregory, who fought in the Wars of the Roses, and was probably an eyewitness to the second Battle of St Albans, himself had difficulty in assessing what actually occurred during the engagement, and provides us only with his unique view of what he saw, in relation to what he thought was worthy of recording for posterity. We are therefore left with one man's experience of the battle amid its confusion, coupled with the very real threat of personal danger when he found himself on the losing side.

Consequently, because this type of problem is common in the chronicles, with a resulting lack of definite information, not only do we need to consider alternative battle sites, but also, because of this confusion, there is a question mark against any battlefield's preservation. In overcoming this stumbling block we have to thank the inquiring minds of modern historians who in many cases may be absolutely correct in their assumptions as to where a battle took place. To the problem itself we have to bow to the chronicles, and also to the letters of the period, and to their lack of information on these highly misinterpreted medieval encounters.

The answer to this alternative battle site problem is not so simple for the conservationist to dismiss, however, and may never be fully resolved owing to this lack of contemporary evidence. But, in my opinion, the first stage in battlefield preservation is to pro-actively interpret a battlefield before any development takes place, pre-empting a possible public enquiry for instance; and secondly, armed with this information, to form independent societies or bodies to keep a close watch on battlefields locally. It may then be possible to enlist higher support a lot earlier and at development planning stage, rather than when the bulldozers are already moving in.

It is a battlefield society's main aim to interpret and thereby preserve a battlefield. It is this new interpretation of battlefields that reminds people that they are there, and along with other plans of action, helps to protect and preserve this heritage for future generations to interpret in their turn.

Here is a comprehensive and detailed work which brings together all the battles and conflicts of the Wars of the Roses in one continuous volume and thus carries on this interpretation into another century for our own children to reconsider. Philip Haigh focuses on these often extremely ruthless and sanguinary encounters with a unique emphasis on the battles themselves, the combatants, and the tactics employed by the commanders. It is uniquely apt in many ways that it should be written by him as his family and children are linked by blood to a commander of the House of Lancaster, who fought and escaped from the Battle of Towton in 1461, 533 years ago, Robert Hildyard.

Andrew W. Boardman
Chairman, Towton Battlefield Society
Leeds 1994

A NOTE
FROM THE AUTHOR

Having been raised near Towton field in Yorkshire, the site of the largest and bloodiest battle of the Wars of the Roses, I visited the scene many times when I was young. I remember being fascinated by the stories of the battle told to me when I visited the Crooked Billet, a nearby pub, which to a young boy was a treasure trove of information about the distant past and the ancient battle.

As I grew older and my interest in all things military grew stronger I eventually became an avid war-gamer. Unfortunately, I was never very good with a paintbrush, and I found that painting the miniature figures used in war-gaming was beyond me, so I cheated and used other people's figures instead. However, there came a time when I decided to master my unsteady painting hand, take the plunge, and purchase some figures of my own. Remembering the interest I had in Towton in my youth, I decided to buy figures from the period of the Wars of the Roses. When it came to painting them it became apparent to me that there was an absence of material about the period, and simply finding information on what the soldiers wore, who fought whom, and even details about the battles themselves, proved quite difficult.

At about this time it occurred to me that the entire subject, particularly the military side of the war, had been somewhat neglected by those who had written accounts of the period. I found myself moving from library to library and book to book in order to discover the information I needed. It was then that I found that one fascination – war-gaming – gave way to another: researching the battles of the period in which I was gaming.

I found various books, both new and old, some better than others, which go to great lengths to describe the political turmoil and the diplomacy of the age. Some even give very good accounts of the more famous battles, Towton, Tewkesbury and Bosworth, for instance, but not one of them chronicles the campaigns and battles of the entire period known as the Wars of the Roses. It is to make good this shortcoming that I decided to write this book.

It is important to understand that this book is a record of the military campaigns of the war, and is not a political history of the period. I have included important political events as an integral part of the text where the politics influenced the way in which battles were fought. However, anything else is secondary to the purpose of the book and I hope that the reader understands this.

The subject of the battles themselves presents perhaps the greatest problem of the book. Most of the accounts of events differ from the others, leaving us sometimes with two or more versions of the same battle. Deciding what is fact and what is not is the cause of much frustration for many an historian, not least myself.

Have I achieved a factual written account in this book? All I can say is that my research has been long and my interest lifelong. I have done my best.

Philip A. Haigh

ACKNOWLEDGEMENTS

I would like to thank the following people for their practical support and contribution towards bringing this book to its conclusion: Graham Shaw, for greatly improving the artwork, and supplying the finished maps; Paddy Hogan, for educating me in the ways of the English language, and making improvements to the text; Andrew Boardman for his foreword, and the continuing debate on who really commanded the Yorkists at Ferrybridge!

And my family and friends, who consistently supported and encouraged me to finish this work, in particular my father-in-law John Claxton, and Tess Walbran; their help over the years is greatly appreciated. Finally, I would like to say a special thank you to Jonathan Falconer and Anne Bennett at Alan Sutton Publishing for their help in bringing the book to publication.

SECTION ONE

CHAPTER ONE

THE ROAD TO WAR

Finding the precise beginning of the Wars of the Roses is difficult – there are many places to start. But to find the principal catalyst we should look no further than Richard Plantagenet, Duke of York, the son of Richard, Earl of Cambridge and great grandson of Edward III. If Henry VI had died before 1453, Richard would undoubtedly have become king, being a direct descendant of Edward III and there being no other living male with such a strong claim to the throne. Being so prominently placed in the royal household, York naturally believed that he should play a significant role in governing the country and at the court of Henry VI. But the king, though not distrusting York, favoured the counsel of Edmund Beaufort, Earl of Somerset. Somerset himself also had a claim to the throne, being the illegitimate grandson of John of Gaunt and Katherine Swynford, his mistress. Although the legitimacy of the claim was questionable, the lineage was legalized by an Act of Parliament.

York's relationship with Somerset was a difficult one. York detested everything about Somerset: his inability to lead, his claim to the throne, his constant bad judgement and advice to the king, and most of all his favoured status. The king, however, could not ignore York, and in 1436 appointed him Lieutenant of France, a role he carried out with vigour, despite having to pay his captains and the men-at-arms under his command out of his own purse. Indeed York committed £26,000 of his own money to support the king's forces in France, and had some success, despite being deprived of funds by Henry VI. In 1447 the king, no doubt on the advice of Somerset, distanced York further from the court, by relieving him of his position in France and appointing him to the post of Lieutenant of Ireland – in doing so imposing on York, by act of office, exile from England. Adding insult to injury, Henry then made Somerset Lieutenant of France, elevated him to the title of duke, and forwarded him an advance of £25,000 to maintain the king's forces overseas. It is important to note that by this time the crown owed York a sum in excess of £38,000 for his services in France. The injustice must have been a bitter pill for York to swallow, the more so because of the funds forwarded to Somerset, who in his own right was not a rich man, and indeed was unable to support the crown financially in any way. In contrast York was a rich man who owned estates throughout the land and had gained considerably from his marriage into the wealthy Neville family, his bride being Cicely Neville ('the Rose of Raby'), sister to Richard Neville, Earl of Salisbury and one of England's richest men.

In August 1450 Somerset returned to England. His time in France had not been a productive one. He had personally surrendered the city of Rouen, an act which

Richard, Duke of York, depicted in a stained glass window in Trinity College Hall, Cambridge

subsequently led to the fall of Normandy to Charles VII of France. However, he was welcomed back to court with open arms by the king and before long had regained – not that he had ever truly lost it – his position as one of the king's chief advisers. But although he was popular with the king, Somerset was among a number of nobles who were distinctly unpopular with the common people. Together with the Dukes of Exeter and Suffolk, he would bear the brunt of the revolt led by Jack Cade in 1450 which was mooted to be the 'voice of the people'. This revolt caused much concern at court and led to the exile and subsequent murder of the Duke of Suffolk.

One must take a moment to ponder York's thoughts at this point. He had had to finance his own royal office, lend money to the state, and stand by and watch his arch-rival not only take his office in France but also manoeuvre himself into a position where he could become a greater contender for the throne than himself. We can certainly understand his bitterness towards Somerset, but we can only imagine what was in his mind when he returned from Ireland in September 1450. He landed in North Wales and travelled straight to London. Whatever his intentions, his arrival caused great alarm to the king and court. Despite an unsuccessful attempt to apprehend him, York nevertheless presented himself to the king as a champion of law and order. With public support firmly behind York, the king, under pressure from his own subjects, was forced to back down. For the moment the status quo was returned between York and Somerset.

In June 1451 Bordeaux in France, and with it Gascony, was lost to Charles VII. York, irked that his own advice on English conduct in France had been blatantly

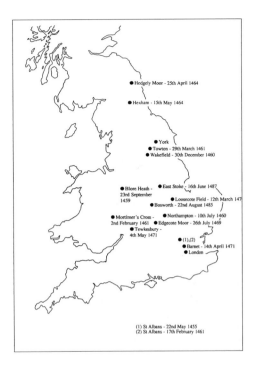

Battlefields of the Wars of the Roses

ignored, was quick to blame Somerset, as the king's chief advisor, for this disaster. And with public support for the king and his advisors at such a low point, York decided to risk everything and in a show of arms force his own decisions on the king and rid him of the source of all this bad advice. Unfortunately he misjudged the support from the other leading lords, and when he raised his army and advanced on London few of the nobility joined with him. Undaunted, however, York continued his advance, and on 3 March 1452 encamped on Blackheath outside London.

The king and his retainers marched out to meet him, but it was decided at a council of war to try to avoid conflict, and a delegation was sent out to parley with the duke. This decision was probably instigated by the Earls of Salisbury and Warwick, both at this point still loyal to the king, even if they were not in full agreement with him, but who understandably did not want to cross swords with their in-law, the Duke of York.

When the two sides met, York stated his terms: he would disband his army if Somerset were put on trial for his disastrous conduct of the war with France. The delegation from the king agreed, and it is said that even King Henry gave his royal assent. With everything agreed, York, being an honourable man, duly dismissed his army. On entering the king's tent, however, York found Somerset in his usual place by the king's right-hand side and himself under arrest. He was held prisoner for three months, and it was not until he swore an oath in St Paul's Cathedral never again to take up arms against the king, that he was released.

To make matters worse from York's point of view, the following October an expeditionary force under Sir John Talbot, Earl of Shrewsbury, recaptured Bordeaux,

Henry VI

and in the spring of 1453 Margaret of Anjou, Henry's queen, announced that she was with child. One by one the doors to the throne were closing for Richard, Duke of York.

The nation's joy at the news from France, however, was short-lived. In August 1453 Talbot was killed and his army routed in the Battle of Castillion in Gascony. This disaster was too much for Henry, who suffered a complete breakdown. We cannot be sure what form his illness took; what we do know is that it so incapacitated the king that he ceased to have any influence at court. Somerset, despite popular opinion, was not stupid: realizing that he could not survive long in power without the king's support, he arranged a meeting of the lords of the land to decide who would rule while the king was sick. He planned to have himself made Protector, and in an attempt to ensure the success of his proposal, did not invite York to the meeting. However, a group of the lords, led by the Earls of Salisbury and Warwick, usurped his position and declared York Protector of England.

This apparent sudden change of allegiance by Salisbury and Warwick dated to June 1453. The king, in his support of Somerset, had granted him by royal decree certain estates in Glamorgan that had previously been held by the Earl of Warwick. Warwick did not take the loss of his estates lightly and harboured a grudge against Somerset, waiting until he could extract his revenge. But this was not the sole reason for Warwick and Salisbury changing sides. In August 1453, shortly before the king's illness, the bridal party of Warwick's brother, Thomas Neville, including his bride, Maude Stanhope, was attacked on its way home by soldiers belonging to the Earl of

Northumberland, Sir Henry Percy. The Percys and Nevilles, even by the standards of the day, had long been bitter rivals, though even bearing this in mind the reason behind the attack is not immediately clear. In fact, the attack had its roots as far back as 1403, when Henry 'Hotspur' Percy had been killed in the Battle of Shrewsbury (see Appendix I), fighting against King Henry IV. Because of this treasonous act the Percy family had been stripped of its earldom and most of its lands. Hotspur's son, also called Henry Percy, served Henry V faithfully for many years and was rewarded with the return of the family earldom. However, some of his former estates remained unrecovered. Two of these, Wressle in Yorkshire and Burwell in Lincolnshire, had been granted to Lord Cromwell, one of Henry VI's ministers. Maude Stanhope, Neville's bride, was co-heiress to the Cromwell estate, and the prospect of Wressle and Burwell passing to the Neville family through inheritance was too much even for the patient Henry Percy. The attack was led by Percy's second son, Lord Egremont, but Neville, accompanied by his father, the Earl of Salisbury and his sizeable retinue, was able to beat off the attackers.

This started a series of 'tit-for-tat' raids by the Percys and the Nevilles against each other's estates. Salisbury and Warwick turned to York, their natural ally, for help. In one of the greatest diplomatic moves of his life, and in return for his support against the Percys, York enlisted their help in his struggle against Somerset. As already stated, Warwick had no love for Somerset, and therefore gladly agreed to this. Thus the Duke of Somerset was outmanoeuvred by Warwick and his father Salisbury when they chose York (even in his absence) as Protector.

For the next fourteen months Richard ruled England. The Duke of Somerset was sent to the Tower on the revised charge of treason for his conduct in France, while the Percys, without royal protection, suffered badly at the hands of the Nevilles. All this came to an abrupt end in January 1455 when the king recovered from his illness, York's protectorate ceased, and Somerset was released from the Tower. Somerset was not the only one relieved at the return of the king; the Percy family, too, must have breathed a sigh of relief, and offered their allegiance to Somerset in exchange for his support (and therefore the king's) against the Nevilles. An understandable case of 'do as you would be done by'!

Shortly after Henry's restoration, aware of the Somerset–Percy pact, York, Warwick and Salisbury left London without taking their leave of the king and travelled to their estates in the North, undoubtedly to gather strength and plan an armed return to power.

Thus the battlelines had been drawn: on one side King Henry, Somerset and Percy (or, as they were to become known, the Lancastrians); on the other, York, Salisbury and Warwick (the Yorkists).

The Wars of the Roses had begun.

CHAPTER TWO

THE BATTLE
OF ST ALBANS
22 MAY 1455

THE CAMPAIGN

While York and his allies gathered their forces in the North, the king and Somerset did not lie idle. The king and his closest advisors met together on 21 April and decided to hold a council, at which all the nobles of the land would be present, in an attempt to resolve the current crisis. The council was due to be held on 21 May, at Leicester, and summonses were sent to nobles throughout the land, including York, Salisbury and Warwick. The wording of the summons read, '. . . that they should meet to discuss the safety of the King against anyone who would threaten it . . .' Suspecting that the council would be a trap, York concluded that the outcome of any meeting of nobles, with no men-at-arms in attendance, would lead to his death.[1] He therefore decided upon a new course of action: his plan was to intercept the king en route to Leicester and take him into his 'protection'. To that end, accompanied by Salisbury and Warwick and three thousand men-at-arms, mostly archers, pikemen and billmen, he travelled south down the Great North Road to London.

On hearing of York's march south, undoubtedly through one of Somerset's many spies, the king dispatched a letter to York stating that if he did not disband his army he would, along with his fellow conspirators, be deemed a traitor and suffer accordingly. On receiving no reply, the king and his retinue (an army of no more than two thousand men-at-arms, again mainly pikemen and billmen) left the capital on 21 May. If there were to be a confrontation with York, the king did not want it to happen near London, where York had popular support. The king's army was clearly under strength. This was probably because of Henry's belief that York would honour the oath he had sworn in St Paul's not to bear arms against the king. Even so, this did not prevent a last-minute military summons, issued on 18 May, to other nobles, ordering them to come to the king's aid.

When the king's army reached Kilburn he received a letter from York. In it York protested that he had not been included in the king's council of 21 April, and stated

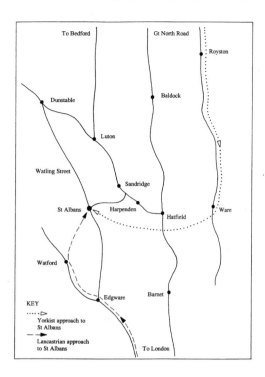

Fig 2.1   Preliminary Moves for the Battle
of St Albans

also that only the removal of Somerset would appease the situation at this stage. The
letter had been signed by York in Royston, Hertfordshire, only the previous day.
Henry continued his journey, and during the night reached Watford and made camp.
At about the same time York reached Ware, only 15 miles from St Albans, and from
here sent a second letter to the king. Its contents were nothing new; again York
protested his innocence and stated that the welfare of the king was his prime concern.
The receipt of this letter caused much concern to the king's party: it showed how
close York was and how fast his army was moving. He was now only 20 miles away.[2]

In the early hours of 22 May the king set out to continue his journey but at
7 o'clock received news that York had reached the outskirts of St Albans. Much
alarmed at the speed of the Yorkist army, the king called an emergency meeting to
decide on what course of action would now be best. The Duke of Somerset, as
Commander of the King's Army, urged the king to stand fast and prepare for battle.
Somerset was undoubtedly counting on the support of Henry Percy, Earl of
Northumberland, and Percy's ally in the North, Lord Clifford of Skipton (who were
both itching at the chance to fight their old enemies Warwick and Salisbury).
However, Sir Humphrey Stafford, the ageing Duke of Buckingham, advised the king
to march to St Albans and parley with York. Buckingham felt that although Somerset
had the support of Northumberland and Clifford, and that the loyalty of men like Sir
James Butler, Earl of Wiltshire (one of the king's favourites), Jasper Tudor, Earl of
Pembroke (Henry's step-brother), Lord Humphrey, Earl of Stafford and Sir Henry
Beaufort, Earl of Dorset (Somerset's eldest son), was not in question, there was good

reason to doubt some of the other nobles. For example, he felt that Sir William Neville, Lord Fauconberg, was unlikely to fight against his relations York, Salisbury and Warwick, while Sir Thomas Courtenay, Earl of Devon, was an old ally of York's. Moreover, if truth were known, Buckingham himself did not relish the prospect of dying on behalf of the Duke of Somerset.

On receipt of this advice, the king promptly replaced Somerset as Commander-in-Chief with Buckingham, who then issued orders to advance to St Albans. Historians believe this act typified the king's state of mind. We shall never be sure. Was it an act of madness that caused the king to change the army's commander at such a late stage, or was it a shrewd move, bearing in mind the dubious loyalty of some of his nobles? Perhaps he believed in Buckingham's ability to parley with York and bring the situation to a peaceful solution. After all, Buckingham was related to York, and was the person most likely to be able to reason with the man.

Whatever Henry's thinking, the Lancastrian army, led by the Duke of Buckingham, reached St Albans at about the same time as the Yorkists, 9 o'clock in the morning. The king raised his banner in the town square, showing that indeed he was ready to give battle. His army took up positions around the town defences, namely the gates on Sopwell Lane and Shropshire Lane. Meanwhile, York's army drew up in a line to the east of the town in Key Field, behind the gardens of the houses of Hollywell Street, the market square and St Peter's Street.

THE BATTLE

The opening positions are shown in Fig. 2.2. York, Warwick and Salisbury gathered their army at the ridge of the hill on which lay St Albans. With York was Sir David Hall, his military advisor; accompanying Warwick was Sir Robert Ogle (a trusted Neville captain), and a contingent of the Duke of Norfolk's men, though Norfolk himself was absent from the battle. With Salisbury was his son, Sir Thomas Neville. On the Lancastrian side, Somerset, Northumberland and Clifford each defended one of the town's east-facing wooden gates. The king remained in the town square, accompanied by the Earls of Devon and Wiltshire, Lord Fauconberg and other nobles. The Duke of Buckingham as mediator probably travelled through the Lancastrian positions but at the time of actual conflict would probably have remained by the king.

The conflict opened with a round of negotiations, but the Duke of York was resolute: only the surrender of Somerset would do. In a message to the king he said '. . . surrender to us such as we will accuse, and not to resist til we have him which deserve death . . .'. The king was equally defiant on the subject of Somerset's surrender, and refused, and in a display of uncharacteristic gallantry cried: 'By the faith that I owe to St Edward and the crown of England I shall destroy every mother's son and they shall be hanged and drawn and quartered.' With this the parley ended and the battle commenced.[3]

The first move came at about 10 o'clock in the morning, when Warwick, Salisbury and York simultaneously attacked the gates on Sopwell Lane and Shropshire Lane (*see* Fig. 2.3). The attack was sudden. York and his allies had watched with increasing impatience as the town's defences, namely the gates and the ditch, had been reinforced as they had parleyed. York had had enough, and though the Yorkists had been within

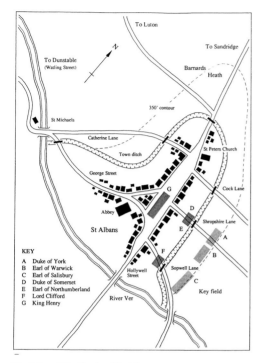

Fig 2.2   The Battle of St Albans

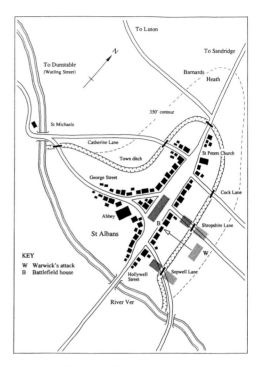

Fig 2.3   The Battle of St Albans

sight of the Lancastrians throughout, the impression is that the Lancastrians were taken off guard. Most of the men-at-arms had expected a peaceful solution, such as the one at Blackheath in 1452, and this sudden rush by the Yorkists nearly paid off. As it became apparent that an attack was under way the gates became heavily manned as more men rushed to defend them, and with the streets being narrow, the Yorkists, even though they outnumbered the Lancastrians, began to suffer heavy losses.

Whether the Earl of Warwick had taken part in the Yorkist attack down Shropshire Lane or not, he managed to return to a contingent of men left as a rearguard at the crest of the hill in Key Field, and led them through the back gardens behind the market square. While his other men, and those under the command of York and Salisbury, kept the defenders of the gates on Sopwell and Shropshire Lanes occupied, he managed to pass undetected and burst through into the market place at what is now called Battlefield House, opposite the king's position in the main street. With a blast of his trumpets and a cry of 'a Warwick, a Warwick', the 25-year-old earl smashed the Lancastrian line in two, and by this act made his mark in military history.[4]

Hearing that the Yorkists had entered the town caused the Lancastrians to panic; the men defending the gates, fearing an attack from the rear, broke their lines and fled, allowing the Yorkists to enter the town via the now undefended gates. The remnants of the Lancastrian forces tried to rally in the market square (*see* Fig. 2.4) round the king (who remained quietly seated under a tree throughout), but were set upon by Warwick's men, who fired arrows at them with devastating effect at such short range.

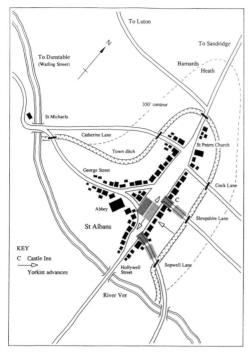

Fig 2.4   The Battle of St Albans

Both the king and the Duke of Buckingham were wounded, the king in the neck, and the duke in the face. The Earl of Stafford, Buckingham's son, and the Earls of Dorset and Wiltshire were also injured but to lesser degrees. All this is testament that the attack by Warwick into the market square had been a complete surprise – many of the Lancastrians had not even had time to put on their helmets.

The remaining conflict was brief, lasting no more than half an hour. Lord Clifford, though managing to make it back to the main street, was killed, hacked to death by the jubilant men under Warwick's command. Northumberland was also killed, trying to fight his way to refuge in the Castle Inn on the corner of Shropshire Lane. The Earls of Devon, Dorset and Pembroke, with the Duke of Buckingham, were captured and spared; the Earl of Wiltshire and Lord Fauconberg made good their escape. The Duke of Somerset was less lucky. After the rout from Shropshire Lane he had managed to find refuge in the Castle Inn. Anticipating his fate at the hands of York if captured alive, Somerset and his remaining retainers decided to fight it out. When the defenders outside the inn were slain, he led a final charge into the main street and killed four men before being felled by an axe.

The victorious Yorkists crowded around the king, who had by now been deserted in the market square, even his standard bearer Sir Philip Wentworth having fled the field. But with the words 'Forsooth, forsooth, ye do folly to smite a king anointed', Henry calmed them, and was led away. He was said to have been taken to a tanner's house near St Peter's Church, but more probably to the abbey, where the Yorkist leaders sought him out.[5] Approaching the king, on bended knee, they asked him for forgiveness, and with an astonishing lack of tact asked Henry to join in the rejoicing at the death of Somerset. The king gave his forgiveness, and everyone seemed to have forgotten his threat to hang, draw and quarter the rebels made some two hours earlier! The Nevilles, too, had reason to rejoice, as both Clifford and Northumberland were dead.

The next day the party returned to London, with York riding on the king's right, and Salisbury on his left, while Warwick rode on ahead, bearing the royal sword. York had achieved in two hours what he had failed to do in two decades, for though Henry wore the crown, it was York who now ruled England as Protector and Defender of the Land, a title that was legalized by Act of Parliament and given royal assent on 19 November 1455.

EPILOGUE TO THE BATTLE

After the battle there was much looting by the Yorkists, and it was probably at this time that the Earl of Wiltshire and Lord Fauconberg made good their escape. It is said that the earl dressed as a monk, and with the aid of this disguise was able to walk unmolested through the Yorkist ranks. It seems likely that Lord Fauconberg did not 'escape' – he had played only a minor role in the battle and it is probable that a blind eye was turned due to his family connections, and that he just quietly walked away.

It is also said that the Duke of Somerset had in the past begged the king never to summon him to Windsor Castle. It seems that a fortune teller had told the duke that he would die in the shadow of a castle, which troubled him so much that as far as possible he kept well away from fortresses. We will never know for certain whether this was simply poetic licence on the part of the chroniclers, to add spice to the tale of Somerset's death in front of the Castle Inn.

Historians say that it was his keen military eye that led the Earl of Warwick to see the gap in the defences and conclude that an attack through the back gardens would be successful. It seems more likely that, because he was unable to proceed one way (via the gates) Warwick simply tried another. The Lancastrians did not have enough men to defend the whole length of the ditch, so we must conclude that the earl was just lucky. Some historians believe that it was Sir Robert Ogle who led the attack and that the earl simply took the credit for it. Lucky or not, the attack launched Warwick's military career and helped to send him down the road towards earning his subsequent nickname of 'Kingmaker'.[6]

CHAPTER THREE

THE BATTLE OF BLORE HEATH 23 SEPTEMBER 1459

THE CAMPAIGN

York's second Protectorate lasted until February 1456, when the king relieved him of his position, claiming before Parliament that he himself was fit and able to take up the reins of power. There is no doubt that this move was initiated by Queen Margaret, who had long been able to influence her husband in affairs of state. After the birth of her son Margaret had begun to increase her involvement in political matters, mainly to protect her infant's birthright. To this end she spent several months during 1456 travelling around the Midlands, gathering support for the Lancastrian cause. In August 1456 she joined her husband at Kenilworth, and during the following two years systematically removed, by political means, Yorkist sympathizers from positions of royal office – men who had been appointed to those positions when York assumed the Protectorate.

After being removed from office York and Salisbury retreated to their estates in the North, and from his stronghold at Sandal York kept a wary eye on Queen Margaret. Warwick had been appointed Captain of Calais (a royal office) by York shortly after St Albans, and returned there, despite attempts by Margaret to remove him, to concentrate on his own affairs in France. But when Margaret installed a Lancastrian sympathizer as Treasurer of England in May 1458, funds to support Warwick's position as Captain of Calais ceased. Unable to pay the wages of the garrison without government assistance, Warwick organized pirate-style raids from Calais on Spanish and Hanseatic shipping to raise capital to pay the troops. Such escapades not only pleased the soldiers but also enhanced Warwick's standing as a swashbuckling hero to many of the common people of England. Claiming that Warwick had overstepped the authority of his position, Margaret instigated legal proceedings against him, and he was charged with treason for his piratical acts. In October 1458 he was summoned to London to answer this charge. On arrival, he and his retainers were set upon by a contingent of the royal guard. In the brawl that followed,

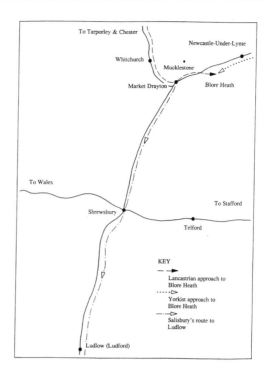

Fig 3.1　　Preliminary Moves for the Battle
of Blore Heath

Warwick escaped and returned to Calais, claiming that there had been a Lancastrian plot to kill him.

The precarious political balance was slowly tilting in the Lancastrians' favour. With Warwick disgraced and York and Salisbury geographically separated (York had by this time moved to Ludlow, and Salisbury had returned to his castle at Middleham in North Yorkshire), Margaret decided to play her final card. A council meeting was held at Coventry in June 1459 to which all the great nobles – except York, Salisbury and Warwick, of course – were summoned. It was here that charges of treason were laid against the Yorkist commanders. With this act Margaret hoped that all Yorkist claims to power would be ended once and for all. However, York realized the similarity between this meeting and the one held in April 1455, and decided to act. He planned his own meeting to be held at Ludlow, where he would be joined by Salisbury with an army of northerners, and by Warwick with a contingent of the Calais garrison. With this combined force he planned to engage the Lancastrians and seize the king (and therefore the throne), as he had done at St Albans five years previously. In September Warwick sailed from Calais, and after landing in England narrowly escaped being intercepted by the new Duke of Somerset, Sir Henry Beaufort (son of the late Edmund Beaufort killed at St Albans), who had been ordered to patrol the Midlands in anticipation of Warwick's arrival. Warwick and his force, however, reached Ludlow unscathed.

King Henry at this time was raising an army in the Midlands under the command of Sir Humphrey Stafford, Duke of Buckingham. His queen had travelled north to

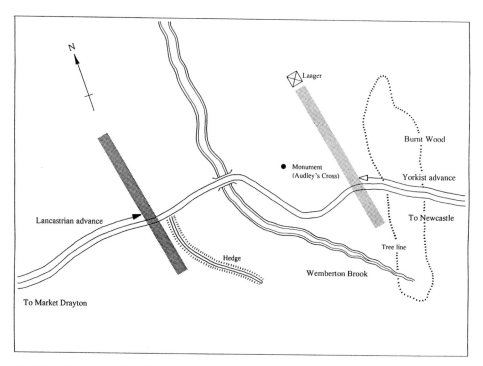

Fig 3.2   The Battle of Blore Heath

Eccleshall, 10 miles south-east of Market Drayton, to join James, Lord Audley's royal army, now approaching Market Drayton. Raised in Shropshire and Cheshire, Audley's force consisted of some ten thousand men-at-arms, including a large cavalry contingent. At about the same time Salisbury left Middleham for Ludlow. With him were his sons Sir John and Sir Thomas Neville, and his captains Sir Thomas Harrington, Sir Thomas Parr and Sir John Conyers. His army consisted of the usual pikemen, billmen and archers, with baggage train, and in total numbered no more than five or six thousand men-at-arms. His route to Ludlow took him west along the road leading from Newcastle-under-Lyme to Market Drayton.

Hearing of Salisbury's departure from Middleham, the Lancastrian army in the Midlands under the command of the Duke of Buckingham made an attempt to block his march, but Salisbury managed to evade it. Realizing the threat posed by a combined Yorkist army, Margaret ordered Lord Audley at nearby Market Drayton to intercept Salisbury, arrest and detain him, and in doing so prevent his army from joining forces with those of York and Warwick.

She also sent a message to the Stanley brothers, Sir William and Lord Thomas, asking them to march to Audley's assistance. The Stanleys had estates in the area and so were well placed to join with Audley and stop Salisbury. However, the Stanley brothers were divided in their loyalties. Lord Thomas sent several messages to Margaret assuring her of his commitment to the Lancastrian cause, and even volunteered to command the Lancastrian vanguard when he made contact with Lord

Audley's army. In the event he kept a safe distance from both Lancastrians and Yorkists – hardly surprising, as he was married to Eleanor Neville, Salisbury's daughter, and any move would compromise either his loyalty to his king or his loyalty to his family.

Sir William was less conscientious, and marched to join forces with Salisbury. Lord Audley and John, Lord Dudley (the Lancastrian second-in-command) and their army left Market Drayton and marched east along the Newcastle road. The two armies, each well aware of the other's presence, met on the morning of 23 September 1459, near Mucklestone, a mile north of the village of Blore Heath and on the heath itself.

THE BATTLE

Detailed accounts of the battle itself are virtually non-existent. We do know, however, that Yorkist scouts advanced along the road to a point parallel to the site where the monument now stands, and, seeing the Lancastrians forming positions beyond the long hedge running from the road south on to the common, returned to the main body of the army and reported the Lancastrian positions to Salisbury. After a brief reconnaissance Salisbury and the main Yorkist army approached Blore Heath. Emerging from the wooded area called Burnt Wood, they took up positions on the ridge before the small stream known as Wemberton Brook.

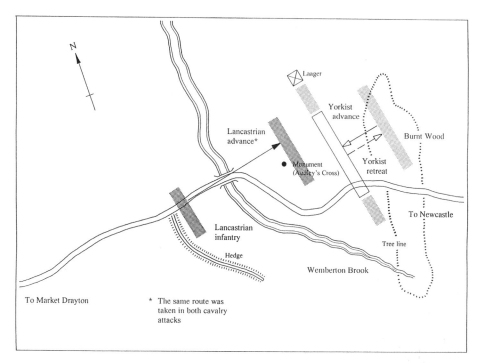

Fig 3.3   The Battle of Blore Heath

The opening positions are depicted in Fig. 3.2. It can be seen from the map that the Yorkists formed their wagons into a laager north of the heath and east of the brook. The Yorkist army, using this laager as an anchor, formed its forces in line south, in a line roughly parallel to Wemberton Brook. The Lancastrians deployed their army in line crossing the road, with half of the line concealed by the hedge and the remainder running north on to the heath, also roughly parallel to the brook. A large proportion of the Lancastrian army was cavalry.

The two armies spent some time squaring up to each other, during which time the Yorkists, realizing that they were outnumbered, strengthened their position by digging a trench to their rear and fixing stakes to their front. At about 1 o'clock the Lancastrian cavalry began to advance. There is some controversy regarding these opening moves and the reason for them. It is said that Salisbury, knowing he was outnumbered, but trusting the strength of his defensive position, ordered his centre to withdraw east beyond the wood. The Lancastrians believed this withdrawal to be a Yorkist retreat in the face of superior numbers, and Audley, mindful of his orders to capture Salisbury, spurred his cavalry forward and was thus drawn into the battle (*see* Fig. 3.3). Their approach was not an easy one. They had to traverse a slope down to the brook, cross the stream (there was a bridge, but the brook was not deep and although a crossing would not be impossible it would certainly be difficult for a large number of armoured cavalry), then climb the bank on the opposite side to engage the Yorkists.

This first attack was met by a heavy barrage of arrows from the Yorkists, who had

Audley Cross: inscription at the battlefield of Blore Heath

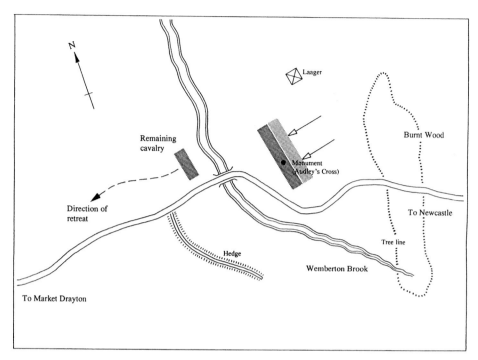

Fig 3.4   The Battle of Blore Heath

returned to their original position as the Lancastrians came within range. The Lancastrians suffered some two or three hundred casualties and were forced to retreat beyond bowshot. A second attack, led by Audley himself, was soon launched, but this too was beaten off, and during the assault Audley was killed. The site where he fell is marked by a memorial cross which can still be seen today. From this we can also establish the exact location of the battle.

A change in leader – with Audley's death Lord Dudley assumed command – led to a change in tactics. A large proportion of the Lancastrian cavalry now dismounted, and a force of some four thousand men advanced towards the Yorkist line on foot. The two armies engaged, and there followed a bitter hand-to-hand struggle which lasted well into the afternoon (*see* Fig. 3.4). The remaining Lancastrian cavalry, watching the mêlée from west of the brook, realized that the skirmish was not going well and left the field, leaving the Lancastrians on foot to fend for themselves. With the expected cavalry support not forthcoming, the Lancastrians began to give ground, some of them, perhaps as many as five hundred men, even deserting to the Yorkist cause. This was the final straw and with it the Lancastrian line broke and the battle was lost. In total some two thousand Lancastrians died, whereas the Yorkists suffered very few casualties: at most no more than five hundred men died in the battle, a very low figure by the standards of the day. It is said that afterwards Wemberton Brook ran red with Lancastrian blood for three days.

EPILOGUE TO THE BATTLE

During the Lancastrian retreat their leader John, Lord Dudley, was captured. Indeed the Lancastrian nobility present at Blore Heath fared badly in the battle, Sir Hugh Venables of Kinerton, Sir Thomas Dutton of Dutton, Sir Richard Molineux of Sefton, Sir John Dunne and Sir John Haigh all being killed. The fleeing Lancastrians were pursued closely by the Yorkists. But as in many battles, the victorious army broke apart as some men went on to loot their dead opponents or gave chase to the survivors of the defeated army. The rout and ensuing pursuit lasted well into the early hours of the following morning. Bearing in mind that it was September, with dark nights drawing in, it is easy to understand how various factions of the Yorkists became separated from the main army.

This was the case with Sir Thomas Harrington, Sir John and Sir Thomas Neville, who, having left the main Yorkist army in pursuit of the defeated Lancastrians, lost their way. Some time in the early hours of the following morning they were unfortunate enough to be caught in a trap while crossing a bridge at Tarporley, manned by a number of Lancastrians under the command of a local squire. These men had remained in the area to try to protect their homes from the victorious Yorkists, who were busy plundering the local homesteads. The three knights were captured alive and eventually taken to Chester Castle, where they remained prisoners for nine months.

It is said that the slaughter of the Lancastrians was greatest during the rout. The heavily armoured knights who had dismounted to fight on foot were hampered by their armour as they tried to flee the battlefield. A great number of them were trapped and killed 2 miles west of Blore Heath on the banks of the River Tern, unable to cross the water because of their heavy armour. This place is still known today as 'Deadmen's Den'.

Although Margaret was not present at the battle she was certainly in the vicinity, probably at Market Drayton. Local tradition tells of her ordering the horseshoes of her carriage horses to be reversed while she made her escape, giving the impression that her entourage was heading in the opposite direction.

Salisbury, although the victor of the day, found his position still quite precarious. There were still two other Lancastrian armies, commanded by Somerset and Buckingham, to deal with. He did, however, manage to reach Ludlow without serious hindrance from the remaining Lancastrians, where he met and joined forces with York and Warwick. It is said that Salisbury encouraged a local Augustinian friar to cover his withdrawal from Blore Heath by firing a cannon throughout the night to confuse the Lancastrians as to the position of Salisbury's army. The friar, when asked about his motives the following morning by Lancastrians drawn to the scene, replied that he had fired the cannon to help keep up his flagging spirits!

From Ludlow the Yorkists sent a letter to the king justifying their actions. The king offered in response a pardon to all who had raised arms against him except those involved in the battle at Blore Heath and those responsible for Audley's death, if they would now surrender to Henry's army. Although the Yorkists had combined their armies the Lancastrians still had the advantage. Margaret learnt the lessons of

Edward flees to Calais with Salisbury and Warwick in November 1469, watched by Henry VI (left)

St Albans and was not about to make the same mistake as Buckingham when he was Commander-in-Chief at St Albans in 1455. Receiving no reply from York, the Lancastrians advanced on Ludlow and reached Ludford Bridge on 12 October. Here they found the Yorkists in a fortified position waiting for them. The king's army had attracted a large number of peers, whereas the Yorkists had failed to attain the popular support expected, and Henry's army outnumbered York's by three to one.

The cream of York's army was the contingent from Calais, led by Andrew Trollope. The Calais army, though effectively controlled by Warwick, was still the only official English standing army, and as such had sworn an oath to the king, which explains why it accepted the king's pardon and promptly changed sides, strengthening the Lancastrian army still further. Andrew Trollope was himself a veteran of the war in France and as such had had access to the Yorkists' plans, and knew the strengths and weaknesses of the current Yorkist positions. His defection meant that the Yorkists' position was now completely untenable, and as evening drew on, York, his two sons, Salisbury and Warwick left the field under the cover of an artillery barrage, stating that they were returning to Ludlow Castle for the night. From here they collected a few personal belongings and then fled, leaving behind them not only their army but also most of their equipment.

The next day, with no commander to control them, the Yorkist army disbanded, leaving the Lancastrians free to plunder Ludlow (a pro-Yorkist town). Meanwhile, the Yorkist leaders had decided to split up: York and his second son, Edmund, travelled to Ireland; Warwick, accompanied by Salisbury and Edward, Earl of March, York's eldest son, began the journey back to Calais.

CHAPTER FOUR

THE BATTLE OF NORTHAMPTON
10 JULY 1460

THE CAMPAIGN

With the disaster at Ludford Bridge most people thought that the Yorkist cause had not only reached the point of no return but had indeed passed it. This would probably have been the case had it not been for the actions of one man – Richard Neville, Earl of Warwick. It was his strength and determination that kept the Yorkist cause alive in the following months.

Warwick, Salisbury and Edward, Earl of March, finally reached Calais on 2 November 1459, where Warwick was reunited with his uncle William Neville, Lord Fauconberg, who had remained in Calais when Warwick had left for England the previous month. The Duke of York and Edmund, Earl of Rutland, reached Ireland at the end of September. On his arrival York was well received by the local people. He was still the official Lieutenant of Ireland and as such had remained popular with the Irish.

Meanwhile, the Lancastrians in mainland England were busy exploiting the Yorkists' flight from Ludford Bridge. They were quick to appoint Sir James Butler, Earl of Wiltshire, as Lieutenant of Ireland, and Sir Henry Beaufort, Duke of Somerset, as Captain of Calais. Though these appointments were, on paper, legal and absolute, putting them into practice was a different matter. The Earl of Wiltshire encouraged the Irish to rebel against York, but all his plots and propaganda came to nothing. The Duke of Somerset also failed to take up his position as Captain of Calais. He sailed for France with an expeditionary force, but on arrival at Calais found the city gates closed before him. He therefore decided to lay siege to the fortress and moved on to Guines, which he made his base and from where he launched daily attacks on Calais. But like Wiltshire's in Ireland, his efforts came to nothing. The reasons for this were many, but the main one was the loyalty shown by the Calais garrison to their leader. Warwick, since his return to Calais, had increased his raids on foreign shipping and as a result had made the rank and file of the garrison considerably richer than they had

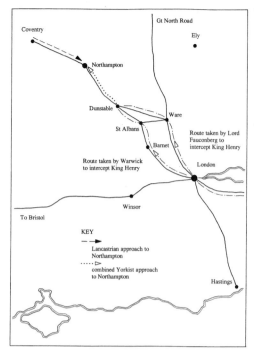

Fig 4.1   Preliminary Moves for the Battle of Northampton

previously been; the men under his command did not relish the thought of Warwick being replaced. The increase in trade that Warwick had encouraged in his time as captain had also made him popular with the occupants of the city.

Realizing Somerset's plight, the Lancastrian government in England organized an army to reinforce him, so that he could storm the city with a far superior force. However, they required ships to transport the army, and therefore a fleet was ordered to be constructed at Sandwich, in southern England, under the command of Sir Anthony Woodville. Warwick was not without his spies in England, and was soon informed of the fleet's construction. He decided that attack was the best form of defence, and on 15 January 1460 led a raid on Sandwich. The raiders took the defenders completely by surprise; they destroyed the ships under construction and sailed away with those already completed, returning to Calais with Warwick's whole fleet intact.

After this the Lancastrians in England, particularly those in the South, feared and expected an invasion by Warwick at any moment. This was not forthcoming, though in March Warwick did leave Calais. However, instead of invading southern England he sailed to Ireland to confer with the Duke of York. He stayed there for two months, and in his absence the attacks on Calais by Somerset increased. But the garrison, left under the command of Salisbury and Fauconberg, remained steadfast. Somerset, finding himself running short of both provisions and money for his army, was forced to ask the king for assistance. The king instructed John, Lord Audley (son of the late James, Lord Audley, Sir James Tuchet), to sail to France with supplies. During the voyage across the Channel his ship was hit by storms and was forced into Calais harbour for safety, where on his arrival Audley was promptly arrested.

At the end of May Warwick sailed from Ireland and returned to Calais. Early in June he led another raid on Sandwich and destroyed another fleet under construction by the Lancastrians. Before returning to Calais he left Lord Fauconberg at Sandwich with a small Yorkist force which was to act as a bridgehead to the forthcoming invasion, planned in Ireland by York and Warwick.

On 26 June Warwick, Salisbury and Edward, accompanied by John, Lord Audley (who had defected to the Yorkists' side), sailed to Sandwich with a force of some two thousand men-at-arms. After marshalling at Sandwich for three days they marched on London. The king and queen were at this time with the bulk of the Lancastrian army at Coventry. The only Lancastrian of note in the London area was Lord Scales, who commanded a small force stationed in London. Realizing that he was outnumbered, and that the city leaders did not plan to resist Warwick's entry into the capital, Scales retreated to the safety of the Tower of London.

Warwick reached London on 2 July. By this time his army had swollen to between twenty and thirty thousand men – on his march to London he had been joined by many of his supporters from Kent, Sussex and Surrey, where he had remained popular throughout his exile in France. On his arrival in the capital Warwick was informed that Lord Scales was at the Tower. The earl did not plan to stay long in London, and so ordered his father, Salisbury, and Sir John Wenlock (one of Warwick's ablest and most loyal captains) to take a contingent of the army and lay siege to the Tower, in order to confine Scales and his force. Once under siege they could not become a threat to Warwick when he and his army marched north.

After two days spent gathering horses and provisions Warwick received reports that the king was en route to safety in the cathedral town of Ely. It appears that Warwick was misinformed. However, on 4 July he dispatched Lord Fauconberg and half his army to intercept Henry; the remainder left London the following day and took the St Albans road on their way to Coventry, a course taken as a precaution in case the information about the king's route was in fact false. The king was actually at this point marching slowly south with the Lancastrian army towards London, having left his queen and son behind at Coventry. The reason for this slow advance was to give the Lancastrian forces in the North, commanded by the Earl of Northumberland and Lord Clifford, time to reach the main Lancastrian army before they engaged the Yorkists. However, the two nobles and their army did not arrive in time.

When Warwick received definite news that the king was indeed travelling south, and that his army, under the command of the Duke of Buckingham, had reached and encamped at Northampton, he sent orders to Fauconberg, who, with the other half of the army, had by this time arrived at Ware, to meet him at Dunstable so their combined force could march on Northampton.

THE BATTLE

Once the king's forces reached Northampton they took up a defensive position outside the city wall, with their backs to the River Nene and their front protected by a ditch filled with water (fed by a channel from the river) and fortified by stakes. The Lancastrian army consisted of some ten to fifteen thousand men-at-arms and a

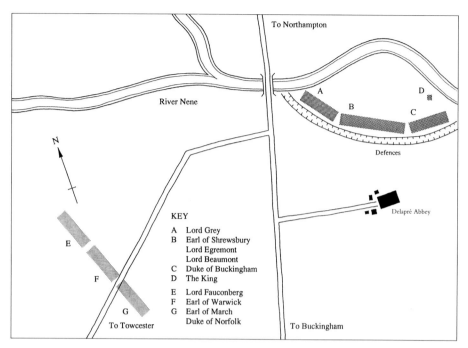

Fig 4.2   The Battle of Northampton

quantity of field artillery (*see* Fig. 4.2). The Duke of Buckingham, Sir Humphrey Stafford, controlled the Lancastrian left flank. The Earl of Shrewsbury, Sir John Talbot, Lord Egremont, Sir Thomas Percy, and Viscount Beaumont, Sir John Beaumont held the centre, while Sir Edmund Grey of Ruthyn secured the right flank.

Warwick sent a delegation, headed by the Bishop of Salisbury with orders to negotiate on his behalf, to the king at Northampton. However, the Lancastrian commander, the Duke of Buckingham, refused the bishop access to the king and sent him back to Warwick with the words: 'The Earl of Warwick shall not come to the king's presence and if he comes he shall die'.[1]

With this, on the morning of 10 July the Yorkists advanced along the Towcester road towards the Lancastrians. Their approach was delayed slightly because of heavy rain which was to last on and off for the rest of the day. During the advance Warwick tried twice more to gain access to the king, but on each occasion, his herald was turned away. The Yorkists took up positions to the west of Delapré Abbey, facing the Lancastrians (*see* Fig. 4.2). Lord Fauconberg commanded the Yorkist left flank or rearguard, the Earl of Warwick held the centre, while the Earl of March and the Duke of Norfolk, Sir John Mowbray, commanded the right or vanguard.

Warwick's first move was to send a message to the Duke of Buckingham which read: 'At 2 o'clock I will speak with the King or I will die'. When he was again refused Warwick gave the command to attack. At about 2 o'clock, with a blast of

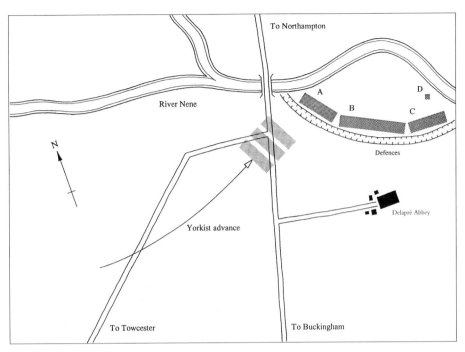

Fig 4.3   The Battle of Northampton

trumpets, the Yorkists began their advance. They approached in column but the rain was by this time falling quite heavily and they found the advance hard going. This, combined with the fierce barrage of archer fire which met the Yorkists as they approached the fortified position of the Lancastrians, stopped them from coming into close quarters with their opponents (*see* Fig. 4.3).

The Lancastrians' strength lay in their artillery and their fortified position. However, the heavy rain put the guns out of action and the treachery of one of the defenders undermined the advantage of their position. The advancing Yorkist column led by Warwick and Edward approached the right flank of the Lancastrian fortification. It was here that Lord Grey, commanding the defenders at this point, ordered his men to lay down their arms and allow the Yorkists access to the camp. The men under Warwick's command had been ordered to spare the lives of all those wearing the livery of Lord Grey (a black ragged staff), the king and the commons, but no others.[2]

The magnitude of Grey's treachery left the Lancastrians in a desperate position; indeed the battle lasted no more than 30 minutes after this. It could be said that Grey's betrayal was the death blow for the defenders, who, unable to manoeuvre within the narrow confines of the fortification, broke and fled as their line was 'rolled up' by the advancing Yorkists (*see* Fig. 4.4). The Duke of Buckingham, the Earl of Shrewsbury, Lords Egremont and Beaumont were all slain while trying to protect the king, as the jubilant Yorkists advanced on Henry's tent. The slaughter of the defeated

Edward kneels before Henry VI after the Battle of Northampton, 1460

was light by the standards of the day, though the nobility suffered badly. Only some three hundred Lancastrians died in the battle, most of whom perished trying to cross the wide but shallow River Nene (probably crushed underfoot in the rout and drowned).

With the death of most of the prominent Lancastrian leaders, and the capture of the king, the mêlée ceased. Once again Henry found himself under the 'protection' of the Yorkists.

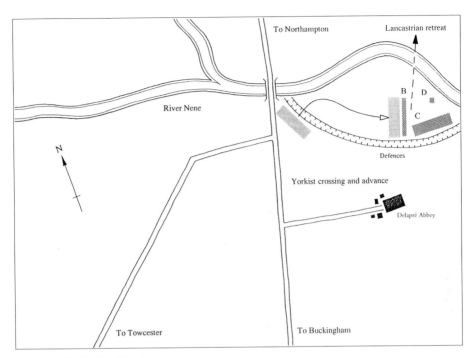

Fig 4.4   The Battle of Northampton

EPILOGUE TO THE BATTLE

Warwick rested at Northampton for three days after the battle before returning to London with the king. On his return to the capital news of his victory at Northampton quickly spread throughout the city. Lord Scales, who had remained besieged within the Tower of London, soon learned that relief for his beleaguered force would not be forthcoming, and therefore agreed terms with Warwick: on 19 July, in return for his life, he surrendered the Tower. His respite was short-lived, however – as he took a boat at Westminster to safety, he was set upon by the boatmen and killed. His body, stripped of clothing, was found dumped on the steps of St Mary's Church at Southwark.

The most unfortunate casualty of Northampton must have been Sir William Lucy. Sir William, who lived near Northampton, heard the artillery fire at the start of the battle and rushed to the king's assistance. But he arrived just as the battle finished, and it is said that a Yorkist knight (reputedly Sir John Stafford), who noticed his approach and recognized him as his rival, took the opportunity to kill him. The motive for this killing was rumoured to be that Stafford was in love with Sir William's wife, and therefore seized the chance to make her a widow, and then, after a respectable time in mourning, make her his wife. Indeed Stafford did marry the widow Lucy the following year.[3]

Profile of Margaret of Anjou on a medallion by Pietro di Milano, 1463

Undoubtedly, the key to the Yorkist victory was Lord Grey's betrayal. We may certainly conclude that this was pre-planned (why else would Warwick have ordered his men to spare all those wearing Grey's livery?). We do not know how Grey got a message to Warwick to plan the event, or why; what we do know is that Grey fared well under the Yorkist government in the years that followed. In 1463 he was made Treasurer of England, and in 1465 Earl of Kent. On top of this his son married into the Plantagenet family.

The disaster at Northampton was, to the Lancastrians, what Ludford Bridge had been to the Yorkists. However, the Lancastrians had their own 'Kingmaker' in Margaret of Anjou, and it would be to her that the remaining Lancastrians would look for guidance in the months to come.

CHAPTER FIVE

THE BATTLE OF WAKEFIELD
30 DECEMBER 1460

THE CAMPAIGN

Warwick returned to London with the king in his custody and his enemies scattered, and set about the task of governing the country. He needed Parliamentary support, and therefore he issued a writ on 30 July summoning Parliament to meet on 7 October. Although he held Henry, nevertheless Margaret of Anjou and her son Edward, Prince of Wales had eluded capture and travelled to Wales. With Margaret still at large, and Somerset still besieging Calais, Warwick and the Yorkist movement were far from being secure.

Warwick's next move was to return to Calais, where the garrison had nervously awaited the outcome of his invasion of England the previous June. With his return and the news of his victory at Northampton the morale of the Calais garrison increased. Consequently, Somerset concluded that his siege of Calais, lacking support from Lancastrian England, could no longer be maintained; his contest had become unwinnable. He therefore came to terms with Warwick: in return for his life and the freedom to go where he wished he would surrender Guines (whence he had conducted the siege) and disband his army. This being agreed, he left for sanctuary in France.

With Somerset and the threat to Calais removed, Warwick returned to England, where rumours concerning the fate of the king were rife. London gossip said that Henry had been murdered and that York or one of his sons would soon be made king in his place. These tales were fuelled by the Duke of York's absence: throughout these events he had remained in Ireland. The rumours ceased when York returned to England. He landed at Chester in the first week of September, and after a leisurely tour of the Welsh Marches proceeded to London. On entering the city he ordered that trumpets be played and his sword be held before him as he marched to Westminster, where the lords of the land were assembled for his arrival. It was clear to all that York had returned to England intent on becoming king. Entering Westminster

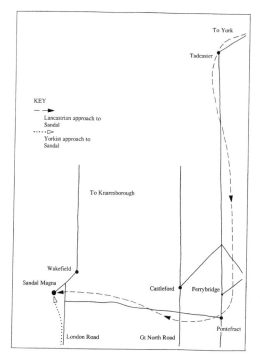

Fig 5.1   Preliminary Moves for the Battle of Wakefield

Hall he walked up to the throne and placed his hand upon it, then turned to the assembled lords. Instead of the rapturous welcome he had expected he was met with a stony silence that was eventually broken by the Archbishop of Canterbury, who approached him and asked if he would like to see the king.

Without the support from the lords for his claim to be king, York, his hopes dashed, set about the task of attaining the throne by legal means. Although his claim was strong in law, he had lost credibility by staying so long in Ireland. This, and the fact that the lords felt that he should honour the oath he had made to Henry in March 1452 not to raise arms against or harm the king, stopped the lords from siding with York and disposing of Henry despite the latter's sorry mismanagement of the country.

However, both the Lords and the Commons, meeting on 7 October, recognized York's position and agreed to a compromise. On 24 October 1460 Parliament passed the Act of Accord, in which it was agreed that Henry would remain king until his death, whereupon the crown would pass to York and his heirs. Though this met with the approval of both Yorkists and Parliament it certainly did not have the approval of Henry's wife, Margaret, who saw it as an affront to her child's birthright. While in Wales she ordered Jasper Tudor, Earl of Pembroke and a staunch Lancastrian and loyalist, to organize resistance to the Yorkist government in Wales. Then she took ship for Scotland in an attempt to gain allies at the Scottish court.

Meanwhile, the Duke of Somerset and the other Lancastrian nobles who had sought sanctuary in France sailed to England and travelled to join Sir Thomas Courtenay, Earl of Devon and those of Somerset's own men who had been under the command of Andrew Trollope during the duke's absence from England. The Lancastrians in the North had not lain idly by; they, too, had begun to organize resistance. Henry Percy, the Earl of Northumberland, together with his allies in the North, Lords Clifford and Roos, had been consistently harassing Yorkist settlements throughout the North, forcing the menfolk of the Yorkist strongholds to join with them or suffer the consequences.

Though the Yorkists knew Somerset had returned to England, his sudden march north with Sir Thomas Courtenay (whose father, also Thomas Courtenay, had previously been a staunch supporter of York) in early November took them by surprise. Somerset and Devon reached the city of York in mid-November and joined forces with Northumberland, Clifford and Roos. Their own ranks had swollen on the march north, having been joined by armies under the commands of the Earl of Wiltshire and the Duke of Exeter, and it was not long before stories reached the Yorkist government in London of a combined Lancastrian army numbering twenty thousand or more men-at-arms, waiting in the North.

York was forced to act. He sent his eldest son, Edward, Earl of March to Wales to suppress Jasper Tudor's Lancastrian uprising. This was Edward's first independent command. Warwick was ordered to remain in London to 'safeguard' the king and contain any French raids (common at that time in the South). York himself and Edmund, Earl of Rutland (York's second son), with the Earl of Salisbury and Thomas Neville (Salisbury's son), travelled north with six to eight thousand men-at-arms to tackle the Lancastrians who had reportedly made Pontefract Castle their base by that time. York's plan was to rendezvous with Lord John Neville (Salisbury's uncle, who had been commissioned to raise an army from the Yorkist shires in the North), and, with their combined forces, rout the Lancastrians in open battle.

York left London on 9 December. The journey was not without danger, and indeed his force was ambushed at Worksop by a contingent of Somerset's men under the command of Andrew Trollope. They managed to beat off the attack and reached Sandal Castle, York's stronghold to the south of Wakefield, on 21 December 1460. But on arrival at Sandal Castle they found it poorly prepared, the keeper of the castle having been prevented from collecting enough provisions for so large an army by the presence of Lancastrian forces. The Lancastrians, under the command of Henry Beaufort, Duke of Somerset, had taken up various positions in open order around the castle itself and the nearby village of Sandal Magna (see Fig. 5.2). To the north of Sandal Castle was Somerset himself with Thomas Courtenay, Earl of Devon. Nearby and also to the north was Sir Henry Percy, Earl of Northumberland; to the west, south of the River Calder, was Sir Henry Holland, Duke of Exeter, accompanied by the contingent of Somerset's men under the command of Andrew Trollope. South of their position, and west of Sandal, was Sir James Butler, Earl of Wiltshire. South of Sandal Castle itself was a great expanse of open land. John, Lord Clifford chose not to expose his army here, and encamped further to the east, south of Sandal Magna village. To the north-east of Sandal, within a great wooded area, encamped Lord Roos. Their combined armies did not amount to more than eighteen thousand men-at-arms, mainly pikemen, billmen and archers. The Yorkists, whose army had increased slightly with men from the local shires, but still numbered no more than eight or ten thousand men, were either directed to foraging patrols or garrison duties in or around the stronghold.

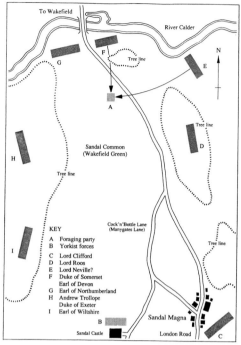

Fig 5.2   The Battle of Wakefield

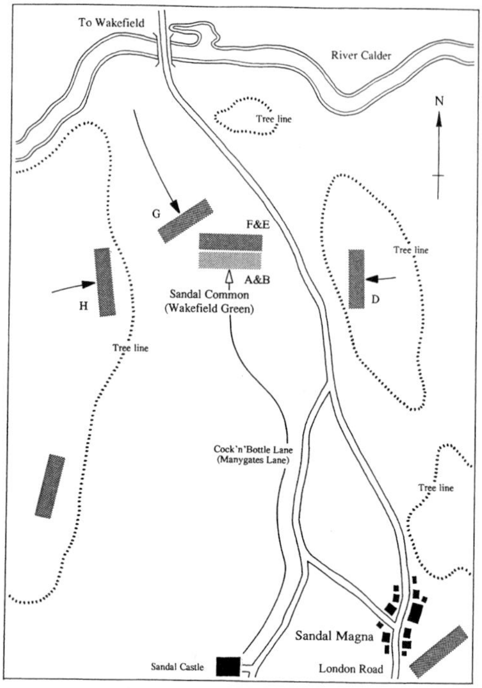

Fig. 5.3   The Battle of Wakefield

However, the Lancastrians, lacking siege artillery, were limited in their response to York at Sandal Castle. They decided to sit things out and await York's move, their plan being to engage him in open battle once he left the castle, and thus decide the issue. They taunted York daily, sending insulting messages to the effect that he was a coward to sit behind the walls of a castle and that he must be afraid of a woman to do so (a reference to Margaret of Anjou, actually at this time in Scotland). Whether York knew their intentions or not, he relied on his captains and military advisors who counselled him to do nothing until reinforcements arrived. He spent a miserable Christmas behind the walls, within the relative safety of the fortress.

THE BATTLE

On 30 December one of the many foraging parties sent out by York to gather food and information from the surrounding countryside was returning to Sandal when it came under attack by men under the command of the Earl of Devon and the Duke of Somerset, who had been encamped by the River Calder, south of Wakefield (Force F on Fig. 5.2). From his vantage point in the castle, York could clearly see the mêlée as it took place before him. Then, to the north-east of Sandal Common, from behind one of the large wooded areas which surrounded Sandal, there appeared a second force which quickly engaged itself in the skirmish (Force E on Fig. 5.2).

Sandal Castle, Wakefield. This was Richard's principal stronghold in Yorkshire. It was destroyed at the end of the English Civil War

Believing that this second army was a relieving force under the command of Lord John Neville (who had been commissioned to raise an army on York's behalf some time previously), which consisted of some four to eight thousand men-at-arms, York decided to take advantage of what he thought was a rear attack on Somerset and Devon. He mustered what troops were prepared within Sandal Castle, led them out of the castle gates along Cock 'n' Bottle Lane (now Manygates Lane), then the main London road, on to Sandal Common (now Wakefield Green), and marched north to engage what he believed to be an encircled Lancastrian force.

Most historians agree on the following points: firstly, that the foraging party, at this point located to the north of Sandal Common, indeed came under attack from a force under the command of the Earls of Devon and Somerset; and secondly, that the Duke of York, accompanied by his son Edmund, Earl of Rutland, Sir David Hall (York's top military advisor), and other prominent Yorkist captains, left Sandal Castle and travelled north to join in the engagement.

It is at this point, however, that controversy begins. Why did York leave the safety of his castle to risk a pitched battle with an enemy that he well knew outnumbered his own forces? There are two possible explanations. The first is that York believed, as already stated, that this second force under Lord John Neville was a relieving force for

Sandal, which had luckily arrived just as Somerset and Devon broke camp to attack the foraging party. This explanation assures that it was just unfortunate for York that he did not realize until too late that Neville had changed sides, and instead of going to the rescue of York's foraging party was in fact assisting in its destruction. The second explanation is based on certain unsubstantiated reports suggesting that the men under Trollope's command had dressed in the livery of the Earl of Warwick and appeared on the scene in an attempt to deceive York into believing that reinforcements had arrived. Accordingly, York left the safety of the fortress to give battle. There is little evidence to support this theory and the fact that the Earl of Salisbury, Warwick's father, was at York's side at the time leads us to believe that such a ploy would have failed anyway, as he would surely have recognized his own son's men and known of his proximity to the castle. Moreover, if Warwick had intended to leave London, he would surely have sent a messenger to York.

Whatever the reason, it was only when York reached the mêlée that he realized that something was amiss. However, proud individual that he was, York was not the type of man to turn tail and run; thinking that the entire Lancastrian force was before him, and that it appeared smaller than he had anticipated, he charged into it, leading his men from the front. The impetus of York's charge took the Lancastrians by surprise and their line almost broke. Indeed, the Lancastrians began to give ground and it was only the timely arrival of the Earl of Northumberland (Force G on Fig. 5.3), who had also been encamped to the north of Sandal Common, which halted the retreat.

It was at about this time that the Lancastrian forces encamped in and around Sandal realized that the confrontation between York's foraging party and the Lancastrian forces was turning into a pitched battle, and began mobilizing and advancing towards the fray. The first to arrive was Lord Roos, who appeared from the wooded area to the east. His men (Force D on Fig. 5.4) moved swiftly to engage the Yorkists on their right flank. With the arrival of Roos, and with York's casualties increasing all the time, the Yorkists slowly began to give ground, with York attempting to retreat in good order towards the castle, some half a mile to the south. Throughout the action York's position was monitored closely by the Earl of Salisbury and the remaining defenders in the castle, who could clearly see the deteriorating situation in which York found himself as it developed on the common before them. Mustering all the available men-at-arms in the castle, Salisbury, accompanied by his son Thomas Neville and the remaining Yorkist captains, sallied forth from the fortress along Cock 'n' Bottle Lane and hurried to his brother-in-law's assistance.

It was at about this time that men under the command of Andrew Trollope and the Duke of Exeter, approaching from the wooded area to the west (Force H on Fig. 5.4), charged York's left flank. Even against such overwhelming odds York managed to hold his army together and for a short time after Salisbury's arrival even halted the retreat. But as more and more Lancastrians arrived, York realized that he would soon be totally surrounded. Accordingly, he placed the care of his son Edmund in the hands of Sir Robert Aspall (formerly Edmund's tutor) and ordered them to flee the battlefield. The death blow came with the arrival of Lord Clifford's men (Force C on Fig. 5.5), who had been encamped south of Sandal Magna village and were therefore the last to arrive. Clifford himself did not join the mêlée but instead gave chase after Edmund and Sir Robert, having witnessed their flight from the field. Finally, totally

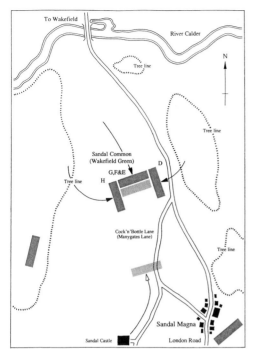

Fig 5.4   The Battle of Wakefield

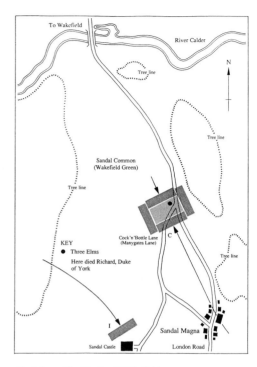

Fig 5.5   The Battle of Wakefield

surrounded, and with his army steadily weakening as casualties increased, York was unhorsed and received a sword wound to his knee. Unable to defend himself efficiently he took up position with his back to a clump of three elm trees by Cock 'n' Bottle Lane. And it was here, in sight of his ancestral home, and after refusing quarter, that Richard Plantagenet, Duke of York, met his death, hacked down under the crushing blows of the Lancastrians who surrounded him.

With York dead all effective Yorkist resistance ended. There then followed the customary flight of the vanquished, hotly pursued by the victors. It was at this point that the Earl of Wiltshire and his men (Force I on Fig. 5.5), who had failed to engage in the battle, took possession of Sandal Castle which had been left unprotected.

Salisbury was captured by a contingent of Andrew Trollope's men and taken to Pontefract Castle, where he was publicly beheaded the following day. More than half the Yorkist army – nearly three thousand men – died in the battle, among them some of the Yorkists' most experienced captains, including Sir David Hall, Sir John and Sir Hugh Mortimer, Sir Thomas Harrington and Sir Thomas Parr. Even Salisbury's son Thomas Neville did not survive the battle.

Local tradition holds that the bodies of the dead were thrown into a huge ditch dug in the field beyond that in which their leader was slain. That same night it began to snow, and in the words of one man who was searching for the body of his father: 'At midnight the kindly snow fell like a mantle on the dead and covered the battlefield with a blanket of white, which when it had finished gave no trace of what had gone before'.[1]

EPILOGUE TO THE BATTLE

There has long been controversy as to whether or not York was tricked at Wakefield; lack of written information is partly to blame for this. Shortly after Wakefield the victorious Lancastrians were themselves to suffer disastrous defeat at Towton, and as dead men tell no tales (nor chronicle them either), we shall never be certain of the facts that presented themselves to York that day and gave him reason to do battle. We do know, however, that York had many advisors with him: Sir David Hall, who had been with York at St Albans; Salisbury, too, who not only advised York but had his own military advisors as well; Sir Thomas Harrington and Sir Thomas Parr, both experienced soldiers who had fought at Blore Heath. With such men to counsel him we can conclude only that the situation must have looked favourable to the Yorkists. But we cannot be sure whether York left Sandal with all his men, or, as stated (and as the author believes), with only a proportion of them, the remainder being left behind under the command of the Earl of Salisbury. The nature of the battle itself may substantiate this belief. It was not a set-piece engagement. It started as a skirmish and only developed into a pitched battle as more participants arrived. The fact that the arrival of the various factions was so staggered (with Somerset, Devon and York

St Mary's Chapel on the Bridge at Wakefield

engaged at the very start, and Salisbury and Clifford arriving some two to three hours later) leads us to conclude that it took time to get the various participants roused from their camps and on the move. The fact that only half of York's men died in the battle leads us to believe that a fair proportion of his army remained on extensive foraging duties, and that when the mêlée started, York left Sandal with whatever force was armed and ready at the time and that Salisbury joined later when the remaining forces in Sandal Castle had been organized and when enough men had returned from foraging duties to be mustered for an armed response.

Salisbury, as already stated, was captured and executed. It is testimony to the hatred felt towards the Yorkist leaders that he was so summarily dispatched (even after it had been generally agreed that he would be held for ransom), and even the presence of his uncle, Lord John Neville, whose timely change of sides was the main reason for the Lancastrian victory, could not prevent this. (After the Battle of St Albans Lord Fauconberg, Salisbury's brother, who had fought for the Lancastrians, had been released unharmed by the victorious Yorkists largely because of his family connections.) This hatred towards York and Salisbury was compounded by the presence of Sir Henry Percy, Earl of Northumberland, Sir Henry Beaufort, Duke of Somerset and John, Lord Clifford, each of whose fathers had been killed at St Albans fighting a Yorkist army commanded by Salisbury and York.

Edmund, Earl of Rutland and Sir Robert Aspall were captured by Lord Clifford at Wakefield Bridge (the bridge and its medieval chapel, with a Victorian reconstructed front, are still visible today), and with the words 'By God's blood thy father slew mine and so will I do thee and all thy kin', Clifford drew his sword and slew them both.[2] This murderous act, in conjunction with Salisbury's execution, set a precedent of summary killings that would follow after every battle, no matter who the victor, for the rest of the war. The heads of York, Salisbury and Rutland were impaled on spikes on Micklegate Bar in the city of York when the Lancastrians returned there shortly after the battle, so that, as many Lancastrians put it, 'York could overlook York'. A paper crown was placed upon York's head in mocking reference to his claim to the throne.[3]

York's eldest son, Edward (later Edward IV), later built a memorial, a simple cross enclosed by a picket fence, to his father at the site of his death, and it was written into the terms of the lease that the tenant who occupied the land must maintain the memorial in the years to come. The condition was honoured, and the memorial survived intact until the English Civil War some 200 years later when it was destroyed, together with the castle, by soldiers of the Parliamentarian army.

In 1897 local residents built a new memorial, in the form of a stone monument decorated with carved white roses. It bears these words: Richard Plantagenet, Duke of York, fighting for the cause of the white rose fell on this spot in the Battle of Wakefield December 30th 1460. The monument can still be seen today, standing within the boundary wall of the local school which now occupies the site.

CHAPTER SIX

THE BATTLE OF MORTIMER'S CROSS 2 FEBRUARY 1461

THE CAMPAIGN

While the Duke of York had spent a miserable Christmas within the walls of Sandal Castle, his eldest son, Edward, spent the new year at Gloucester. The young Earl of March (aged only 17) had left London the previous December and travelled towards Wales on his first independent command with the intention of suppressing reported uprisings inspired by Lancastrian sympathizers and bringing Wales back under the reins of Yorkist control.

In the middle of January he received news of the disaster at Wakefield and the death of his father, brother, the Earl of Salisbury and the young Thomas Neville. After learning the grim news of the fate of the Yorkist army at Sandal, and realizing the potential threat that Warwick must by now be facing, he prepared to return to London with troops he had raised in the Welsh Marches and confer with Warwick to decide what would now be the best course of action. In his retinue were a number of staunch Yorkist supporters, many of whom had served with his father, among them Walter Devereux (the Duke of York's steward of his Welsh lordship since 1452), Sir William Herbert of Raglan (who had been York's steward in Caerleon and Usk), and Sir William's brother, Sir Richard Herbert. Also present were some new recruits to the cause: John Milewater and the young Lord Audley (whose father had been defeated and killed by the Yorkist army at Blore Heath, but who had defected to the Yorkists the previous year), Lord Grey of Wilton and the future Yorkist Earl of Devon, Humphrey Stafford).

As Edward prepared to travel east, news of a hostile army to the north, including the Lancastrian Owen Tudor, caused him to change his plans. Owen had been a squire at the court of Henry V, and after Henry's death in 1422 had become clerk to the wardrobe of Henry's widow, Catherine of France. In 1429 Tudor married Catherine in secret, and they had two sons, Edmund, Earl of Richmond (father of the future Henry VII) and Jasper, Earl of Pembroke. As Henry VI's stepfather, Owen was Margaret's

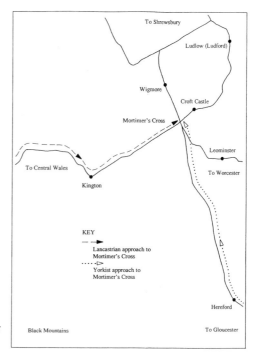

Fig 6.1   Preliminary Moves for the Battle of
Mortimer's Cross

natural ally, and when she had reached Wales, following Henry's defeat at Northampton, she had encouraged him to organize resistance against the Yorkist government before she took ship to gain allies for Henry VI in the Scottish court. It was Owen's son Jasper, Earl of Pembroke who was to lead this resistance, and his army consisted mainly of followers from the Tudor estates at Pembroke and Carmarthen. He was not alone. Sir James Butler, Earl of Wiltshire had travelled to Wales by ship, landed in the south-west and moved towards Worcester with a large force of mercenaries, mainly Bretons, French and Irishmen. He had then joined forces with Pembroke, and together the two were marching on Hereford when Edward received news of their advance.

We do not know whether Edward's march on Hereford was made in order to stop the Lancastrian army in Wales from advancing into England and uniting with Margaret's force, or whether the threat of a Lancastrian army to his rear while he was marching to London together with his lack of intelligence concerning the location of the victorious Lancastrian army from Wakefield, was a situation he simply could not ignore. Whatever the reason, Edward turned his army north from Hereford and marched 17 miles to intercept Pembroke's army at Mortimer's Cross, not far from the Yorkist castle and estate at Wigmore, on or about 2 February.

Edward approached Mortimer's Cross along the old Roman road which leads into central Wales. He deployed his army to the west of the River Lugg in a generally north–south line either side of the road at the point where it was crossed by the Wigmore–Hereford road (*see* Fig. 6.2). His army consisted mainly of Welshmen, retainers of the Herbert brothers and his own supporters and numbered no more than

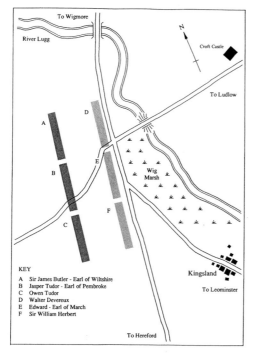

Fig 6.2   The Battle of Mortimer's Cross

eleven thousand men-at-arms. The army formed up into three separate wards, with the right flank or vanguard commanded by Walter Devereux, the centre by Edward himself, and the left flank or rearguard by Sir William Herbert. There was no field artillery.

The Lancastrians deployed for battle early on the morning of 2 February, with a force of some eight thousand men-at-arms in a north–south line facing the Yorkists. The Lancastrian left flank was under the command of Sir James Butler, Earl of Wiltshire, the centre under Jasper Tudor, Earl of Pembroke, and the right flank under the joint command of Owen Tudor and Sir John Throckmorton.

THE BATTLE

For several hours the two armies squared up to each other, and some time passed during which both adjusted their lines. Finally, at about midday, the Lancastrians made the first move. The whole of their line began to advance. The Earl of Wiltshire's army, on the Lancastrian left, engaged with Edward's right flank, while the Earl of Pembroke engaged Edward's centre. However, the Lancastrian right flank under Owen Tudor, instead of marching forward to engage the Yorkists' left, tried to encircle it, and moved in a wide arc towards Kingsland in an attempt to approach it from the rear.

These opening moves had mixed results for the Lancastrians. The Earl of Wiltshire, commanding the more experienced and professional mercenaries, managed after a fierce struggle to push Edward's right flank back across the road, with its rear to the

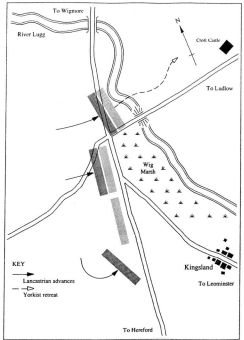

Fig 6.3   The Battle of Mortimer's Cross

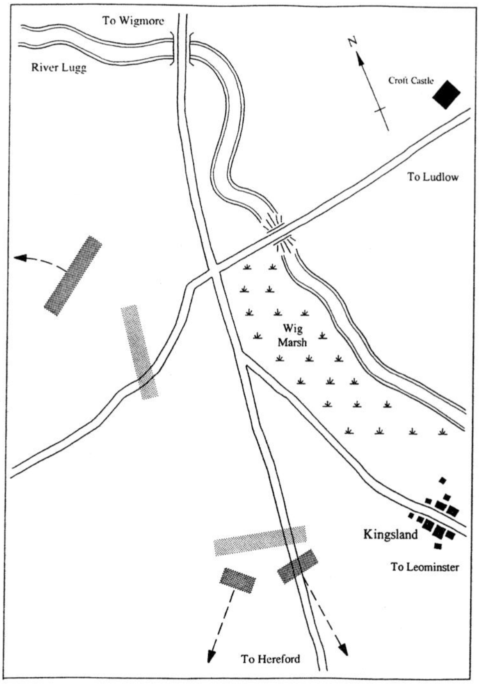

Fig 6.4   The Battle of Mortimer's Cross

river, so that Devereux's force of relatively inexperienced men, left with little chance of recovery, broke and scattered across the river towards Croft Castle (see Fig. 6.3). Pembroke, however, was less fortunate. His force clashed with Edward's, and for some time it seemed that neither side would yield, but gradually Pembroke's men began to give ground, and as the Yorkists, confidently led by the young Edward, gained the upper hand, the Lancastrians suddenly broke and scattered westward. Owen Tudor, in his attempt to encircle the Yorkists, exposed the left flank of his army to the front ranks of Herbert's force (see Fig. 6.4). Herbert was quick to take advantage of this, and thrust his men forward into Tudor's flank. The effect of this attack was devastating: Tudor's men, already in open order on the move, could offer little resistance, and though Tudor tried to rally and reorganize them, his attempt to turn them failed, and they quickly broke and scattered, mainly towards Hereford.

Meanwhile, the Earl of Wiltshire, having by now regrouped his mercenaries, tried in vain to bring them to close quarters with Edward's centre. By this time Edward had all but beaten off Pembroke's attack, and with Tudor's army in the process of being attacked by Herbert, it was clear the battle was almost certainly lost for the Lancastrians. Reputedly, on learning this, the mercenaries calmly sat down to await the outcome of the closing moves.

Half an hour later it was all over (see Fig. 6.4). Pembroke's forces had broken and retreated westward, while Tudor's had been routed southward. As for Wiltshire's mercenaries, to his despair they left the field. With no victors to pay their wages they must look elsewhere for their keep.

Showing the triple sun phenomenon, shining through three golden crowns. Edward is saying: 'Lord, what will ye that I do?'

EPILOGUE TO THE BATTLE

The Earl of Pembroke made good his escape, as did again the Earl of Wiltshire, perhaps the greatest escaper of his day! However, many Welsh Lancastrians died on the battlefield. The jubilant Yorkists pursued the remnants of Owen Tudor's army all the way to Hereford, where after a brief fight Owen Tudor and the remaining Lancastrian captains were captured. Tudor, his second-in-command Sir John Throckmorton, and eight other nobles were, on Edward's own orders, executed in the market square. It is said that Tudor did not believe that he would be executed until he actually saw the axe and block. He is quoted as saying: 'That head shall lie on the stock that was wont to lie on Queen Catherine's lap'. With these few words he went to his death. Afterwards a mad woman placed his head on the top step of the market cross, washed the blood from his face and combed his hair.[1]

After the battle had ended Edward claimed that a meteorological phenomenon – three rising suns – seen at dawn on the day of the battle, had been a good omen and a sure sign of victory. So convincing did he find the sign that from that day onward

Edward took as his emblem a sunburst, thus creating his favourite badge, 'the golden sun of York'.[2] Whatever Edward saw on the morning of the battle must have appeared in a very graphic form (although a meteorological phenomenon is not out of the question, it was more probably the reflection of daybreak on the wetlands to the east of Edward's position). However, to the young and impressionable Earl of March, now indeed the new Duke of York, doubtless he believed it to be a sign from God that not only was this the morning of a new day but also the beginning of a new age. Had followers of the Yorkist cause been able to see two months into the future they would probably have agreed with him.

CHAPTER SEVEN

THE BATTLE OF ST ALBANS 17 FEBRUARY 1461

THE CAMPAIGN

While Richard, Duke of York had marched north towards Sandal, and Edward, Earl of March had travelled to Wales, the Earl of Warwick remained in London to protect the king and to guard the south coast against possible French raids. It was rumoured that France was set to invade the Isle of Wight, and so he commissioned Geoffrey Gate, its governor, to construct a fleet to guard against this possibility. Although the French never made such a move, Gate was fortunate enough to capture Edmund Beaufort, brother of the Duke of Somerset, when Beaufort's ship was captured by Gate's fleet. Afterwards, because it was felt to be the safest place to put him, he was given into the security of the Calais garrison.

Warwick spent Christmas 1460 in London, where early in the new year he received news of events at Sandal. It is said that though he was physically stricken with grief at the loss of his father, brother, uncle and cousin, within a few days of receiving the news he had set about gathering his forces in readiness to meet the Lancastrian horde, which had united with Queen Margaret's Scottish mercenaries at York on or about 20 January and was now advancing south. The Lancastrian army, flushed with the success of Wakefield, was an ill-disciplined combination of Scottish and French mercenaries, Welshmen and northerners who brought great destruction to the towns through which they passed on their steady advance towards London. The towns of Grantham, Stamford, Peterborough, Huntingdon and Royston, all located on the Great North Road, suffered particularly heavily, because of their Yorkist connections. News of this destruction went before the Lancastrians, and in London panic set in. The citizens, it is said, began boarding up their homes and burying their possessions; the streets became deserted as an air of fear settled over the city. But the dread this northern horde brought upon the South worked in favour of the Yorkists. Though Warwick had already sent the Duke of Norfolk to East Anglia to raise men-at-arms, and Lord Bonville and Viscount Bouchier into southern England to do the same, great numbers

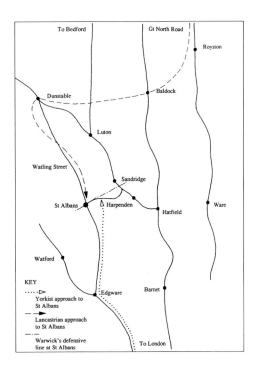

Fig 7.1   Preliminary Moves for the Battle of
St Albans

of armed men had begun to arrive daily in London, without waiting for a summons, in order to join the one man whom they believed could save the South: the Earl of Warwick.

Warwick himself seemed in no rush to leave the capital, and though reports stated that Margaret's army was only a week's march from the city, and even that all the Yorkist leaders had reunited in London with their retinues, before the end of January Warwick made time to have his brother John Neville created Lord Montagu. At the same time, and with great pageantry, he elected himself, Sir John Wenlock, Lord Bonville and Sir Thomas Kyriel to the Order of the Garter.

By 12 February Warwick was at last ready to leave the city. He commanded an exceptionally large army, numbering some twenty-five thousand men-at-arms. His main supporters were Sir John Mowbray, Duke of Norfolk, Sir William Fitzalan, Earl of Arundel and Sir John de la Pole, Earl of Suffolk. Even the Duke of Burgundy had sent a contingent of handgunners to London to help the Yorkist cause. Also among the Yorkist ranks were Lords Montagu, Fauconberg, Bonville and Berners, Sir John Wenlock, and Captain Lovelace, a survivor of the Battle of Wakefield who had brought to Warwick in London the news of his father's death.

The Lancastrian army was equally impressive, with Queen Margaret and her son Prince Edward at the head of an army of more than twenty-five thousand men-at-arms under the command of Sir Henry Beaufort, Duke of Somerset. Exact figures are impossible to calculate since much of the Lancastrian army was no more than a rabble, but in its ranks were included the retinues of Sir Henry Percy, Earl of Northumberland,

Sir Henry Holland, Duke of Exeter, Sir John Talbot, Earl of Shrewsbury, and Lords Roos, Grey of Codnor, Clifford, Greystoke, Wells and Willoughby. They marched slowly southwards, with the white ostrich feather of the young Prince of Wales as their emblem. Upon reaching Royston, however, the Lancastrian army suddenly turned west and headed for Dunstable. There is some confusion as to why they did this. What is known is that Warwick reached St Albans on 13 February; what is not known is whether the Lancastrians turned west to take up a better position from which to attack Warwick or whether Warwick heard of their change in direction before leaving London and instead of marching up the Great North Road to intercept them made for St Albans. What is certain is that Warwick was not sure exactly where the Lancastrians were: he was still receiving reports of Lancastrian troop movements south of Royston (though these reports were probably of breakaway contingents of looting mercenaries). Because of this Warwick decided to opt for the more defensive tactic of deploying his army over a 2 mile front slightly north of St Albans in a line that covered all main roads leading south.

The opening Yorkist positions are depicted in Fig. 7.2. The left flank of Warwick's army, under the command of Lord Montagu, Warwick's brother, was split into two groups: a garrison of Yorkist archers in the town of St Albans, and to the north of their position, on Barnard's Heath, the major part of Montagu's command, including a contingent of men from Kent under the control of their Captain Lovelace. To the north of Barnard's Heath (not shown on the map), at an area known as 'No Man's Land', were the Yorkist centre and reserve under the command of the Earl of Warwick himself. One mile to his north, beyond the town of Sandridge, was the Yorkist right flank led by the Duke of Norfolk. This extended front was ultimately to be the Yorkists' undoing, as communications between the various contingents along the network of narrow lanes were at best difficult.

Having arrived at St Albans on 13 February, Warwick had spent the subsequent three days reinforcing the Yorkist position and setting traps for the Lancastrians. There were also to be seen, for the first time in England, some new military inventions. The Burgundian handgunners had weapons that could shoot iron-tipped arrows or pellets of lead. The Yorkists made great use of nets across gaps in the hedgerows; these nets, each being about 24 ft in length and 4 ft wide, could not be passed over by man or beast without injury from nails attached to every second knot, which stood upright when the nets were in place. The archers had barricades with covered openings that could be tilted horizontally to allow them to fire and placed back vertically to protect those behind them. Devices known as caltraps (which no matter how they were laid on the ground always had a spike facing upwards) were spread abundantly over the routes the Lancastrians were expected to take; a hazard which was to men and cavalry what mines are to infantry today.

It would seem at first glance that the well dug-in Yorkist army must have the edge over the Lancastrians. Warwick, however, was still unaware of the exact location of the queen's army. Though he sent out scouts they failed to locate the enemy, so Warwick, believing that her army was further away than it actually was, remained settled in this defensive position.

The first indication that something was amiss came late in the evening of 16 February, when Warwick received news that the Yorkist outpost at Dunstable,

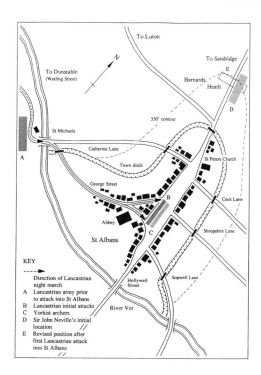

Fig 7.2   The Battle of St Albans

containing two hundred men-at-arms under the command of Sir Edward Poynings, had been overrun by the Lancastrians earlier in the day and that every man in Poyning's command had been killed or captured. Because the accuracy of this report was questionable, and because Warwick believed that the Lancastrian army had not yet reached Dunstable, he decided not to act upon the information. This was perhaps the greatest miscalculation the earl was to make in the entire campaign, and it greatly affected the events that followed.

THE BATTLE

The information concerning the Lancastrian attack on Dunstable that Warwick had received that evening was in fact correct. After Queen Margaret's attack on the town her army stopped a while before beginning a night march of 12 miles down Watling Street towards St Albans (*see* Fig. 7.2). They arrived at St Michael's Church on the outskirts of St Albans, west of the Ver river, some time between 6 and 7 o'clock on the morning of 17 February. After another short break, during which the Lancastrians made their final plans for an attack, the advanced guard of the Lancastrian army, led by Andrew Trollope, moved down George Street into St Albans. Their arrival took the Yorkists completely by surprise: even the gates on George Street at the town ditch had not been closed; apparently the gates were not even manned. The Lancastrians moved on into the market square, where they came upon the Yorkist archers, who though taken by surprise, managed to stem the Lancastrian advance in the narrow confines of the streets. After a fierce fight in which the Lancastrians suffered heavy casualties, the Yorkist archers managed to push the Lancastrians back the same way as they had arrived, along George Street (*see* Fig. 7.2).

Alarmed at the unexpected arrival of the Lancastrians at such an early hour, especially as the last reports of their whereabouts had placed them some 12 miles away at Dunstable the previous night, somehow the Yorkist leaders had now to turn their battleline to confront the enemy: their current positions were facing the wrong way. The first group to react was the remainder of the left flank under the command of Lord Montagu; their location on Barnard's Heath meant they were the first to realize that the Lancastrians were upon them. Montagu roused his men from their camp and brought them away from their prepared positions and into formation on a line crossing the Sandridge road in a roughly east–west direction, facing St Albans (*see* Fig. 7.2).

The Lancastrians, having been forced back as far as St Michael's Church, held a hurried council of war at which it was decided to send scouts to discover whether there were any unguarded routes into the town. As Warwick had managed to find one in the first battle some five years earlier, so now did the Lancastrians, the scouts returning with the news that Catherine Lane was unguarded. The Lancastrian field commander, the Duke of Somerset, ordered another attack into the town using this route as well as George Street in a pincer movement to trap the defenders (*see* Fig. 7.3). This second attack caught the Yorkist archers, now assembled in the market square, on both sides, and though greatly outnumbered they offered a resolute defence worthy of their reputation. However, they were eventually overpowered, and with them out of the way the Lancastrian commanders ordered the remainder of their army into the town.

With the successful occupation of St Albans the first part of Margaret's operation was complete. The Lancastrians took time off to reorganize and refresh themselves: they had been on the road some 24 hours and badly needed to rest before attacking the Yorkists for the third time that day. But by noon the queen's army was facing the remainder of Warwick's left flank, which having by now turned towards St Albans, had become the Yorkist front line (*see* Fig. 7.3). Lord Montagu, commander of the Yorkists on Barnard's Heath, sent a message to Warwick asking for the men from Warwick's centre and reserve to be sent to his assistance with all possible haste, since the entire Lancastrian army was about to assault his position. However, the tall hedgerows and narrow lanes that were so important to the Yorkist defensive position proved to be a hindrance to Montagu's messengers, and it took them some time to locate Warwick and give him the message. Shortly after noon the Lancastrians advanced on Montagu's position. Montagu, who had drawn up all his men in line, put up a bitter defence, and it took some time for the numerically superior Lancastrians to make any impact. But under sheer weight of numbers Montagu's line began slowly to give as his men were gradually pushed back down the slope on which St Albans is situated, and on to Barnard's Heath itself (*see* Fig. 7.4).

It was early in the afternoon before Warwick learnt of the attack on St Albans and the precarious situation his brother must now be facing. He at once ordered an advance towards the town but once again the narrow roads and hedgerows proved a hindrance to the Yorkist infantry, and their advance towards the town was pitifully slow. In his haste to reach the mêlée Warwick ordered his cavalry to leave the infantry

A contemporary drawing of fifteenth-century mercenaries

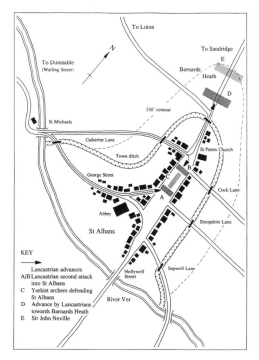

Fig 7.3   The Battle of St Albans

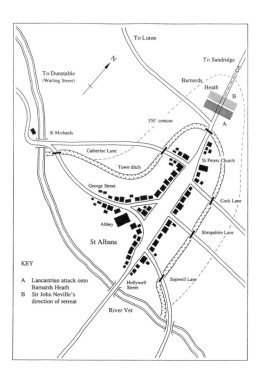

Fig 7.4   The Battle of St Albans

behind, and personally led the charge across country in an attempt to reach Barnard's Heath before it was too late. Meanwhile, Montagu's situation was reaching crisis point; by this time his army had fought alone for several hours without reinforcement, but the many anxious Yorkist glances eastwards offered no sign of salvation. Then, just as Montagu must have thought the situation was at its worst, treachery raised its monstrous head and cast a death blow on Montagu's position: Captain Lovelace chose that moment to change sides and throw in his lot with the Lancastrians. With the loss of the men from Kent, the already battered Yorkist morale sank and their line broke.

When Warwick finally reached the heath it was too late: the Yorkist left wing was routed, his brother had been captured, and the Lancastrians were advancing in his direction. Although there were still pockets of Yorkist resistance on the heath, Warwick ordered his cavalry to retreat, and he returned to his infantry. His plan was to rally his troops out in 'No Man's Land', form a line, and offer resistance to the Lancastrian army, by now in hot pursuit of the fleeing Yorkists. It was now early evening and news of the defeats earlier in the day had by this time reached the columns of Yorkist infantry still marching towards St Albans. This, and the scenes of panic they witnessed as they marched past the survivors, sapped the morale of the Yorkist infantry, and many of the rank and file took advantage of the night, which was now drawing in, and the absence of the Earl of Warwick (who had not yet returned to their position), to disappear. Though the Earl of Warwick managed to rally some of his troops (a remarkable achievement, all things considered), he found it prudent to leave the field of battle with what forces he had left rather than stay to fight the Lancastrians the next morning.

In all the Yorkists lost some four thousand men slain upon the field that day and the Lancastrians half that number, but the greatest loss to the Earl of Warwick personally was his pride: he had suffered his first defeat in battle.

EPILOGUE TO THE BATTLE

As night descended upon the battlefield the rout and subsequent pursuit of the remaining Yorkists continued. It was at about this time that King Henry (who had accompanied the Yorkist army to St Albans) was liberated by the Lancastrians. The king had been found peacefully seated under a tree, deserted by all except Sir Thomas Kyrill and Lord Bonville (who had stayed at his side only after reassurances from Henry about their future safety). He was then taken to the more dignified quarters of the abbey where he was reunited with his queen and his son Prince Edward. The king then formally knighted his son, who in turn knighted Andrew Trollope and many others. Trollope accented the honour with mock modesty, claiming that he did not deserve such a reward – he had slain only fifteen men as a result of an injury inflicted by a caltrap during the battle. After this there followed the by now customary trial and execution of the captured enemy leaders. Lord Bonville and Sir Thomas Kyrill were sentenced to death – despite Henry's promise of safety – on the instructions of Queen Margaret (who gave the honour of issuing the order to her eight-year-old son, Prince Edward), and were taken out and summarily executed there and then.

Lord Montagu's life was spared, however, largely because the Duke of Somerset feared for the life of his own brother, by now a 'guest' of the Earl of Warwick in Calais; the execution of the Earl of Warwick's brother would surely have meant his own brother's death too. In consequence Montagu was sent into captivity in the city of York.

The king was approached by the abbot of St Albans Abbey who asked Henry to call a halt to the plundering of the town by Margaret's Scottish mercenaries. But the king was by now no more than a spectator to the events going on around him, and was powerless to stop the pillage that had started even before the end of the battle. It is fair to say that throughout the campaign the royal army was under the command of the queen, who in turn left the actual tactics and control of its movements to the Duke of Somerset. It is also true that Andrew Trollope had been a major influence on any decisions made by Somerset.

The reason for Lovelace's defection stemmed from the Battle of Wakefield. Apparently he had been captured by the Lancastrians at Sandal but had not escaped as first thought. His life had been spared on condition that he betrayed the Yorkist movements, and it was information from him about Warwick's plans and positions that had caused Queen Margaret to change direction at Royston, march on Dunstable, and from there launch a flank attack on Warwick's positions at St Albans. However, this betrayal was confirmed only by people close to Warwick himself, and it has been suggested that Lovelace, a man about whom little is known either before or after the battle, was used as a scapegoat to cover for Warwick's disastrous mismanagement of the

St Albans campaign. Indeed, some historians believe that the story of Lovelace's actions was no more than clever Yorkist propaganda to cover up their errors in the battle, and even that Lovelace himself was simply a figment of Yorkist imagination!

It is rumoured that Warwick left his brother to fend for himself and fled the field fearing for his own life. This may be discounted for two reasons: first, it does not accord with what we know of Warwick's character, and second, his absence from the thick of the fighting was much more probably an attempt by him to muster the centre and right flank of his army into a position from which he could resist the Lancastrian onslaught. The fact that no Yorkist leaders (apart from the nobles executed after the battle) were slain is testament to the fact that poor communications between the Yorkist ranks meant that the greater part of the Yorkist army, and the earl himself, never came into battle.

CHAPTER EIGHT

THE BATTLE OF TOWTON 29 MARCH 1461

THE CAMPAIGN

On 19 February Edward Plantagenet (now calling himself Duke of York), heard of Warwick's defeat at St Albans, and with great haste began moving his army eastwards from Wales towards London. If he had moved as swiftly a few days earlier, he might have been in a position to save Montagu's force. However, he joined forces with Warwick on 22 February. The exact meeting place is not known, but is believed to have been either Chipping Norton or Burford in the Cotswolds. Four days later, on 26 February, Edward, Warwick and their army marched into the capital. They were well received by the Londoners, who cheered as the young Duke of York entered the city. The outcome of the second Battle of St Albans did not have the military consequences at first feared, but it did, however, create a whole new political perspective; since July 1460 the Yorkists had had the king himself in their custody, which gave them, through Henry's name, legal authority in the land. However, all this had now changed: without control of the king's person, the Yorkists could not assume the obedience of his subjects.

This fact explains Edward's accession to the throne. In the light of current events, the Yorkists needed their own king. The young duke was, as quoted by one chronicler 'by the grace of God, of England, France and Ireland a true and just heir', which indeed he was under the Act of Accord of 1460.[1]

On Wednesday 4 March, after hearing a Te Deum in St Paul's Cathedral, Edward made his way to the Palace of Westminster, where in the Great Hall the king's robes were placed upon him and he took the oath before those assembled; he was then formally acclaimed King of England. The official coronation was postponed until later, as there were more pressing issues to deal with – mainly a Lancastrian army with its own king at its head on the march somewhere north of the capital. Edward's popularity was at this point at its highest, largely as a result of clever Yorkist propaganda; from every quarter people flocked to his banner.

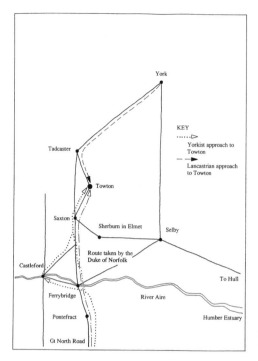

Fig 8.1   Preliminary Moves for the Battle of Towton

On 6 March the young Yorkist king issued two proclamations: first, he called upon thirty-three English counties to accept him as king and to offer no help to his adversaries; second, he announced that any followers of Henry who submitted within ten days would receive pardon, with the exception of men listed by name, and those who enjoyed an income of more than 100 marks a year. This last move was a clever attempt at winning the support of the common people and isolating the Lancastrian lords.

Meanwhile, the Lancastrian army, having rescued King Henry from Warwick at St Albans, had become virtually immobilized because of his chronic indecision – and his army would not move without a royal command. When a decision was finally made the order was given to advance towards the capital. The road to London was open but Henry's army stopped at Barnet while negotiations with the Londoners for entry into the city proceeded. Nevertheless, even after assurances by the Lancastrians that the capital would not be plundered, and the withdrawal of the army to Dunstable in an attempt to appease the Londoners, the gates of the city remained firmly closed against them. With this Queen Margaret advised the king to retreat to the safety of the Lancastrian heartlands in the North. The actual date of the withdrawal to Dunstable is unknown, but it must have been before 26 February, as this was the date on which Edward and his army marched unchallenged into London. Meanwhile, the Lancastrian army moved slowly northwards, plundering as they went, and after several days' march crossed the River Aire and made camp at and around the city of York.

On the day after Edward's coronation, Sir John Mowbray, the ailing Duke of

Edward IV, *c.* 1516

Norfolk, left London and travelled to his homeland of East Anglia to raise troops on Edward's behalf. Likewise, Robert Horne and John Fogge travelled to Kent for the same purpose. On 7 March Warwick left London for his estates in the Midlands. On his way he travelled through Coventry, where he had the good fortune to capture the two illegitimate sons of Henry Holland, Duke of Exeter, whom he believed had been personally responsible for the execution of his father, the Earl of Salisbury, at Pontefract Castle. His vengeance was swift. Both were beheaded.

On 11 March Lord Fauconberg left London at the head of an army made up of men from the Welsh Marches and his own followers from Kent. This force was to become the vanguard of Edward's army, which left London with the Yorkist King at its head on 13 March. Edward's own force contained not only the Burgundian handgunners, but also a contingent of men-at-arms supplied by the Duke of Burgundy, under the banner of the Dauphin of France.

On 18 March Edward arrived at Cambridge. His advance was deliberately slow to allow his captains in the field, recruiting men-at-arms on his behalf, to catch up and unite with him. Even so, it was not until he had crossed the River Trent that Warwick and Fauconberg effected a union with Edward's army. The Duke of Norfolk had so far failed to arrive, though a message was received by Edward that Norfolk was advancing towards his position. The decision was made to press on without him. With Warwick now leading the vanguard they arrived at Pontefract on the morning of Friday 27 March. Scouts sent out by the Yorkists came back with reports that the Lancastrian army (under the command of the 25-year-old Duke of Somerset) had taken up a position north of the River Aire on a small plateau between the villages of Saxton and Towton, some 15 miles south-west of York.

Later that same day Warwick and the advance guard occupied the crossing over the River Aire at Ferrybridge. The crossing was not taken easily, the north bank being held by a small but determined force of Lancastrians, and Warwick had to force the crossing via the bridge, which had been destroyed by Lancastrian forces on their way to York several days earlier. Warwick's men had to use planks to bridge the gaps and in doing so his men suffered many casualties; the biting cold of the river was to claim as many lives as the Lancastrian archers. When the Lancastrians retreated Warwick set his men to repairing the bridge, and by evening, with the bridge rebuilt, Warwick had established a camp on the north bank of the river. However, his labours had not gone unnoticed, and the following morning his camp came under attack by a large force of Lancastrians led by Sir John Clifford and Sir John Neville (the Earl of Westmorland's brother, Warwick's great-uncle), who had left the main Lancastrian force and under cover of nightfall moved into a position to ambush Warwick's camp just before dawn. Surprise was total. Lord Fitzwalter, Sir John Radcliffe, Warwick's second-in-command at the camp, was mortally wounded while trying to rally his troops in the confusion of the attack. He died a week later. After a fierce struggle Warwick managed to lead the surviving Yorkists back across the bridge to safety, in the process receiving an arrow wound to the leg.

Their retreat back to the main Yorkist position at Pontefract was chaotic, and was seen as a bad omen by the rank and file of Edward's army. It was at this point that Warwick, aware of the growing dissent within the Yorkist ranks, and fearing that the entire Lancastrian army was upon them, in an attempt to restore the Yorkist morale reputedly drew his sword and, with the words, 'Flee if you will but I will tarry with he who will tarry with me', slew his own horse. By this gesture he hoped to prove to the men around him that he was prepared, as they should be, to fight or die. In the event, although Warwick did not know it at the time, the Lancastrians never ventured further south than the river.[2]

By midday on 28 March Edward's army had reached the bridge, but Lord Clifford had totally destroyed the repairs made to it the previous day and was holding the north bank in force. Warwick, remembering the cost of his attack over the river, and perhaps having learnt from Queen Margaret's flank attack at St Albans, despatched his uncle Lord Fauconberg, with a large body of mounted archers, to travel 3 miles upriver to Castleford, where they could cross the ford unhindered. Clifford was not without his own spies, and soon got wind of Fauconberg's manoeuvre. Realizing that his position would soon be overrun he began to withdraw towards the main Lancastrian position at Towton. However, Fauconberg was too quick for him, and his cavalry's speedy advance caught Clifford's force in the open south of Dintingdale. There then followed a fierce struggle in which Lord Clifford was killed, felled by an arrow through the neck. Sir John Neville (the turncoat of Sandal) was also to die in the retreat, together with most of the Lancastrian force (*see* Fig. 8.2).

Shortly after this Edward began to move across the river, and by late evening had managed to transport his entire army north of the Aire. They made camp a little south of Saxton village and prepared to spend a cold night, with food in short supply, bivouacked less than a mile from the Lancastrian position.

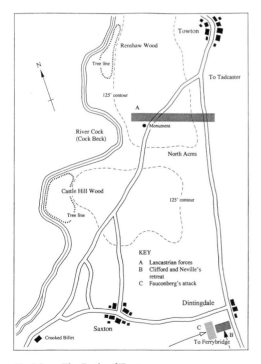

Fig 8.2   The Battle of Towton

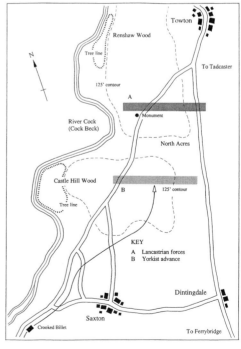

Fig 8.3   The Battle of Towton

THE BATTLE

The following morning was grey and bitter, and the snow began to fall and blow into the faces of the Yorkists as they stirred from their camp and advanced northward towards the Lancastrians, who had formed up in line about half a mile south of Towton village at a point where the windings of the River Cock narrowed their front.

The Lancastrians, under the command of the Duke of Somerset (the king, queen and prince having remained in York), had among their ranks most of the surviving nobility of England. The banners of Sir Henry Percy, Earl of Northumberland, Sir James Butler, Earl of Wiltshire, Sir Henry Stafford, Duke of Buckingham, Sir Henry Holland, Duke of Exeter, Sir Thomas Courtenay, Earl of Devon and Sir John Talbot, Earl of Shrewsbury were held high above their retinues as they grimly awaited the arrival of the young 'pretender' Edward of Rouen, self-styled King of England. The Lancastrian army numbered more than forty thousand men-at-arms, an exceptionally large force for the time but a figure not hard to believe when it is remembered that the country had been under arms for nearly two years. To bolster their ranks even more, the Lancastrian force contained no fewer than sixty knights of various degrees of wealth and power, of whom perhaps Sir Andrew Trollope, Sir Anthony Woodville, Lord Scales, Sir Richard Woodville, Earl Rivers and Robert Hildyard of Winestead are worthy of mention.

The Yorkists did not run to such nobility: with the exception of Edward, Warwick and Fauconberg the only other noble of any rank was the Duke of Norfolk (who, although he had made up some time on his march north, had still failed to effect a union with the Yorkist king). The Yorkists were also outnumbered. Their army consisted of some thirty-six thousand men-at-arms, but it included the likes of John Lord Clinton, Sir William and Thomas Lord Stanley, experienced captains like Robert Horne, John Fogge and Sir John Wenlock, who had all witnessed the scenes of devastation at Yorkist settlements left behind when the Lancastrians had retreated north. Hardened in their resolve by their experiences, fired with the confidence of their leaders – the famous Earl of Warwick and Lord Fauconberg – and in the hope of future prosperity offered by the energetic new King Edward, they faced the Lancastrians in high spirits.

More than four hours elapsed while the two forces adjusted their ranks, and waited for stragglers to arrive, before the battle began. In the stillness of the morning air the bells of York Minster could be heard summoning people to the service on that cold Palm Sunday morning, 29 March 1461. The two armies had drawn up in line facing each other, separated only by the shallow valley of Towton Vale (*see* Fig. 8.3). The Yorkist army was split into three lines. The vanguard was commanded by Lord Fauconberg, the middle line by the Earl of Warwick, and the rearguard and reserve by Edward himself. The exact positions of the Lancastrian leaders are unknown, though it is believed that they also drew up their army in three lines, with the vanguard under the command of Sir Andrew Trollope and the Earl of Northumberland, the middle line under Lord Dacre, and the rearguard under the Dukes of Exeter and Somerset.

At about 9 o'clock the wind shifted direction and began to blow the still falling snow into the faces of the Lancastrians. This was all the encouragement that Lord

Detail of the medieval head incorporated into Lord Dacre's Cross, commemorating the Battle of Towton

Fauconberg needed, and with it he ordered his archers forward into the valley. The change in wind direction not only added range to the Yorkist archers but also blinded their Lancastrian counterparts; Fauconberg took advantage of this to order his men to fire volley after volley of arrows deep into the cramped Lancastrian ranks. The Lancastrians replied, but in the harsh weather conditions, with the wind blowing towards them, their arrows fell short, landing harmlessly in front of the Yorkists. The quick-thinking Lord Fauconberg then ordered his archers, who had spent most of their own arrows, to advance to the spot where the Lancastrian arrows had landed, pluck them from the snow, and fire them back! After this second barrage of archer fire the Duke of Somerset realized that his men could not sustain this damage for long, as the effect of the Yorkist archer fire was not only inflicting heavy casualties but was also having a severe effect on morale. He came to the conclusion that his only course of action was to advance upon the Yorkist position and engage in close-quarter combat (see Fig. 8.4). With this the order was given, and the entire Lancastrian army began to advance into the valley towards the Yorkist positions. When Fauconberg saw the oncoming Lancastrians he ordered his archers to return to the ranks of his main army, though not before firing one last volley into the oncoming Lancastrians. (He also gave the order to leave some of the Lancastrian arrows in the snow to act as obstacles for the oncoming enemy.)

Once the Lancastrians engaged with the Yorkist army the sheer weight of numbers caused the Yorkist line to give way slightly, but the soldiers of Edward's army fought grimly on, and up and down the line great numbers of soldiers on both sides began to fall, cut down under sword, halberd and axe blows. Warwick had by this time made his way to the centre of the Yorkist front line, and it was this centre that was to take the brunt of the attack. But the earl, surrounded by his household, fought valiantly on, his very presence in the thick of the fighting giving confidence to his troops.

The young King Edward rode up and down the entire line, dismounting from his horse and joining in the battle wherever the line looked like giving way, committing soldiers to it from the reserve when it looked like breaking. As the hours passed and the fighting continued, in some parts of the field the troops on both sides were obliged to stop fighting and pull the bodies of their dead comrades aside to get at one another, so great was the slaughter. (Before the battle the order had been given on both sides not to give or ask for quarter, as the commanders of both armies were determined to settle the issue that day.)

However, under sheer weight of numbers the Yorkist line began gradually to give ground. The Lancastrians had concealed a force of men in Castle Hill Wood, which, when committed to the battle (see Fig. 8.5), almost caused the collapse of the Yorkist left flank, and exhausted the Yorkist reserve, which had had to be committed to stem the break-up of the Yorkist flank.

In the middle of the afternoon news of Norfolk's arrival reached Edward. By this time the Yorkist army had been pushed back to the very ridge of the plateau over which they had marched that morning to confront the enemy. At once Norfolk's men, a force of several thousand, were ordered to engage the Lancastrian left flank (see Fig.

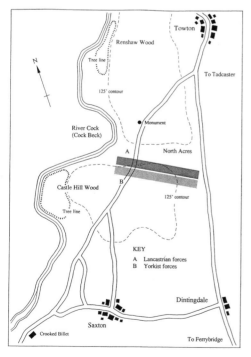

Fig 8.4   The Battle of Towton

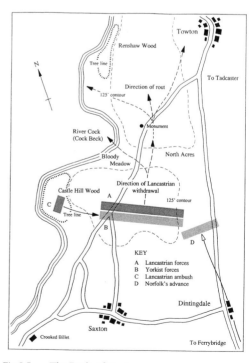

Fig 8.5   The Battle of Towton

8.5). So great were the Lancastrian numbers that it was some time before Norfolk's force could make an impact but gradually the roles were reversed: the Lancastrians, after several hours' fighting, were exhausted, while the Duke of Norfolk's men were relatively fresh. By late afternoon the Lancastrians were grudgingly giving more and more ground whereas the Yorkists, cheered by the arrival of Norfolk's men, fought with a determination befitting what was at stake. Within an hour the Lancastrian line was faltering, and then, suddenly, it broke in two as thousands of men began fleeing the field. With this the battle ended and the rout of the Lancastrians began.

Somerset's right flank retreated towards the little River Cock, but the steep slope leading down to it (which had so well protected their original position), was to be their undoing. As the men in heavy armour tried to traverse the slope, made treacherous by the snow and slush, they found themselves slipping and sliding down the hill to be either crushed underfoot by the men behind them or slain by the pursuing Yorkists. Of those who made it to the river many were to drown in its icy waters – turned from a large stream into a torrent by the snow – unable to cross it in their heavy armour. It is said that the crush made by so many people trying to cross in one place caused the bodies to accumulate in such numbers that it was possible to cross from one bank to the other by walking over them. The scene of this slaughter is now known as Bloody Meadow.

As for the rest of Somerset's army, they were pursued all the way into Tadcaster, where some of them tried bravely but unsuccessfully to make a stand. At the beginning of the rout orders had been given to seek out the lords and spare the commoners. As a result, the nobility was to suffer greatly. The Earl of Northumberland, the Duke of Buckingham, Sir Andrew Trollope and Lord Dacre of Gilsland, together with many other knights and squires, lay dead upon the field. From the Yorkist nobility only Robert Horne was killed on the field of battle.

The Duke of Somerset, the Duke of Exeter, Lord Roos and Sir John Fortescue (then Chief Justice) managed to escape to York, whence they accompanied the king and queen to safety in Scotland. However, by the end of the day more than forty-two captured knights had been executed although many were spared. The Woodvilles (Sir Anthony and Sir Richard) were granted pardons. Many others were to spend time as prisoners of the Yorkists. In all more than twenty-eight thousand men died on the field of Towton, the single largest loss of life ever to occur on English soil.

EPILOGUE TO THE BATTLE

Due to the larger number of combatants, the fighting had at times actually to be stopped in order to clear the bodies of the slain so that the antagonists might continue to fight. At such times men on both sides, especially those wearing heavy armour, had to withdraw from the front in order to regain their strength. It was during one of these periods that Lord Dacre of Gilsland removed his helmet, and having done so was shot in the neck by a crossbow bolt and killed. His assassin is reputed to have been a Yorkist sniper who recognized him as the man who had killed his father, and from his vantage point in a bur tree, in an area of the field known as North Acres, took the opportunity to exact his revenge. Though the truth of this is questionable, Lord Dacre did indeed die at Towton.

The tomb of Ralph, Lord Dacre of Gilsland, killed at the Battle of Towton

The idea for the ambush from Castle Hill Wood was born of the tactics used by Queen Margaret at St Albans. She favoured flank attacks rather than the more traditional practice of face-to-face combat. This tactic would later be widely adopted, but at the time was viewed as extremely unethical and unchivalrous.

Among the captured nobility there were found the sons of both Lord Clifford and Sir Henry Percy. Though revenge was uppermost in everybody's mind (Clifford had murdered Edmund of Rutland at Wakefield Bridge the previous December), the young Clifford's life was spared, and he was given into the custody of a humble shepherd, where he remained until restored to his rightful title and lands by Henry VII some twenty years later. As for the young Henry Percy, he was to spend the next nine years as a prisoner in the Tower of London before being restored to his rightful status and regaining the family earldom of Northumberland. He was later to become one of Edward's leading supporters, and later still he would support Richard III when he claimed the throne in 1483.

After his victory at Towton Edward travelled to York, where he immediately ordered the removal of the heads of his father, brother and the Earl of Salisbury from above Micklegate Bar so that they could be formally buried. While in York he also released Lord Montagu from captivity and presided over the trial and execution of some of the lesser nobles captured in the battle.

Some historians have questioned why Edward did not await the arrival of the Duke of Norfolk's force before starting the battle. The answer to this is simple: the Yorkist commanders did not know when Norfolk would arrive, and Edward's army was short of both food and supplies. While waiting for Norfolk to catch up, the Yorkists would have probably lost more men to the harsh weather conditions and to desertion than they would have gained by waiting for his arrival. This leads to the actual reason for the duke's delay. Norfolk was by this time an old man, and terminally sick. His army could therefore travel only as fast as the ailing duke's condition would allow. His health was in such a poor state that it is questionable whether he was actually present on the field of battle at all. It is more likely that the duke's cousin, Sir John Howard, led the men into battle, Norfolk himself remaining in Pontefract.

The Crooked Billet public house which today stands near the battlefield is rumoured to have taken its name from an earlier inn on the site which was the resting place of the Earl of Warwick on the night before the battle. The emblem of both Warwick and Fauconberg carried the Neville badge of crossed sticks, in old Yorkshire dialect, 'Greukt Billets' or 'Crooked Billets'. However, some believe (the author included) that the name of the inn is derived from the badge of the Warwick household which was a ragged or crooked staff. This, and the fact that Warwick chose the inn as his billet for the night, is perhaps the real source of the unusual name. Whatever the case, the inn still incorporates the Neville emblem on the sign that hangs over its door.

Much of the credit for the victory at Towton is attributed to the command and direction of the Earl of Warwick. But the role that Edward played must also be taken into account. The young king stood 6 ft 4 in in his armour, and his presence on the field of battle, together with his steady display of courage, must have played no small part in keeping up the flagging spirits of the Yorkist army before the arrival of the Duke of Norfolk. He should surely receive at least equal recognition with Warwick and Lord Fauconberg for the Yorkist victory at Towton.

The blood that was spilled at Towton is rumoured to have caused the Towton rose (*Rosa Spinosissima*), a flower which grew in that area, to develop red spots. The plant survived in this form until recent times.

SECTION TWO

CHAPTER NINE

THE WAR
IN THE NORTH

With the Battle of Towton decisively won by the Yorkists, it would appear at first glance that Edward's position as King of England would be secured. However, it would not be until the summer of 1464 that the young king could claim to be ruler of all England and Wales. There were, despite the crushing losses of the Lancastrian nobility at Towton, many survivors who would not give up the fight so easily, and the next three years saw many Lancastrian-inspired revolts throughout the land. The majority of these revolts, and those causing most concern to the new Yorkist government, had their roots in the Lancastrian strongholds of Northumberland.

After his victory at Towton Edward stayed at York for three weeks before moving north to Durham. He arrived in the city on 22 April and spent a week there before travelling to Newcastle. His arrival there on 1 May was in time to preside over the trial and subsequent execution of Sir James Butler, Earl of Wiltshire, who, though notorious for his ability to escape, had been finally captured while fleeing to the North from the battlefield of Towton.

In Northumberland the strongholds of Warkworth, Alnwick, Dunstanburgh and Bamburgh were held by retainers of the Percy family loyal to the Lancastrian cause. Although he was advised to travel into Northumberland with his army, Edward instead returned south through Lancashire, Cheshire and the Midlands towards London. This was in order to make preparation for his coronation and the opening of Parliament, where he could pass an act of attainder against the remaining Lancastrians. He chose at his departure to leave the Earl of Warwick and Warwick's brother Lord Montagu to subdue the turbulent North.

Margaret of Anjou, King Henry, Prince Edward and many of the surviving Lancastrian nobility had fled to sanctuary in Scotland after their defeat at Towton. In May, only two months after the battle, a combined army of Scots and Lancastrians moved over the border and laid siege to Carlisle. At this point consideration must be given to Scottish politics at this time, because Scotland was to play a pivotal role between Yorkists and Lancastrians in the months to come. Since 1456 King James II of Scotland had taken advantage of the political turmoil in England to harass the troubled border between the two countries in an attempt to make territorial gains in England. To this end he led raids into England in 1456 and laid siege to the town of Berwick in 1457. In 1460 he personally led over the border the largest invasion force he had yet

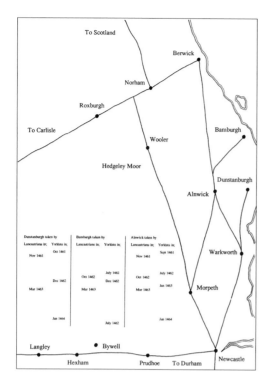

Fig 9.1   Siege Warfare in the North

assembled, and laid siege to Roxburgh Castle. His moment of glory was short-lived, however. On 3 August 1460 one of the siege cannon fired to celebrate the arrival of his wife, Mary of Guelders, at the Scottish camp at Roxburgh, exploded and killed him instantly.

With James II's death his eight-year-old son became king, with the dowager Queen Mary as head of a regency council set up until the boy was old enough to assume the kingship in his own right. As with most regency councils there appeared a division: on the one side a group led by Queen Mary, known as the 'Young Lords', and on the other the 'Old Lords' led by Bishop Robert Kennedy of St Andrew's. Each group had its own opinions on home affairs and foreign policies, as a result of which Queen Margaret and the exiled Lancastrians found it difficult to appease both factions and gain military and political support for their own cause. However, when Margaret offered to cede major English border towns in return for military aid she did find some sympathy with the Scottish court. She ordered the town of Carlisle to be handed over to the Scots. The citizens of Carlisle, however, were not as enthusiastic as Margaret to hand over the town, and she was obliged to lead a joint Scottish–Lancastrian army over the border in order to take it by force. Once Warwick learnt of Margaret's advance on Carlisle he ordered Lord Montagu to march north and raise the siege on the town. Upon the arrival of Montagu's force the Scots withdrew across the border.

In June another raid, this time led by Lord Roos, Lord Dacre and Rougemont Gray, crossed the border and advanced deep into Northumberland, arriving at the Earl of Westmorland's castle at Brancepeth near Durham. Here the Lancastrians raised the royal standard of King Henry (who had accompanied them on their journey south) but found support for Henry's cause negligible; they quickly returned to the safety of Scotland when word reached them that the Earl of Warwick was advancing upon their position.

These somewhat alarming events caused Edward to bring forward his coronation to 28 June 1461 so that he could personally travel north. But even as Edward prepared for his journey events in Wales led him to change his plans. After the Yorkist victory at Towton, Jasper Tudor, Earl of Pembroke had remained in Wales and garrisoned the fortresses of Denbigh, Harlech and Pembroke for Henry VI against Edward. Revolt in Wales had boiled over, and Edward was forced to travel to the welsh marches in person to suppress the risings. Accompanied by Sir William Herbert, Sir Henry Bourchier, Earl of Essex and Sir Walter Devereux (promoted to the title of Lord Ferrers in Edward's coronation honours), Edward arrived at Hereford early in September. Here Edward decided to leave the actual campaigning in Wales to his trusted captains, and moved on to Ludlow, where he remained until returning to London for the opening of Parliament on 4 November. Meanwhile, his commanders in the field managed to capture the main Lancastrian stronghold of Pembroke on 30 September 1461. On 16 October Sir William Herbert and the main Yorkist army in Wales fought a small skirmish with a Lancastrian force led by Jasper Tudor and Sir Henry Holland, Duke of Exeter at Twt Hill just outside Caernarvon. The Lancastrians were totally routed. With this the Welsh Lancastrians lost heart. The defenders of Denbigh Castle finally surrendered the fortress to the Yorkists at the end of January 1462, leaving only Harlech Castle opposing Yorkist rule in Wales.

While Edward was concentrating on events in the South and Wales, Warwick and Montagu steadily moved throughout Northumberland during the months of August and September eradicating pockets of Lancastrian resistance as they went. Edward had bestowed upon Warwick the title of Warden General of both East and West Welsh marches at the end of July, legalizing Warwick's position in the North and giving him royal permission to raise levies and the command of all military resources in Northumberland. By the end of September the Percy-held castle of Alnwick had surrendered to Warwick, who subsequently manned it with one hundred men-at-arms loyal to him. At the beginning of October the coastal fortress of Dunstanburgh was personally surrendered to Warwick by Sir Ralph Percy, and it seemed to the Yorkists that their struggle for control of the North would soon be over.

But this military success was to be marred by the personal misjudgement of Edward himself. After the surrender of Dunstanburgh, he instructed Warwick to retain Sir Ralph Percy as constable of the castle. This decision was to backfire on the king when another raiding party from Scotland, led by Sir William Tailboys, recaptured Alnwick Castle. They then marched on to Dunstanburgh where Percy, having reverted to his original allegiance, opened the gates to them. To make matters worse a simultaneous raid into England by Lord Humphrey Dacre took Naworth Castle (east of Carlisle), proving to all that the North was far from secure for the Yorkists.

The Yorkist leaders concluded from these events that as long as the Lancastrians had a Scottish base to work from they could never eradicate Lancastrian opposition to their government in Northumberland. It was decided to attempt diplomacy where armed aggression had failed, and Warwick arranged for a meeting to be held between himself and Mary of Guelders. Though Warwick received some sympathy from Mary and the Young Lords, the Old Lords led by Bishop Kennedy (whose resistance was obviously fuelled by Margaret's interference) refused to take a pro-Yorkist stand. The meeting achieved little other than an agreement to meet again, and between the two meetings Warwick stepped up the pressure by increasing Yorkist raids into Scotland, while Edward put pressure on Mary's uncle, Philip, Duke of Burgundy (a Yorkist ally), to induce Mary to adopt a more pro-Yorkist attitude. The pressure on Mary led her to seek a breathing space for herself, and when Margaret of Anjou asked for money to pay for passage to France (where she hoped to engage in diplomacy with the French court on Henry's behalf), Mary readily agreed, hoping that in Margaret's absence the Old Lords (without Margaret to fuel Bishop Kennedy's ambitions), would be less resistant to her own suggestions for peace with Edward's government.

Without Margaret's presence to influence the Old Lords, and perhaps because of Scotland's own domestic problems in the North and the regency council's unwillingness to fight on two fronts, the Scottish and Yorkist governments made an Anglo-Scottish non-aggression pact, which it was agreed would last from June to the end of August 1462. With the ceasefire imminent Edward ordered Yorkist reinforcements north to challenge the Lancastrians. By mid-July Lord Dacre had surrendered his force at Naworth to Lord Montagu. Tailboys, who was holding Alnwick (having recaptured it the previous November), surrendered it after a short siege to a force under the command of Lord Hastings, Sir John Howard and Sir Ralph Grey. At the same time Bamburgh Castle was captured for the Yorkists by Sir William Turnstall.

Meanwhile, Margaret had achieved her own diplomatic victory in France. Having promised to cede Calais to King Louis XI in an agreement made in June, the king in return agreed to lend Margaret money and the services of Pierre De Breze, a competent French commander, to lead an expeditionary force of French soldiers to England. Margaret, De Breze and eight hundred men-at-arms soon sailed for England, their voyage taking them first to Scotland, where Henry VI joined them. They then sailed for Bamburgh, where they landed on 25 October. The castle soon opened its gates to the queen's army, which was given into the command of the Duke of Somerset. With Sir Ralph Percy still holding Dunstanburgh for the Lancastrians this meant that the queen could now concentrate her efforts against the defenders of Alnwick Castle, whose garrison, starved of supplies, soon capitulated to her army.

Five days after Margaret's army landed at Bamburgh the Yorkists struck back. The Earl of Warwick, in London when Margaret landed, travelled north. By 4 November the king himself was taking the road north with an army that consisted of most of the nobility still remaining in Yorkist England. It is claimed that two dukes, seven earls, thirty-one barons and more than fifty knights, accompanied by an army in excess of forty thousand men-at-arms, escorted Edward by the time he reached York. In the face of such overwhelming odds, and because her own cause had received little popular support (even after King Henry's standard had been raised at Bamburgh Castle), Margaret decided to flee to the relative safety of Scotland, taking Henry with her. On her departure she vowed to return with an army equal to Edward's in order to relieve the beleaguered garrisons of Dunstanburgh, Bamburgh and Alnwick, which she left adequately manned to repel the advancing Yorkists.

Bamburgh Castle, Northumberland. Besieged by Lord Montagu and the Earl of Warwick in 1464, its commander, Sir Ralph Grey, was seriously injured by a cannon ball fired during its bombardment. He eventually surrendered

Edward left York and travelled to Durham, arriving there on 16 November, only to be stricken with measles and confined to bed, leaving the Earl of Warwick to lead the forthcoming campaign. Meanwhile, Margaret was beset with her own misfortunes when her small fleet of four ships was caught in a winter storm after setting sail from Bamburgh on 13 November. Her life, and those of Henry and De Breze, was saved by a fisherman who rescued them from their stricken ship and sailed them to the safety of Scottish-controlled Berwick on board his own vessel. Her army of some six hundred men was not so lucky: forced to disembark at Lindisfarne on Holy Island, most of its members were either killed or captured by the local inhabitants.

By early December the Earl of Warwick had managed to organize his resources and was laying siege to Alnwick, Bamburgh and Dunstanburgh. Lord Montagu had command of the forces laying siege to Bamburgh, which was being defended by a garrison under the command of the Duke of Somerset. Accompanying Montagu were Lords Ogle, Strange and Say, and Sir Ralph Grey. Lord Fauconberg (who had recently been given the title of Earl of Kent), along with Lord Scales and the Earl of Worcester, Sir John Tiptoft, were placed in command of the force besieging Alnwick, which was defended by a garrison under the command of Lord Hungerford. Dunstanburgh, defended by Lancastrians under the command of Sir Ralph Percy, was left to the Lords Scrope, Greystoke and Powis to subdue.

The entire operation was commanded by the Earl of Warwick, who from his headquarters at Warkworth Castle (which housed the reserve, a force of some seven thousand men-at-arms) daily toured the three engagements giving advice on strategy and directing supplies as needed. The supplies themselves arrived daily in Newcastle, coming both by sea and overland, and were distributed to the separate castles within Warwick's command by the new Duke of Norfolk, Sir John Mowbray (who had inherited the title when his father died shortly after the Battle of Towton), placed in command of the town when the Yorkists marched north. The logistics of the operation were an outstanding achievement by the Earl of Warwick and a far cry from his fiasco at St Albans in 1460. His efforts soon reaped rewards for the Yorkists.

The defenders of Bamburgh Castle, faced with such overwhelming opposition, were the first to capitulate when the Duke of Somerset sought terms for surrender. On 26 December the soldiers of Somerset's army were allowed to quit the castle, leaving their weapons behind. Two days later Sir Ralph Percy and the Dunstanburgh garrison followed them. Though the men-at-arms were allowed to go free, pardoned after taking an oath of allegiance to King Edward, Percy and Somerset were taken to Edward at Durham, allowing Warwick then to concentrate his efforts entirely on the defenders of Alnwick and on a Scottish army led jointly by De Breze and the Scottish Earl of Angus that was reported to be coming to their relief.

The Scottish relief force appeared before Alnwick on 5 January. Though forewarned of its existence, Warwick seemed almost startled by its appearance and immediately ordered his army's withdrawal from their prepared position. Surprised and perplexed by Warwick's withdrawal, Angus and De Breze halted their army below the castle, suspecting a trap, and as the two armies squared up to each other the garrison of Alnwick, led by Lord Hungerford, promptly took the opportunity to join with their

The keep gatehouse of Dunstanburgh Castle, Northumberland, which with Alnwick capitulated to the Earl of Warwick and Lord Montagu in 1464

allies and marched out of the castle in full view of Warwick's army. Once united, the Scottish army and their Lancastrian allies withdrew towards Scotland, and next morning Warwick occupied the vacated castle. With this Edward achieved complete control of the North, all its principal castles and fortresses being now in his possession. But though his military position was formidable, yet again his personal misjudgement of others was to let him down. After receiving Sir Ralph Percy and the Duke of Somerset at his court in Durham, Edward allowed Percy to return to his lands in the North, and once he had sworn loyalty to Edward and the Yorkist cause he was also retained as lieutenant of Dunstanburgh and Bamburgh Castles. With this, and the appointment of Sir Ralph Grey as constable and Sir John Astley as captain of Alnwick, Edward left Durham for the South as soon as Warwick had joined him from the siege at Alnwick.

It is worth noting that at this point even the Duke of Somerset had been taken into King Edward's favour, a surprising event in view of Somerset's recent history, and perhaps one that highlights Edward's repeated attempts at reconciling the two opposing factions. Indeed Somerset, who had travelled with Warwick and had stood with the Yorkists before Alnwick when they faced De Breze and the Earl of Angus, was to become one of the King's favourites in the weeks ahead, and accompanied both Warwick and Edward when they returned south for the formal burial of Edward's father, the Duke of York, at Fotheringhay on 30 January and the Earl of Salisbury, Warwick's father, at Bisham Abbey on 15 February.

It was during March 1463, while both Edward and Warwick were in the South, that Queen Margaret chose her moment to cross the border once more into England. With Margaret's arrival at the head of a joint Lancastrian and Scottish army Sir Ralph Percy decided to revert to his original allegiance for the second time, and handed over the castles of Bamburgh and Dunstanburgh to the Lancastrian cause. At about the same time Sir Ralph Grey (until this point a loyal Yorkist) also decided to change sides, and after tricking Sir John Astley into opening the gates of Alnwick Castle, allowed a force under the command of Lord Hungerford unopposed entry. Though Percy's change in allegiance is not difficult to understand – his father having died at the hands of the Yorkists at the first Battle of St Albans, and his brothers at Northampton and Towton, meant that he would always be a Lancastrian at heart – the reason for Sir Ralph Grey's defection is not at first clear. It appears that Grey felt that his appointment as constable of Alnwick Castle was marred by the appointment of Sir John Astley to the more senior role of captain. Because of this Grey felt that he had been treated unfairly by the side for which he had been fighting and as a result transferred his allegiance to the opposite camp.

It seemed that the Yorkists must go through the labours of the previous winter once again, but even if the castles were retaken there could obviously be no guarantee that they would remain loyal to the Yorkist cause. The only long-term solution to the problem was the permanent representation of the Yorkist government in the North, and as the Earl of Warwick was Warden General of the East and West Welsh marches he was the obvious candidate for the job. However, the earl was not the sort of man to be content with the rule only of the North, and Warwick had his own plans which needed his presence in the South. In pursuit of these the earl's brother, Lord Montagu, was created Warden of the East March on 26 May 1463. The appointment came as no

Alnwick Castle, one of the Northumbrian strongholds held for Henry VI, which surrendered to the Earl of Warwick in 1464

surprise to many of the Yorkist hierarchy, as Montagu had spent much of the last two years in Northumberland. However, as it was an emergency, Warwick was once again sent north to assist his brother in gaining control of Northumberland, and left London on 3 June accompanied by his brother-in-law, Thomas, Lord Stanley.

By July Warwick and Montagu were at the head of a large army heading into the heart of Northumberland. On arrival Warwick found the situation so serious that he sent word to Edward in London urging him to come north with all haste with reinforcements as the Lancastrians were now supported by a full-scale Scottish invasion. This force had crossed the border in June, with Mary of Guelders, King James III, King Henry and Margaret herself among its ranks, and had managed by mid-July to lay siege to Norham Castle.

Edward headed north with his usual vigour and energy, but his plans were upset when he reached Northampton. News of his arrival in the town spread quickly. Unfortunately for Edward he had chosen to take the Duke of Somerset with him, and when news spread that Somerset was within the town rioting broke out (proving that old hatreds die hard). By the time the rioters reached Edward's party only the presence of the king himself saved Somerset from the hands of a lynch mob. The king decided to send Somerset to the relative safety of North Wales, and never ventured further north in the campaign. Instead he decided to remain at Northampton and await news of events in the North.

Though the Scottish invasion force had all the 'great ordinance' of Scotland with it, and was protected by the garrisons of Dunstanburgh, Alnwick and Bamburgh to its rear, the campaign ended in utter disgrace for the Scots when they were surprised by the arrival of Montagu and Warwick's relieving force, who had managed to reach Norham without being detected. At the news of the Yorkists' arrival the Scots panicked, dispersed and fled, leaving the Scottish border undefended and at the mercy of the Yorkists, who took full advantage of the situation to launch a retaliatory raid over a wide area of Scotland, penetrating some 60 miles into the lowlands, burning and pillaging as they went, returning to England only when they ran out of supplies. In the panic Margaret of Anjou and her young son Prince Edward, with De Breze, made good their escape to Berwick, while King Henry made his way first to Scotland and then to Bamburgh Castle. The rout of the Scots from Norham was to be a decisive victory for the Yorkists in the campaign for control of the North. It was clear to Margaret that even though she had promised Bishop Kennedy the Archbishopric of Canterbury and the cession of several English counties to the Scots in return for Scottish assistance in the June raid, with its failure she was no longer welcome in Scotland. Margaret took the next available ship from Berwick to France, taking her son with her but leaving Henry behind. He was never to see his wife or child again.

By late autumn the Scots were eager to make their peace with Yorkist England. King Edward reached York on 3 December 1463 and was met by a Scottish envoy six days later. A truce was signed between the two countries to last until October 1464, with a further agreement to hold Anglo-Scottish talks in the coming year, aimed at a more lasting peace. Though Alnwick, Dunstanburgh and Bamburgh were still held by Lancastrian sympathizers, this truce ruined any remaining hope for the Lancastrian cause in the North.

CHAPTER TEN

THE BATTLE OF HEDGELEY MOOR 25 APRIL 1464

THE CAMPAIGN

Early in 1464 civil unrest in more than fifteen counties throughout the land, from Kent to Cornwall and as far north as Leicestershire, caused Edward temporarily to turn his attentions away from the North and concentrate on the South. Severe unrest in Cambridgeshire and Gloucestershire caused Edward to postpone the state opening of Parliament, due to be held in York, so that together with the Earl of Warwick and two senior justices of the peace, he could visit these counties to assist in the suppression of what were obviously Lancastrian-inspired revolts.

At about the same time, but unknown to Edward, the Duke of Somerset, who had been sent to North Wales the previous year after Edward had personally saved him from the hands of a lynch mob, was at this time in secret correspondence with King Henry VI at Henry's court-in-exile in Bamburgh. Early in the new year Somerset decided to show his hand openly and declare for Henry, and without taking leave of King Edward left Wales. Somerset's first intention was to travel to Newcastle, where as fate would have it Edward had sent Somerset's retainers (a force of some two hundred men-at-arms) the previous year when he had sent Somerset to Wales. These retainers had been sent to bolster up the garrison of Newcastle which had become a vital supply link for the Yorkists with their armies in the North. Somerset's initial plan was to use his retainers in Newcastle to surprise the Yorkist element of the garrison and take the town by force. By then declaring for Henry, he could both hamper the flow of supplies to the Yorkist forces in the North while at the same time giving the Lancastrians in Northumberland the advantage.

However, troops loyal to Edward got wind of Somerset's plan, took the initiative and interned his men before Somerset's plan came to fruition. When Edward heard of Somerset's betrayal, and the attempted takeover of Newcastle, as a safeguard against further risk to the town, he appointed Lord Scrope of Bolton as captain of the town and reinforced it with men loyal to the Yorkist cause.

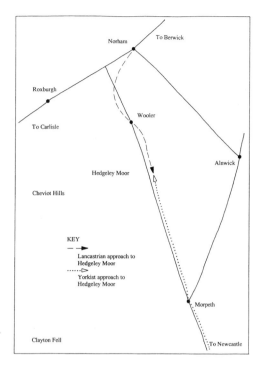

Fig 10.1   Preliminary Moves for the Battle of
Hedgeley Moor

With the failure of his planned takeover of Newcastle, Somerset changed direction and set out for Bamburgh to join the remaining Lancastrians still at large. His journey was not without danger, and he narrowly avoided being caught at Durham by Yorkist sympathizers when he was surprised while sleeping, escaping barefoot and wearing only his nightshirt.

Meanwhile, Edward and Warwick, having successfully suppressed revolts in the South, returned to London to make diplomatic contact with the envoy of the Duke of Burgundy, Jean de Lannoy.

In March news reached London of Somerset's arrival at Bamburgh and of the subsequent increase of Lancastrian activity in Northumberland. On his arrival at Bamburgh Somerset had been joined by two other rebel lords, Sir Humphrey Neville of Brancepeth and Sir Henry Bellingham, who, like Somerset, had been pardoned by Edward the previous year, only to revert to his original cause at the first opportunity. These knights, together with Sir Ralph Percy, Lords Hungerford and Roos and the Yorkist traitor Sir Ralph Grey, went on the offensive and in an extensive military campaign, which was to last from early February to late March, managed to secure for the Lancastrians the castle of Norham as well as the towns of Prudhoe, Bywell, Langley and Hexham. To make matters worse for the Yorkists the staunch Lancastrian Clifford family managed to retake its family home at Skipton in Craven, Yorkshire at about the same time.

With Lancastrian uprisings occurring almost nationwide the Yorkist government was forced to act. However, at this point the most urgent priority as far as Edward was concerned was the threat from marauding Lancastrians to the Anglo-Scottish talks due to be held in Newcastle on 6 March. Because of the increase in Lancastrian activity these talks, a continuation of those which had taken place the previous December, were postponed to 20 April, and for safety's sake the venue was moved to York. On 27 March 1464 Edward made a public announcement stating that he would be personally travelling north to put an end to the troubles once and for all.

In mid-April Lord Montagu was despatched by Edward to meet the Scottish envoys, who were awaiting escort at the border near Norham, and take them to York through what was now Lancastrian-held territory. The journey was not without risk – a force of some eighty men-at-arms and some archers, under the command of Sir Humphrey Neville, was detached from the main Lancastrian army with orders to move forward and take up positions from where they could ambush Montagu's party on the road to Newcastle. However, Montagu's scouts detected the ambush and by using an alternative route they reached Newcastle unharmed. Throughout the journey supporters had been attracted to Montagu's banner, and by the time he left Newcastle he had collected a force of between five and six thousand men-at-arms. En route to the border his army encountered the main Lancastrian force, consisting of some five thousand men under the command of the Duke of Somerset, with Sir Ralph Percy, Lord Roos, Hungerford and Grey also in attendance. The two armies clashed some 9 miles north-west of Alnwick, at Hedgeley Moor on 25 April 1464.

THE BATTLE

Exact details of the battle are scarce. What is known is that Montagu's force came upon the Lancastrians, who were aware of the Yorkists' presence, and were already formed up for battle in open line (*see* Fig. 10.2). The location of the nobles present is unknown, but there are vague suggestions that Sir Ralph Percy held the Lancastrian right wing or vanguard; Somerset, Bellingham and Grey the centre; Hungerford and Roos the left wing or rearguard.

Montagu's force, arriving at Hedgeley Moor, formed up almost directly opposite the Lancastrians. For some time both sides adjusted ranks separated by only 1,500 yards of open moorland.

The battle opened with the customary exchange of archer fire. This was followed by the advance of Montagu's entire force. As the Yorkists crossed the open ground towards Somerset's position the Lancastrians suffered a major blow to their chances of victory when the left flank, under the command of Lords Hungerford and Roos (some two thousand men-at-arms), faltered, broke and scattered before Montagu could bring his force into close combat. Somewhat surprised at this unexpected departure of a third of the Lancastrian army, Montagu was obliged to halt his force for a short time while the Yorkists readjusted their lines and consolidated their front to allow Montagu to bring up the bulk of his force against the remaining Lancastrians, by now marching forward to engage with the Yorkists (*see* Fig. 10.3).

As the two armies clashed the Lancastrians, their force already depleted by the departure of Roos and Hungerford, gave way under the impetus of the Yorkists' advance. Either in the ensuing mêlée or perhaps even just before the final engagement Sir Ralph Percy was deserted by all, including the Lancastrian commander Somerset,

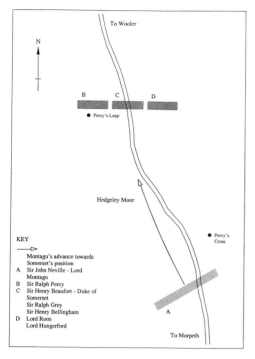

Fig 10.2   The Battle of Hedgeley Moor

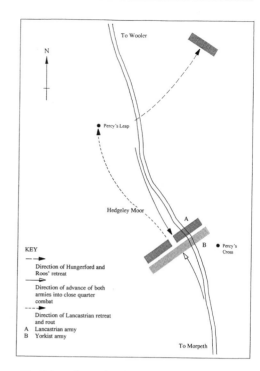

Fig 10.3   The Battle of Hedgeley Moor

except his own household retainers. The remaining Lancastrians put up a brave fight but were hopelessly outnumbered. The battle did not last long, Percy himself and most of the remaining Lancastrians being soon slain by the vastly superior Yorkist force.

EPILOGUE TO THE BATTLE

It is almost certain that low morale among the Lancastrian troops led to the collapse of Roos' and Hungerford's wing when it was confronted by the more optimistic Yorkists, and that, left all alone, Percy and his force held their ground only because they were in his homelands. Left only with his household retainers, where could he go? Tradition says that before the battle Percy had a vision of his own death, and that his demise would be the result of the desertion by Hungerford and Roos. Vision or not, this is exactly what happened, but the tale is probably the result of some chronicler's poetic licence.

As he died Percy is reputed to have cried: 'I have saved the bird in my bosom'.[1] The exact meaning of these words is unknown, gone with Percy, but it was later interpreted to mean that he had always remained loyal to the Lancastrian cause.

It is also said that Percy made one last leap for freedom and escape after receiving his death blow. The distance he covered is said to have been some 12 yards, a remarkable feat for someone mortally injured and dressed in full battle armour! Again, like the

The Percy Cross, Hedgeley Moor battlefield. The shaft is carved with the family heraldic badges of a crescent and shackle-bolt, and the 'luce' or pike fish from the Percy arms

vision, this is more probably some chronicler's poetic licence. However, the place and distance known as 'Percy's Leap' is marked by two boulders which can still be seen to this day.

Precisely at what point the Lancastrian Commander Henry Beaufort, Duke of Somerset decided to leave the field is unknown. It may be assumed that with Sir Ralph Percy the only noble killed on the field, Somerset and the remaining Lancastrians either left with Hungerford and Roos or quit the battlefield shortly afterwards when it became clear that the odds in favour of victory for Montagu were overwhelming. With the battle won, Lord Montagu remustered his forces and continued his journey to the border to meet the Scottish envoys at Norham. He then escorted them safely south to York.

The site of the Battle of Hedgeley Moor is marked with a square stone pillar set on a round base bearing the Percy heraldic badges. The marker, known locally as 'Percy's Cross', is still standing.

CHAPTER ELEVEN

THE BATTLE OF HEXHAM
10 MAY 1464

THE CAMPAIGN

While Montagu was making his way to York with the Scottish envoys, King Edward himself was making preparations to fulfil his promise of 27 March and advance north to put paid to the remaining Lancastrians once and for all. On 16 April Edward gave orders for the preparation of the 'great ordnance' of England and to this end the great guns 'Dijon', 'London', 'Newcastle', 'Richard Bombartal' and 'Edward' were made ready for the journey north. Letters bearing the royal seal were sent to sheriffs in more than thirty English counties, ordering the mustering of all able-bodied men to Leicester, whence the king would personally lead them north.

The Lancastrians, who had regrouped at Alnwick after the disaster of Hedgeley Moor, received news of the size of Edward's force now converging on Leicester and knew that only a swift military victory in the North could save them from the might of this army. With King Henry VI at their head they left Alnwick and marched south into the Tyne Valley, hoping that with Henry to lead them support for their cause would increase and that people would flock to his banner.

Though the Earl of Warwick had already left London with his usual vigour, en route to Northumberland, Edward himself did not leave the capital until 28 April. His journey north was delayed a short while when on 1 May he left the royal party at Stony Stratford and travelled alone to the residence of Earl Rivers at Grafton Regis. Earl Rivers and his son had fought against Edward at the Battle of Towton and had afterwards been pardoned by him. The reason for Edward's journey was not, however, to parley with the earl, but to visit his daughter Lady Elizabeth Woodville, the widow of Sir John Gray, who had died fighting for the Lancastrians at the second Battle of St Albans in 1461. As the chronicler Gregory wrote: 'Now take heed what love may do, for love will not nor may not foresee fault nor peril in no thing'.[1] On that day Edward Plantagenet, King of England, took the Lady Elizabeth for his wife, and unknown to any man made her Queen of England by this marriage. It would have devastating consequences in later years.

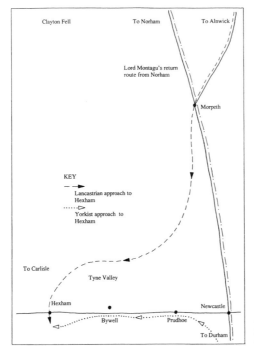

Fig 11.1   Preliminary Moves for the Battle of Hexham

While Edward was marching north and King Henry and the remaining Lancastrians south, Lord Montagu had delivered the Scottish envoys to York and returned to Newcastle, where he received news that the Lancastrian army had reached Hexham. Their presence so close to Montagu's location was sufficient encouragement for the courageous lord, and without waiting for reinforcements from the South he immediately set out with all his retainers for Hexham. His army included the former Lancastrians Lords Greystoke and Willoughby, who had remained loyal to Edward despite so many of their former allies having reverted to the Lancastrian cause, even after taking an oath of allegiance.

The Lancastrians had reached Hexham on 14 May, and made camp 2 miles south of the town, by a stretch of river known as 'Devil's Water' in a meadow called the 'Linnels'. While the troops and soldiers slept in the open air King Henry was made comfortable in the nearby estate at Bywell.

On the morning of 15 May the Yorkist army marched past Bywell on its way to Hexham. Whether any of King Henry's party saw it and tried to warn the main Lancastrian army will never be known; it is known that it was only the warning given by Lancastrian scouts, as Somerset's troops were stirring from their camp, that saved Henry's force from being totally surprised by the Yorkists' arrival.

THE BATTLE

Actual details of the battle, as with Hedgeley Moor, are, at best, scarce. We do know that Somerset, warned of Montagu's presence by his scouts, managed to rouse his men from their camp in the Linnels and form them into line ready for battle. With the Yorkists almost upon him Somerset had no chance to move to a more advantageous position, but was obliged to form his line on an area of flat land at the base of the hill on which Montagu's force had already taken up position.

The opening positions are depicted in Fig. 11.2, from which it may be seen that Somerset's force, with the Devil's Water to its rear, had drawn up in line with Somerset himself commanding the centre, Lords Roos and Hungerford the right flank, and Lords Grey and Neville the left. The Yorkists, looking down on Somerset's force from the brow of the hill, had also arranged themselves in line. Lord Montagu commanded the largest position of the Yorkist force and held the centre, with Lords Willoughby and Greystoke commanding the flanks. With Lancastrians to his front and former Lancastrians to his side it is not surprising that Montagu (probably remembering his experience at St Albans in 1461), chose to lead the lion's share of the Yorkist force himself.

It was still early in the morning when Montagu seized the initiative. His centre advanced in a rapid downhill charge and smashed into the ranks of the Lancastrians, engaging in fierce hand-to-hand combat with Somerset's centre. The Lancastrians gave only slightly under the impetus of Montagu's charge, but it was enough. With their

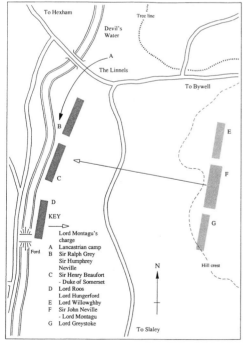

Fig 11.2   The Battle of Hexham

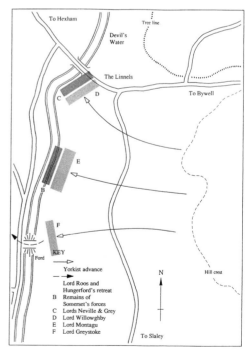

Fig 11.3   The Battle of Hexham

backs already to the water Somerset's men could retreat no further and the precarious nature of the location on which he had been forced to make a stand became all too evident. As the men of Somerset's force tried in vain to reorganize themselves, a degree of panic now arose within the Lancastrian line. As the front ranks gave ground, many at the back were pushed into the water, drowning under the weight of their armour. Others, clinging desperately to the bank, were simply crushed to death.

Montagu's charge was soon followed by the remainder of his army, enabling the Yorkist force to engage the whole length of the Lancastrian line. The hand-to-hand conflict that followed was fierce, if brief (*see* Fig. 11.3). Somerset strove to rally his army but to no avail. His centre had been smashed. He managed to organize and engage his left flank, but when he turned his attention to his right flank he found that Lords Roos and Hungerford had repeated their actions of Hedgeley Moor and had taken advantage of the chaos – and the ford to the rear of their position – to quit the field of battle, taking with them most of their men.

The left flank was to fare no better than the centre, and the morale of the remaining Lancastrians waned and finally broke along with their line. Soon the Lancastrian soldiers (along with their commanders Sir Ralph Grey and Sir Humphrey Neville), were fleeing for their lives, hotly pursued by the victorious Yorkists, some say as far as Hexham itself. With this the battle ended as the remaining Lancastrians, mostly Somerset's own retainers, were rapidly overpowered. The duke himself was taken prisoner.

EPILOGUE TO THE BATTLE

The destruction of the Lancastrians on the field of battle was completed with the execution of Sir Henry Beaufort, Duke of Somerset in Montagu's presence the following day. Lords Roos and Hungerford, captured in a wood near Hexham, were taken to Newcastle and executed two days later.

It seems ironic that the once mighty Duke of Somerset should die so ignominiously when it is remembered that his family had held such high positions in King Henry's court of old. We should, however, bear in mind that the duke was lucky to have lived so long, especially after falling into Warwick's hands – it was Somerset who commanded the Lancastrians at the Battle of Wakefield in 1461, where both Edward's and Warwick's father and brother had died. Indeed, Somerset had had many escapes, typically at Durham early in 1464 and at Northampton in 1463. With reference to the latter, as one chronicler put it, 'The commons of the town of Northampton and of the shires about rose upon that false traitor the Duke of Somerset and would have slain him within the King's palace, and then the King with fair speech and great difficulty saved his life for that time, and that was a pity for the saving of this life caused many a man's death soon after'.[2] How right he was! It seems fair to conclude that Somerset had made too many enemies in his life, and that by the time he had reached the North he was already on borrowed time. At Hexham, his luck finally ran out.

By 19 July more than two dozen other Lancastrian activists had been captured and executed on the orders of Lord Montagu and his brother the Earl of Warwick, who had now joined Montagu in the North. Left to their own devices these two were far less compassionate than King Edward in dealing with captured enemy nobles. The last of the summary executions came when another prominent Lancastrian, Sir William Tailboys, was captured (along with 2,000 marks from King Henry's war chest) while hiding in a coal pit and was taken to Newcastle and beheaded on 20 July.

After the Battle of Hexham, Lord Montagu learned of the presence of King Henry at Bywell Castle. Though he immediately despatched men to Bywell in the hope of capturing Henry, by the time they arrived he had already gone. On entering the chamber where he had spent the night all they found were some of his clothes and his coronated helmet, overlooked by Henry's servants in their haste to vacate the castle.

Two weeks after his victory at Hexham, Lord Montagu received his reward for his many years' service in Northumberland on King Edward's behalf. At York, before a host of other nobles, including his brothers Richard, Earl of Warwick and George, Bishop of Exeter, Montagu was elevated by Edward himself to the much coveted (and financially rewarding) Earldom of Northumberland.

The defeat of the Lancastrians at Hexham signalled the end of Lancastrian resistance to the Yorkists in Northumberland. All that remained hostile to Edward's rule in the North were the garrisons of Alnwick, Dunstanburgh and Bamburgh. Though the Earl of Warwick was anxious to return south, leaving the new Earl of Northumberland to tackle these nests of rebels, Edward persuaded him to remain in the North to help finish the job, while Edward himself went on to ratify a truce with the Scottish envoys (whom Northumberland had brought to York after the Battle of Hedgeley Moor). This truce was to bring peace between England and Scotland for the next fifteen years.

The Yorkists advanced first upon Alnwick. Its fortress, like those of Bamburgh and Dunstanburgh, was filled with survivors of the defeated Lancastrian armies that had fought at Hedgeley and Hexham, who had little stomach for further conflict. When Warwick's herald approached the castle and offered terms for its surrender (which included a full pardon for the defenders) they readily agreed. Warwick and Northumberland occupied Alnwick on 23 June. Two days later Dunstanburgh capitulated without a struggle when its defenders were given the same offer as the garrison of Alnwick.

Bamburgh was left as the last Lancastrian foothold in England to be overcome. Warwick's herald approached Bamburgh and offered the defenders the king's pardon if the castle were surrendered immediately. Though the garrison would probably have complied, its commander was the turncoat Sir Ralph Grey, who together with Sir Humphrey Neville was excluded from the offer of pardon, and therefore remained defiant. Grey sent Warwick's herald away with a message for the earl: 'I am determined to stay, and to live or die in this place'.[3]

Warwick's herald tried once more to secure a peaceful outcome, and returned to the castle to repeat the offer. On a more aggressive level he also added a personal message to Grey from Warwick himself: 'We will besiege this castle seven years if necessary. For every gunshot that hurts a wall of this royal stronghold, this jewel, a Lancastrian head shall fall'.[4] But Grey, doubtless aware of the fate awaiting him at Warwick's hands if he should surrender, was determined to stay. There then followed the only set-piece siege of a fortress, using cannon, of the entire war. Before long the king's great cannon were in place, and as they fired on the castle its once mighty walls began to crumble. In one attack a ball from the great gun 'Dijon' landed on the ceiling of the block that housed Grey's chambers, and Grey himself was knocked unconscious by the falling masonry. In the words of one chronicler, cannon fire 'passed through his chamber often times'.[5] With Grey incapacitated,

Harlech Castle, held for the Lancastrians during the Wars of the Roses, it was besieged by Lord Herbert and finally surrendered after many years in 1468

his second-in-command Neville negotiated a ceasefire and agreed terms (which included his own pardon) for surrender. The gates of the castle were opened and the fortress occupied by the Yorkists. Sir Ralph Grey, who was badly injured, was tied to his horse and taken to Doncaster, where he was tried before the constable of England, the Earl of Worcester, sentenced to death for high treason and hanged on 10 July.

By the end of the summer of 1464 Edward could claim to be King of all England and Wales, with the irritating exception of Harlech Castle, which was to hold out against him for several more years before it, too, finally capitulated. The following years of Edward's reign brought relative peace and prosperity to the land. As far as the Yorkists were concerned this was the reward for several long years of hardship which had started with the opening bowshots of the first Battle of St Albans in 1455 and ended with the surrender of Bamburgh Castle some nine years later in 1464. But it would be many years yet before the Wars of the Roses could be said to be finally over.

The Lancastrian King Henry managed to stay at large for another twelve months before being finally captured in a wood called Clitherwood near the small town of Clitheroe in Ribblesdale, Lancashire. At the time of his capture Henry was accompanied only by his squire Ellerton, and by two chaplains, Dr Thomas Makin and Dr Bedon. He was sent to the Tower of London, where he remained in relative comfort, alone in his piety, for most of what was left of his troubled life. As for his queen, Margaret, and his son Prince Edward, they remained in exile in France, supported by the charity of Margaret's father and surrounded by a few loyal retainers, planning for better days.

SECTION THREE

CHAPTER TWELVE

THE SEEDS OF REBELLION

Without doubt Edward Plantagenet sat on the throne of England and Wales not only by the grace of God but also in no small part through the efforts of Richard Neville, Earl of Warwick, known as 'the Kingmaker'. This being so, it is difficult to believe that by April 1471 Edward would be facing his one-time greatest ally, by then in command of a Lancastrian army, in battle at Barnet.

To understand this change in Warwick's allegiance it is necessary to explain the reasons for it. There were three main reasons. Firstly, Warwick was furious at Edward's clandestine marriage to Elizabeth Woodville, and the subsequent rise in fortunes of the Woodville family. Secondly, there was a serious difference in opinion between Warwick and Edward regarding England's foreign policy towards France and the Duchy of Burgundy. Thirdly, Warwick disliked Edward's increasing independence (of Warwick) and was irritated by the king's refusal to allow his brother Richard of Gloucester to marry Warwick's daughter Anne. Although it could be said that any of these reasons would give sufficient grounds for Warwick to bear a grievance against Edward, few thought it possible that open hostility might develop between the king and his most powerful noble.

'Now take heed what love may do . . .' wrote the chronicler Gregory, 'for love will not, nor may not foresee fault or peril in no thing.' These were his words on the subject of Edward's marriage to Elizabeth Woodville.[1] Elizabeth was by birth related on her mother's side to the emperor Charlemagne. Her father, however, belonged only to a minor English family. Elizabeth was the widow of Sir John Grey (son of Sir Edward Grey, Lord Ferrers of Groby), a Lancastrian noble who had died at St Albans fighting for Queen Margaret. As such she was considered unsuitable both as bride for Edward and as Yorkist queen. Edward, well aware of this, kept the marriage secret for more than four months and let it be known only when Warwick announced his plans for a diplomatic marriage between Edward and a French princess. Warwick, accompanied by Lord Wenlock, had in March 1464 pushed forward a truce with France, which was signed on 14 April. At this meeting he made plans for the discussion of a long-term truce, scheduled for 21 April, to be agreed and signed at St Omer, and which Warwick hoped would be ratified by a royal marriage. The announcement of Edward's marriage caused acute embarrassment for Warwick at the French court, and he was forced to take a different approach. The St Omer meeting

Queen Elizabeth Woodville, wife of Edward IV. Portrait in Queen's College, Cambridge

was postponed, and by the end of October Edward's secret marriage was common knowledge in Europe as well as in England.

Whether Warwick was more annoyed that Edward had chosen to marry a commoner and then to keep the marriage secret (even when Warwick had discussed with him the possibility of the diplomatic marriage), or because he had chosen not to discuss his plans with Warwick, is a matter for surmise. What is clear is that with the announcement of Edward's marriage an even greater problem presented itself to Warwick – the Woodvilles themselves. In a letter to Jean De Lannoy, Lord Wenlock summed up his own and probably Warwick's feelings on this subject when he wrote: 'We must be patient despite ourselves'.[2] Angry Warwick certainly was, but also sensible enough to accompany the Duke of Clarence in escorting Lady Elizabeth when she was publicly introduced at the royal court at Reading Abbey on Christmas Day 1464. The Lady Elizabeth did not arrive alone: when she came to court she brought with her five unmarried brothers, seven unmarried sisters, and her own two sons from her previous marriage. As members of the royal entourage, for appearance's sake the Woodvilles had to be elevated to a more respectable status than their background could justify.

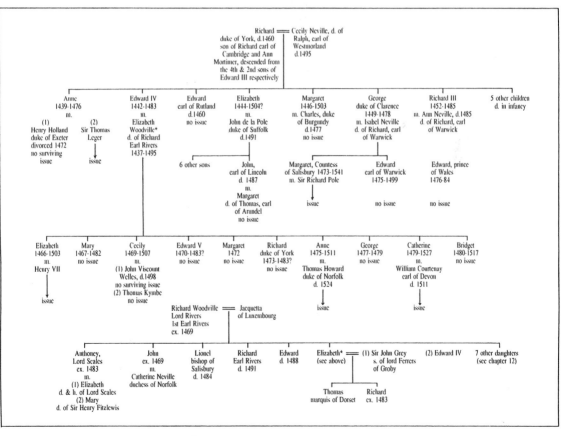

The House of York and Woodville

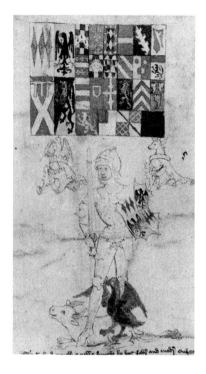

Richard Neville, Earl of Warwick, 'The Kingmaker', from the Rous Roll

This caused Edward much concern. It was no longer possible for him to bestow on the Woodvilles lands and titles which he had taken from the Lancastrians, as these had already been allocated to loyal supporters for services rendered. The only answer was to marry off these assorted Woodvilles into respectable families. The betrothals and marriages began even before the queen's coronation (which was by all accounts a splendid affair). Between 1464 and 1466 marriages of the various Woodvilles included: Margaret to Thomas, Lord Maltravers (Warwick's nephew and heir to the Earldom of Arundel); John to the Dowager Duchess of Norfolk, Katherine Neville (Woodville aged 20 and Katherine 65); Mary to William Herbert, son of Lord William Herbert; Katherine to Henry Stafford, grandson and heir to the Dukedom of Buckingham; Anne to William, Viscount Bourchier; and Eleanor to Anthony Gray, son of the turncoat of Northampton (*see* Chapter 4), heir to the title of Earl of Kent. Finally, in October 1466, Queen Elizabeth paid the Duchess of Exeter – Edward IV's sister – 4,000 marks in order that her eldest son by her first marriage, Thomas Grey, should be allowed to marry the duchess's eldest daughter, Anne Holland, even though she was already betrothed to George Neville, the Earl of Northumberland's son and Warwick's nephew.

Most of these marriages offended Warwick to some degree. He took most offence, as did many others, at the exploitation of his aunt, the Duchess of Norfolk (who, ironically, outlived her groom, though years his senior). The marriage of Thomas Grey to Anne Holland was nothing less than a direct family insult, and Warwick took great outrage at the Woodville/Herbert union when the young Herbert was granted the title of Lord Dunster, a title that Warwick had coveted for himself.

By 1466 most of the eligible bachelors of the kingdom had been taken by the Woodvilles. Warwick, quite apart from concerns already outlined, now faced the question of to whom could he marry off his own daughters? Both Isabel and Anne Neville were approaching marriageable age, and to Warwick it seemed that the only potential bridegrooms remaining were Edward's two surviving brothers, George, Duke of Clarence and Richard, Duke of Gloucester. It was due perhaps to Warwick's hope for his daughters (for having no sons of his own it was with them that his dynasty's future lay) that he suffered the setbacks of the previous two years. This important prospect of Warwick's own children marrying the king's brothers had first been raised at Cambridge in 1464. Even then Edward had been opposed to it, but Warwick, believing that he had the ability to manipulate his young cousin, persisted in the idea. So he again approached the king, once the Duke of Clarence had reached a suitable age, but despite the fact that Clarence was as keen on the match as Warwick, Edward angrily refused, claiming that the royal bachelors would better serve their country by marrying foreign brides, a rather hypocritical statement, in view of his own marital actions.

With the Woodvilles married to respectable partners, Edward turned his attention to the diplomatic needs of the kingdom. But here, too, was an area in which Warwick and he were to disagree. By May 1468 Edward had secured treaties with Aragon, Castile, Denmark, Scotland, Naples, Brittany and Burgundy. Warwick had been a close friend of King Louis XI of France for many years, during which time he had convinced Louis that since Edward had been king England's policy was in fact Warwick's own. The French had for some time been in dispute with Burgundy, and Louis had asked Warwick to convince Edward to side with France against it. But Edward's Anglo-Burgundy treaty was further evidence of how little control Warwick had over the young Yorkist king. Once again Warwick was made to look a fool.

To his great dismay, on 3 August 1468, and despite all Warwick's advice to the contrary, Edward signed an agreement to send English men-at-arms to serve with the Duke of Burgundy against France. This decision had a great effect on Edward's popularity with the common folk of England, who rallied behind the king whom they now saw as a second Henry V, taking up arms against their age-old enemies, the French. With the whole of England behind him Edward refused to change his mind, and for the time being rode along on the ever-increasing tide of support, apparently ignoring the fact that he lacked the backing of the one man who had done most to put him on the throne, Richard, Earl of Warwick.

By September the expeditionary force under the command of Lord Mountjoy was almost ready. With its departure imminent the first doubts about his own role in Edward's court must have entered Warwick's mind. It was clear to everybody that he was being pushed to the fringes of Edward's close circle of advisers, and that many of the Woodvilles and Herberts were taking his place. This must have been a bitter pill for Warwick, made the more difficult to swallow by the increasing power being bestowed on the Woodvilles. Since their arrival at court, hardly a week passed in which one Woodville or another failed to achieve advancement of some sort. Richard Woodville (Lord Rivers), the queen's father, had been created 1st Earl Rivers (and was later to replace the Earl of Worcester as treasurer of England); Sir Antony Woodville, the queen's brother, was created Lord Scales and given the wardenship of the Isle of

Wight, with its strategically placed Carisbrooke Castle. Though Warwick thought little of the title and lands, what cut deepest was the fact that he no longer held the king's confidence.

The widening divide between Warwick and the king was becoming increasingly evident also to those who opposed him and sought his downfall. Over the years, Warwick had made many enemies and those who hoped to prosper from his fall from favour were quick to fuel the fires of discord. Particularly damning was a rumour spread at court that Warwick was in league with Lancastrians-in-exile against the king. This rumour, though dismissed by most, was given credence by a messenger captured in Wales by men under the command of Lord Herbert. Sent by Margaret of Anjou to the besieged garrison at Harlech (still holding out for the Lancastrians), he was quick to agree that Warwick was indeed in contact with the Lancastrians. Edward called upon Warwick to come to London to answer the charge, but Warwick refused to travel to the capital for so ridiculous an accusation. The captured messenger was then sent to Warwick, and, once in his presence, withdrew his earlier statement.

This attempt to discredit Warwick had obviously been instigated by Lord Herbert, who saw Warwick as a major threat to the Herbert family's property in Wales. Although it failed it must have been a clear indication to Warwick of what the future must hold, since at first even the king had been prepared to go along with it. In order for Warwick to survive as a major power in England the king had to go, or, at the very least, the close circle of advisors that now surrounded Edward had to be broken. On which of these alternatives Warwick was working at this stage it is impossible to say. But what is clear is that to achieve either he needed an ally, though not as Herbert would have had people believe, a Lancastrian ally. Warwick's new protégé was a lot closer to home: no less a person than Edward's own brother, George, Duke of Clarence.

CHAPTER THIRTEEN

THE BATTLE OF EDGECOTE MOOR 26 JULY 1469

THE CAMPAIGN

In February 1469 Warwick was commissioned by Edward to cross the Channel to Calais and 'survey the boundaries of English territories'.[1] Unknown to all save Warwick's own supporters, by this time his plans for taking control of the country with Clarence were already well in hand. The seeds of rebellion had already been sown in the north of England, where one of Warwick's captains, Sir William Conyers, was busy stirring the common people into armed insurrection. Conyers was actually related to Warwick, by virtue of having married his niece, and could therefore be trusted. He had been instructed to raise an army (not a mob, for Warwick could still remember the damage done to Margaret's cause by her unruly northern army prior to Towton), and to await orders before coming out into the open.

Meanwhile, plans were in hand, secretly arranging Clarence's marriage to Warwick's daughter Isabel. To this end Warwick arranged for a dispensation to be granted by the Pope in Rome to make the marriage legal; the arrival of this dispensation in England set off a chain of events which would lead once again to armed conflict.

While the Duke of Clarence was being entertained by the prior at the convent of Christ Church in Canterbury, Warwick returned to England on or about 7 June, and made his way to Windsor to attend a chapter meeting of the Order of the Garter in honour of Edward's brother-in-law, the Duke of Burgundy. Edward had agreed to cross the Channel to visit Calais himself, but as he made plans to travel south news reached him of rebellion in the North. Warwick's men had already caused trouble when Conyers mistimed the rebellion and acted before Warwick was ready, forcing the earl of Northumberland to show a force of arms to put the rebels to flight. (The earl had allowed the leaders to escape, however, ensuring that the rebellion could rise again when the time was ripe.) On this occasion the revolt came not from Warwick's men but from the men of

Holderness, under a leader who took the name Robin of Holderness, and was fundamentally a local minor matter concerning a tax in the form of corn thraves levied by St Leonard's Hospital in York. However, it is alleged that these men of Holderness then began to demonstrate for the reinstatement of Henry Percy (a prisoner in the Tower of London since his capture at Towton) as Earl of Northumberland. This was a direct threat to Warwick's brother, Sir John Neville, who now held this title, and who was quick to crush the movement when the rebels reached York.

With unrest on this scale the king decided to postpone his trip to France, and on 6 June he left Windsor and began a slow march northwards. At the same time Warwick travelled to Sandwich for the official launching of his ship, the *Trinity*, after it had undergone a refit. Also present at this ceremony was Archbishop George Neville, Warwick's other brother, who was able to advise him of the arrival of the dispensation from Rome.

The Duke of Clarence left Canterbury on 9 June and also made his way to Sandwich. After the ship had been blessed by Archbishop Neville on 12 June, Clarence stayed in the company of the Duchess of York for four days (while she made an unexpected visit to a nearby abbey), before returning with Warwick to the duke's castle at Queensborough in Kent, there doubtless to finalize plans for the forthcoming rebellion. Things began to happen quickly. In the capital there were rumours, spread by Warwick's agents, that King Edward was illegitimate and that the Duke of Clarence

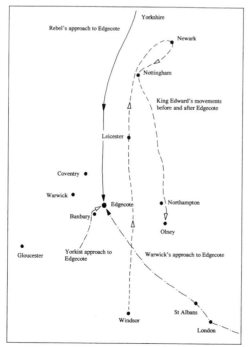

Fig 13.1   Preliminary Moves for the Battle of Edgecote Moor

was the true heir of the Duke of York and therefore to the throne. In the North, on Warwick's orders, Conyers had come out into the open while the Earl of Northumberland was busy putting down the rebels under Robin of Holderness. Conyers took the name Robin of Redesdale, and claimed that he had the support of the common people; he issued a 'popular petition' (actually written by Warwick) which compared Edward's government to those of Edward II, Richard II and Henry VI and called on the king to rid himself of his evil advisors, namely the Woodvilles, Herberts and Staffords.

With these events as a backdrop, on 28 June Warwick travelled to London, and then wrote to the mayor of Coventry informing him of the forthcoming marriage of his daughter to Edward's brother, the Duke of Clarence. Three days later, on 1 July, Warwick succeeded in obtaining a licence for the marriage from Archbishop Bourchier. Returning to Canterbury, he joined his brother George and Clarence before all took ship for Calais on 6 July. Five days later George, Duke of Clarence married Isabel Neville in Calais. The ceremony was performed by Archbishop George Neville and was witnessed by many lords and several knights. It was presided over by Warwick himself.

At about this time Edward had reached Newark, only to learn there of Robin of Redesdale and the seriousness of the situation in the North. Believing at first that the revolts there would be easily put down, he had mustered only a small force, including the Duke of Gloucester, Earl Rivers, Lord Scales and several other Woodvilles. Now he became aware that Redesdale's force outnumbered his. He turned south towards Nottingham to recruit reinforcements. But the king's popularity had waned somewhat over the last four years, and by now many of the common people of England had come to believe that their king was just a hedonistic individual who paid for his luxuries out of their taxes. The response to his call to arms was poor, as much of England favoured the petition and wanted change.

At Nottingham Edward waited patiently for the arrival of Sir William Herbert, Earl of Pembroke and Sir Humphrey Stafford, new Earl of Devon. For their own safety Edward thought that the Woodvilles should travel further south; accordingly Earl Rivers and his young son Sir John Woodville were sent to Wales and Lord Scales to Norfolk. By this time Edward had abandoned the idea of going north to deal with the rebels; ably led by Sir William Conyers and numbering many thousands, the rebels were approaching Nottingham, and were in fact dangerously close to outflanking Edward and cutting him off from the reinforcements heading in his direction.

On 12 July Warwick, Clarence and the others in their party, including the Earl of Oxford, who had travelled to Calais with Warwick, issued a manifesto declaring their support for the northern rebels and claiming that they sought 'a remedy and reformation'. Attached to the manifesto was a copy of the rebels' petition which also included a grievance about 'the exclusion of the Princess of the blood royal from the king's secret council in favour of the disceivable covetous rule and guiding of certain seducious persons'. These were named as most of the Woodville family, the Herberts, the Earl of Devon, Lord Dudley and Sir John Fogge, who were directly blamed for 'his [Edward's] realm to fall in great poverty of misery, disturbing the ministration of the laws, only intending their own promotion and enriching'. The manifesto also included a summons to all who wished to aid them, to come to Canterbury on 16 July.[2]

When Warwick reached Canterbury he and his party were well received, and when they left the city on 18 July, heading for London, he was at the head of a sizeable force. In London also they were well received (largely because the Londoners had received no word from Edward and because Warwick was a skilful and persuasive orator). They were allowed access to the city, and were even offered a loan of £1,000 to aid their cause. Warwick did not stay long in the capital and soon made off towards Coventry to join forces with Redesdale, undoubtedly planning to confront the king.

THE BATTLE

Author's note: Due to the turbulent nature of the period immediately before the battle, and the events that followed it, it is not possible to report the movements of the mêlée itself in any detail. Even by the standards of the day, because of the confusion faced by the chroniclers of the time, actual reference to the battle is scarce. No attempt has been made to re-create events and support them with diagrams. Instead, what is recounted is the best written reconstruction of the battle that can be made based on the information available today.

Edward must by now have been aware of what Warwick and Clarence were up to, yet strangely did nothing! While Warwick was assembling an army in the South and Redesdale was advancing on his position, Edward stayed motionless at Nottingham. The only possible explanation for this is that Edward, confused by recent events, deemed it prudent to stay put and await Pembroke and Devon before venturing into what he must have classed as unfriendly territory.

Robin of Redesdale, aware that Warwick was marching north to join him, deliberately bypassed the king at Nottingham, not only to speed up his union with the earl but also to cut Edward off from London. However, he was unaware of the whereabouts of Pembroke and Devon, and the two armies, unknown to each other, were on a collision course.

By all accounts the two forces became aware of each other on the night of 25 July. However, earlier that evening (before the presence of Redesdale's army became known to them) Pembroke and Devon had had an argument about the billeting arrangements for their respective parts of the army, when they made the decision to camp for the night at Edgecote, near Banbury. It appears that the Earl of Devon withdrew his portion of the army some miles from their current location and moved nearer to Banbury, while Pembroke's force made camp to the south of the little River Cherwell. As night fell scouts reported the arrival of the rebels to the north, and as it was too late in the day not only to do battle but even to bring up Devon's portion of the king's army, both forces decided to make camp for the night separated by the small river.

Early next morning the rebels launched an attack against Pembroke's force, apparently centred around the crossing of the river. The Welshmen of Pembroke's force, though well disciplined, were hampered by the absence of Devon's archers, and despite putting up brave resistance came off the worse, having to retreat from the

William, Lord Herbert, 1st Earl of Pembroke, and his wife Anne Devereux, kneeling before Edward IV

crossing and pull back some distance. Later in the day the Welshmen, still awaiting the arrival of the Earl of Devon, again came under attack. The struggle was particularly hard-fought, but they once again put up a brave defence. At about 1 o'clock Pembroke received news that the Earl of Devon had arrived and that his army was about to join the battle. At the same time an advanced guard of Warwick's army (whose main body was still on the road from London) came to reinforce the rebels. This mounted troop was led by Sir William Parr, Sir Geoffrey Gate and the Neville captain, John Chapman. Although this troop was only a small part of Warwick's army it did much to raise the confidence of the rebels, who believed that the rest of his force would soon be with them. The king's army, on seeing the arrival of men wearing Warwick's livery, concluded that the whole of his army was upon them. Their courage failed and it is uncertain whether Devon had the opportunity to commit his force to the battle before the king's army broke ranks and fled.

With this the conflict was over. It is said that on the field of battle some two thousand Welshmen lay dead. But the rebels also took heavy casualties, particularly among their leaders. Sir William Conyers (Robin of Redesdale himself) plus several other rebel captains lost their lives that day. The Earl of Pembroke and his brother Sir Richard Herbert were taken prisoner, though Devon managed to escape (which strengthens the conjecture that the earl might never have fought at all). On Sir William Conyers' death his brother Sir John took command of the rebel army. As steward of Warwick's castle at Middleham he was a high-ranking officer in the Neville household. In later years it was suggested that he was the original Redesdale, but there is some evidence that proves that he took the name only after his brother's death.

EPILOGUE TO THE BATTLE

The Earl of Warwick had by now arrived at Northampton where the day after the battle the two Herbert brothers were brought to him. With no legal justification, they were both executed on Warwick's orders, guilty of nothing other than loyalty to their king and the thwarting of Warwick's ambitions in Wales.

Meanwhile, the king, who had remained at Nottingham throughout these events, and who by all accounts was still unaware of the fate of his army at Edgecote, left the city on 29 July and headed towards Northampton, hoping to be reunited with the Earls of Pembroke and Devon. En route to the town he was brought news of the defeat at Edgecote and the destruction of the royal army. At this point it appears that he was deserted by the remnants of his army, abandoned by all except a few loyal retainers, including Richard, Duke of Gloucester and Lord Hastings.

Warwick was making for Coventry when he heard of Edward's fate, and not wanting to show force of arms at once ordered his brother George to go and intercept the king. The archbishop found Edward on the Northampton road near Olney with only his few loyal retainers at hand. After dismissing the Duke of Gloucester (who at sixteen was thought to be of no importance) and Hastings (who was Warwick's brother-in-law, and whom Warwick hoped to win over at a later date), Neville suggested to Edward that he should allow himself to be escorted to Warwick at

Coventry. The king, with no other obvious choice of action open to him, duly agreed, and was taken into the 'protection' of the Earl of Warwick.

The following August Earl Rivers and Sir John Woodville were captured on the banks of the Severn and were taken on 12 August to Coventry, where they were duly executed at Warwick's command. The Earl of Devon, who had been lucky to escape Edgecote with his life, was killed by a mob in Somerset who had recognized him while he was trying to make good his escape. With Devon, the Herberts and the senior Woodvilles all dead, and with Edward Warwick's prisoner, the Kingmaker had achieved his goal – reinstatement as the most powerful noble in the land.

CHAPTER FOURTEEN

THE BATTLE OF LOSECOTE FIELD 12 MARCH 1470

After his capture at Olney, Edward was taken first to Warwick Castle and later to the Neville stronghold of Middleham in the North. For his capture, he had only himself to blame: his indecision at Nottingham and his apparent faith in the ability of Devon and Pembroke alone to crush the 'rebels', were certainly the major contributing factors to his downfall. But if Warwick was pleased that he had been able to capture the king entirely by his own devices, then his satisfaction must have been short-lived. Though he had gained control of Edward almost single-handedly, it seemed that he would also have to govern the country single-handedly as well, for the fact was that he did not have the support of the realm's other leaders. From the outset this lack of support from his fellow nobles limited his ability to run the country. Warwick helped himself to the offices made vacant by Pembroke's death, but even bestowing the office of Chamberlain of South Wales on William, Lord Hastings failed to win him over to his camp. As to what to do with the king, it was clear at this point that Warwick had no evil intentions towards Edward, though at one stage it was reported (by the Milanese ambassador in France) that Edward would be publicly declared a bastard and that the throne would pass to the Duke of Clarence. It appears that this was not the case, but as time went by it became clear to Warwick that Edward would not allow himself to become a puppet monarch. In London Warwick's victory over the king (and the absence of any royal authority) signalled the start of violence, as people began a campaign of rioting and plundering in the capital. It was only the intervention of the city authorities, with the backing of the Duke of Burgundy, who published a message promising his goodwill to the people of England if they remained loyal to Edward and the Burgundy alliance, which put a halt to the disturbances.

Elsewhere in the country lack of royal authority led to the resumption of personal feuds between the nobles. Nothing better illustrates the lack of order in England at this time than the Duke of Norfolk's attack on the Paston-owned castle of Caister in August 1469. Though Warwick sent Archbishop George Neville and the Duke of Clarence to act as mediators between Norfolk and the besieged Pastons, all efforts to bring peace to the county failed. There were similar disturbances in Gloucestershire between the Talbots and the Berkeleys, and in Lancashire between the Stanleys and the Harringtons. Even the king's brother, Richard, came to blows early in 1470, when violence broke out in Yorkshire between the young duke and Thomas, Lord Stanley.

This breakdown of Yorkist law and order led to fears of Lancastrian uprisings, fears that were soon realized when Sir Humphrey Neville of Brancepeth and his brother Charles raised the standard of Henry VI along the border with Scotland. Warwick, unable even to maintain law and order, much less to raise on his own a royal army to march north to deal with the Lancastrians, became painfully aware that he needed the king's authority to command the obedience of the people of England. The king, still at Middleham since his arrival there in August, was allowed to leave the castle and duly appeared in public at York on 10 September 1469. With his royal backing Warwick was able to muster a force, and set off north to deal with the Neville-backed Lancastrian uprisings. The two Neville brothers were soon captured and taken to York, where they were tried and executed on 29 September.

This brief taste of freedom was all that Edward needed to re-impose his control over the country. He summoned his brother Richard, the Earls of Arundel, Essex and Northumberland as well as William, Lord Hastings and other members of the king's council to travel from London into his presence. Once surrounded by his own men, Edward declared that he was returning to London. In the middle of October he entered the capital in full state. The Earl of Warwick, anxious to associate the Neville name with the king's return, ordered Archbishop Neville to march into the city alongside Edward. However, while Neville, accompanied by the Earl of Oxford, tried in vain to catch up with the king's entourage, they were intercepted by a messenger from the king, with a message that when the king wanted them he would send for them. Warwick's success and subsequent rule was at an end. Once again Edward was his own man and King of England.

Warwick's failure to exert control stemmed largely from the lack of support from his fellow nobles. Even though Edward was unpopular both with them and among the common people, he was still king. The support Warwick had received from Robin of Redesdale and his followers went only so far as freeing the king of the 'evil council' of the Herberts and Woodvilles, not to rid England of the king himself. The idea of replacing Edward was not one that people would openly support. It became clear that Warwick could not rule without Edward, so Edward was allowed to go free, but, as the king was about to find out, just as Warwick could not rule without him, neither could he rule without Warwick.

As an air of uneasy peace settled over the kingdom, Edward was careful not to offend Warwick. However, in order to fill the power vacuum in Wales created after Pembroke's death, Warwick was relieved of the titles he had taken for himself the previous summer, and these were then passed to Edward's brother, the Duke of Gloucester.

Warwick's success of 1469 had failed to bring about the results he had wanted. Though he had managed to remove the Herberts and some of the Woodvilles as the king's councillors, he found that he was not yet in a position to formulate policy for Edward and England. His daughter's marriage to the king's brother had brought his family closer to the throne, should Edward die without leaving a son, but Warwick was still left wanting. He had tried to rule England with Edward as a puppet king, but this had failed. On the surface, Edward acted as if nothing had happened, but Warwick knew that he was just waiting for the right moment to exact his revenge. The only counter-move open to Warwick was to rid himself of Edward before his queen bore him a son. Once this was done Clarence would become king and Warwick's daughter would be queen. With Clarence as king, England would be governed as Warwick wished.

To bring all this about Warwick needed only a catalyst. While there was peace in England his plans would not bear fruit, but he knew also that there would not be peace for long. All he had to do was to wait. Peace in England was (as Warwick had guessed) short-lived: trouble flared up again early in March 1470. The spark that lit the fire this time was a feud between Sir Thomas Burgh of Gainsborough and a leading landowner in Lincolnshire, Richard, Lord Welles. During the winter of 1470 Welles, accompanied by his son Sir Robert Welles and his brothers-in-law Sir Thomas de la Lande and Sir Thomas Dymmock, had led a group of men-at-arms to Burgh's manor house, attacked it, driven Burgh's family from the shire and carried off all his possessions. But Burgh was Edward's Master of Horse, and Edward decided to march to his assistance. He also summoned Lord Welles and Sir Thomas Dymmock to appear before him at Westminster, where they were questioned and though subsequently pardoned for their acts (owing to their prompt arrival at Westminster), were nevertheless detained in London at the king's pleasure. This dramatic intervention startled Sir Robert Welles and those members of his family who had remained in Lincolnshire, and caused him to seek equally powerful allies. It was only natural that he should turn to the Earl of Warwick, who by chance was Welles' second cousin. With this windfall the earl (and Clarence) gladly agreed to help. Warwick left the subsequent planning of the forthcoming armed response to the Duke of Clarence, in an effort to improve Clarence's status with Welles' supporters (later to be classed as 'rebels'). Clarence sent his chaplain into Lincolnshire with a message for Welles to muster his forces but not to act until the Earl of Warwick had left London.

The king had called for an army to be mustered at Grantham on 12 March. This time Edward was taking no chances, as he could recall only too clearly the events of the previous summer. Edward had planned to leave the capital on 4 March, accompanied by forces led by the Dukes of Norfolk and Suffolk, the Earls of Wiltshire and Worcester, and Lords Hastings and Howard, but as he was making ready to leave, he was told that his brother Clarence had arrived in the city and wished to see him. The two met at Baynard's Castle on the 6th. If Edward had any suspicions about his brother he did not show them, and seemed to be satisfied when Clarence told him he was travelling west to see his wife, and would not therefore be going with the king. Only afterwards did Edward learn that Clarence had come to London with the intention of delaying Edward's departure from the city, to allow time for Welles to raise his army. No sooner had Edward left the capital than Clarence rode off to join Warwick, who had by now left London.

The news of the king's intention to march into Lincolnshire to quell the unrest was misinterpreted (no doubt fuelled by wild rumours from Welles) to mean that the king intended to hold a bloody assize and would not uphold the general pardon issued to those former rebels from Lincolnshire (of whom there were a great number) who had joined with Robin of Redesdale the previous year. It was reported that the king's intention was to: 'Come thither and utterly destroy those that late made commotion there', and that: 'The King's Judges would sit, and hang and draw a great number of the commons'.[1]

At this (and perhaps also with some encouragement from Warwick and Clarence), Sir Robert Welles set himself up as a 'great captain' of the commons of Lincolnshire. On 4 March he had arranged for notices to be posted in every church in Lincolnshire, with a call to arms and an appeal for men to meet him at Ranby Hawe near Lincoln in order to resist the king. On 7 March the king, by now at Waltham Abbey, heard of Welles' call to arms and moved to Royston, arriving there the following day.[2] While he was there Edward received the alarming news, from Lord Cromwell's steward of Tattershall Castle, that the 'rebels' were heading for Stamford and had been joined by men from neighbouring shires, particularly Yorkshire, and now numbered some hundred thousand men-at-arms. On the same day Edward received letters from Clarence and Warwick stating that they were joining the king on his journey north and would soon be with him to help him put down the rebels, since these rebels had been able to gather such a great host. The king, though surprised at this offer of aid, did not yet suspect Warwick's or Clarence's loyalty, and, being unaware of their involvement, issued commissions of array which included Warwick, so that Warwick began assembling his own forces with the king's blessing. Next day Edward pushed on the 21 miles to Huntingdon. Here, Edward was joined by the captives Lord Welles and Thomas Dymmock (whom he had ordered to be brought to him after he had heard of Sir Robert Welles' call to arms). Upon their arrival Edward interrogated them, separately, and both confessed to their parts in the revolt but not to Warwick's or Clarence's involvement. With this, Edward ordered Lord Welles to write a letter to his son demanding his submission and informing him that, if Sir Robert failed to comply with the instructions in the letter, his father and Dymmock would be put to death.

On Sunday 11 March, by which time Edward had reached Fotheringhay, he received news that the rebels had changed course and were heading for Leicester. Later the same day he learnt that Warwick and Clarence were also heading for Leicester. Receipt of this news must have forced Edward to conclude that Warwick, Clarence and Welles were in league with one another, and that the two forces were heading for a rendezvous. If Edward continued on his way he would be cut off from London and caught between two enemy forces, that of Warwick and Welles to the west, and the Yorkshire element of the rebels who had answered Welles' call to arms to the north-east. It was rumoured the latter were led by Sir John Conyers and Lord Scrope of Bolton.

It appears that, the following day, Sir Robert Welles received his father's letter and turned back towards Stamford, without joining up with Warwick, in an attempt to save his father's life. Edward, moving more confidently since Warwick had lost Welles' force, and because his own army was being joined by many who had answered his call to arms, reached Stamford at the same time as did Welles. As Edward made camp in Stamford he received word from Warwick and Clarence that they had reached Leicester en route to coming to his aid. Edward, if privately doubting Warwick and his brother, kept his thoughts to himself and maintained an outward confidence in their avowed intentions.

Edward ordered his scouts ahead to find the exact location of the rebel army, and they soon returned with news that it had moved towards Empingham, some 5 miles west of Stamford, and that it was arrayed and awaiting battle. With this, Edward ordered his army westward, and when Edward's force met that of Welles it, too, lined up for battle. As the two armies faced each other Edward ordered the summary execution of both Lord Welles and Sir Thomas Dymmock in front of the assembled armies. With this the rebels, their force consisting mainly of infantry, began their advance. Led by their 'Captain of footmen', Richard Warren, and with cries of 'a'Warwick, a'Warwick', and 'a'Clarence, a'Clarence' (confirming Edward's suspicions), they marched towards the king's forces. The rebels, it is said, numbered some thirty thousand men, but the king's army, though outnumbered, was more highly trained. After an initial barrage of royal cannon fire, Edward ordered his men to charge, and what followed was more a rout than a battle, for even before the two armies came to blows the rebel army broke and fled the field, jubilantly pursued by Edward's men.

Many of the men under Welles' command were wearing livery jackets of the Earl of Warwick and the Duke of Clarence. It is said that as they fled the field these jackets were discarded by their wearers, who doubtless had no desire to be caught wearing such incriminating evidence. This shedding of garments gave the battle the name of 'Losecote Field'.

Among those captured after the battle were Sir Robert Welles (still wearing the livery of Clarence), Sir Thomas de la Lande and Richard Warren, but the most important capture was another man also wearing the livery jacket of the Duke of Clarence. He turned out to be the duke's envoy to Sir Robert Welles, and who had in

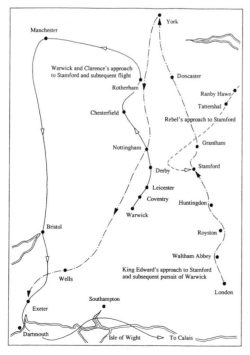

Fig 14.1 Preliminary Moves for the Battle of Losecote Field

his possession a casket of letters from the duke, the contents of which confirmed the king's fears that his brother and Warwick were in league with the rebels. It had, as far as Edward was concerned, been a close-run thing. If the experienced forces of Warwick's army had joined with the rebels then the outcome could have been very different. The following day, Edward wrote to Warwick and Clarence reporting his victory and instructing them to disband their army and to come to him at Stamford with no more men than was appropriate to their status. On the same day he wrote to Sir John Neville with a commission of array instructing him to deal with the Yorkshire element of the rebel army, which had indeed been led by Sir John Conyers and Lord Scrope of Bolton, and which had failed to reach Empingham.

The Earl of Warwick and Clarence were at this time in Coventry, and the king's letter must have seemed like an invitation into a trap. Warwick knew that his force was too small to take on the might of the king's army, so he wrote back to the king informing him that he and Clarence would disband their army and meet him at Stamford as instructed. However, instead Warwick kept his army together, and wrote to his Yorkshire supporters asking them to meet him at Rotherham with as many men as they could muster. Warwick and his army then marched via Burton-on-Trent and Derby to the Warwick-controlled town of Chesterfield, where they arrived on 19 March.

Edward, on hearing of Warwick's march, wrote another letter, again commanding him to disband his army and to come to his presence to answer charges of involvement in the revolt. Warwick and Clarence this time agreed on condition that they were given guarantees of safety and clemency. Edward, however, refused to treat them as equals, and so Warwick continued to travel towards Rotherham while the king himself moved his army to Doncaster, where he arrived on or about 19 March. While he was here the Earl of Shrewsbury, who had been supporting the Duke of Clarence, defected and marched towards the king's army at Doncaster, taking many of Clarence's north midland supporters with him. It was also at Doncaster that the captives Sir Robert Welles and Richard Warren were tried and executed before the assembled army on 19 March. They had now confessed not only to their own but also to Warwick's and Clarence's involvement in the revolt, and had acknowledged that it was the primary intention of the revolt to place Clarence on the throne. At this time Edward issued an offer of pardon and safe passage to any who would desert Warwick and Clarence. It seems that one of Warwick's captains Sir William Parr (who had led the cavalry at Edgecote) took up the offer and marched into Edward's camp. During Edward's later reign he became a prominent member of the royal household, and his grand-daughter Katherine Parr was later to marry Henry VIII and become Queen of England.

Edward travelled from Doncaster to York, arriving in the city on 22 March. Here he received Sir John Conyers, brother of the late Sir William Conyers, Lord Scrope of Bolton and Robert Hildyard, 'Robin of Holderness', who had all submitted to the king on the promise of safe passage. Edward was true to his word and issued them all with pardons and forgave them for their involvement in both the previous year's and the current uprising.

On 24 March Edward issued a proclamation stating that if Warwick and Clarence did not surrender before the 28th of the month they were to be treated as traitors and would suffer accordingly. Also at the end of March Edward reinstated Henry Percy (a Yorkist prisoner since his capture and his father's death at Towton in 1461) to the title of Earl of Northumberland. Sir John Neville, who had previously held this title, was created instead Marquis of Montagu (*see* Appendix II), and to offset any insult to the Neville pride John Neville's son, George, was given the title of Duke of Bedford and became betrothed to Edward's eldest daughter, Elizabeth.

Meanwhile, Warwick was still on the move. Having reached Rotherham to find only a handful of supporters willing to join him, he marched into Lancashire to try to enlist the aid of the Stanleys. Finding that the Stanleys, too, were unwilling to help, Warwick was forced to retreat south. When he reached Bristol he still retained some five thousand men-at-arms, but, realizing that he could not possibly hope to win in battle, accepted that his coup had failed. Abandoning their artillery at Bristol, Warwick and Clarence travelled to Exeter, arriving on 3 April. They then moved on to the Clarence-held town of Dartmouth, where they boarded ship and left England to seek exile abroad in France.

Edward had failed to take up the pursuit with vigour (because of shortages of food and provisions he had detoured to York in order to re-supply his army before heading south), and did not reach Exeter until 14 April. His arrival in that city via Nottingham, Coventry and Wells came after a 290-mile march lasting nineteen days.

Edward, mindful of the events of 1460, attempted to prevent Warwick from using either Ireland or Calais as a base by replacing Clarence as Lieutenant of Ireland with the Earl of Worcester, and by writing to Warwick's deputy in Calais, Lord Wenlock, with strict instructions to refuse them entry into the city.

As Warwick and Clarence headed for Calais, accompanied only by a few hundred retainers, the Countess of Warwick and the (now heavily pregnant) Duchess of Clarence sailed east along the south coast of England. Warwick, keen to strengthen his fleet, raided Southampton in an attempt to capture his flagship, *Trinity*, plus several other vessels moored there. But Anthony Woodville, the new Earl Rivers, was waiting for him there with the royal fleet, and Warwick did not have it all his own way. He failed to capture the ships and some of his own men were captured, among them Sir Geoffrey Gate. Though Gate was spared, many of the common soldiers were cruelly put to death by Edward's new Constable of England, John Tiptoft, Earl of Worcester, who ordered that the captured men be hanged, drawn, quartered and beheaded. Their bodies were then hung upside down and a sharpened stake with the head on one end was impaled into their buttocks. This act, as one chronicler put it, caused the earl to become 'greatly behated among the people'.[3]

Warwick arrived at Calais on 16 April, but when his ships approached the harbour they were fired upon by the cannon in the fortress. Edward's message to the city had arrived only hours earlier and though Wenlock was still a loyal Warwick supporter the majority of the garrison, including their commander, the Marshal of Calais, Gaillard, Lord Duras (a Gascon exile), sided with Edward. Warwick sent an angry message to Wenlock ordering him to allow him entry into the city. Wenlock politely refused. He was later to send a secret message to Warwick informing him that Calais was a 'mousetrap'. With a Burgundian army to its rear, camped at St Omer, and with Lord Howard fast approaching it with the English fleet, Wenlock advised Warwick that it would be better for him to sail on, rather than be besieged within the city. Though many believe that Wenlock betrayed his royal master, as one chronicler put it: 'No man showed such great loyalty as Lord Wenlock'.[4]

Warwick decided to sail towards the relative safety of French soil west of Calais, but before he could set sail Isabel went into labour. With no medicinal herbs or wine aboard to help, the Countess of Warwick became concerned for her daughter's well-being. Warwick sent a message to Wenlock asking compassion for his daughter, and Wenlock ordered two casks of wine to be taken to Warwick's ship. The birth was a difficult one, and though the mother survived the baby died and was buried at sea before Calais.

Warwick left Calais on 20 April. As his small fleet sailed into the English Channel it was lucky enough to fall in with a large fleet of Flemish merchant ships. Warwick, always keen to indulge in profiteering, engaged the merchant fleet in combat and captured some sixty of their number. It is said that when this was reported to Duke Charles at the Burgundy court, he flew into a great rage and travelled in person to the port of Sluys to oversee the mobilization of his own fleet which would later sail to seek out the Earl of Warwick and avenge the loss of the Flemish merchant ships.

As Warwick sailed further west his fleet was sighted by the English navy under the command of John, Lord Howard. Howard was quick to engage Warwick's fleet, and in the fierce battle that followed managed to recapture some of the ships that Warwick had taken previously. But when Warwick sailed into Honfleur he was still at the head of a powerful naval force, and when he sent a message to the King of France asking for protection he also sent a personal note to Louis in which he claimed that he, Warwick 'the Kingmaker', was ready to reinstate the House of Lancaster on the throne of England. At first stunned by Warwick's total change in allegiance, Louis XI was nonetheless quick to take advantage of it. To him a Lancastrian king on the throne of England, with Warwick by his side, meant an Anglo-French alliance against the Duke of Burgundy, with the prospect of realizing his ambition to retake the Somme towns for the kingdom of France.

Unfortunately for Louis (and Warwick), Warwick's attacks on Flemish shipping had so incensed Charles of Burgundy that the Burgundian fleet, under the command of Admiral Henrik van Borselen, had now joined forces with Lord Howard's fleet, and both were determined to destroy Warwick's, whose own fleet continued to raid Dutch shipping throughout the month of May. As a result of this, combined Anglo-Burgundian raids were launched against Norman coastal towns in reprisal for Louis' giving sanctuary to Warwick's fleet.

At the end of June threats of a Hanseatic raiding party to the east caused the English fleet to return to England to protect its coastline, and van Borselen took the opportunity to return to his home port to refit his ships. With the Channel free of hostile shipping, Warwick ordered his fleet to sail farther down the coast to Barfleur and La Hogue, while Warwick himself (with Clarence) made his base inland at nearby Valognes.

In the meantime Louis was making plans on Warwick's behalf to reinstate the House of Lancaster to the throne of England. Out of his own purse he paid for the meagre court of Margaret of Anjou to be moved from the family home at Saumur in Anjou to Angers, where Louis visited her in order to enlist her support and that of the Lancastrians-in-exile for Warwick's planned invasion of England. It took all of Louis' considerable diplomatic skills to convince Margaret that she could now trust the one man who had done the most to bring ruin to her household. It was only Louis' promise of support and aid which persuaded her to even consider talking to Warwick at all. Finally, on 22 June 1470, Margaret agreed to meet Warwick at Angers in northern France. When they met, it is said, Warwick went down on one knee to ask the queen for her forgiveness, and that Margaret kept him there for a good twenty minutes before finally agreeing to pardon him for the sake of restoration of the Lancastrian cause to the throne of England. In political terms the plan was simple: in return for Margaret's aid, Warwick would lead an invasion force (paid for by French money) to England, overthrow Edward, and return the Lancastrian King Henry VI to the throne. As for Warwick, all he wanted in return was the marriage of his youngest daughter Anne to Henry's son Prince Edward. Warwick no doubt intended to have young Edward made king as soon as possible upon their return, and that any children the couple should bear, the future monarchs of England, would be Warwick's grandchildren. Prince Edward and Anne Neville were solemnly betrothed in Angers Cathedral on 25 July and married on 13 December. The Warwick and Lancastrian alliance was finally cemented.

Meanwhile, in England, Edward was not unaware of Warwick's plans, and set about preparing the country for invasion. In the South he promoted Sir William Fitzalan, Earl of Arundel to Constable of Dover and the Cinque Ports. (He personally visited the defences they were building in June 1470.) To the north the recently reinstated Earl of Northumberland, Sir Henry Percy, and the Marquis of Montagu, Sir John Neville were patrolling as a safe-guard, but as the English fleet, once again blockading the ports in France where Warwick's ships were berthed, was his best defence against invasion, Edward reinforced their position with another naval squadron under the command of Sir Anthony Woodville, Earl Rivers.

Part of Warwick's plan to invade England involved a diversion to the north of the country, so drawing Edward's attention (and, Warwick hoped, Edward as well) away from the South. The majority of Warwick's captains, like Conyers and Gate, had been captured after the previous uprisings, so Warwick turned to one of his brothers-in-law for help. He wrote to both Lord Fitzhugh, who lived in North Yorkshire, and Richard Salkard, until recently Constable of Carlisle, with instructions to instigate the revolt on his behalf.

By the beginning of August 1470 news of northern uprisings was once again being heard in London. Edward, weary of these northern revolts, and somewhat puzzled both at Northumberland's inability to deal with the rebels and Montagu's similar lack of resolve, made the decision to travel north in person to deal with the revolt. In later years he was greatly criticized for this serious error of judgement. With his naval blockade of Warwick's ships still in place he felt it was a risk worth taking. By 14 August Edward was at York; two days later he was at Ripon, where the rebels dispersed as quickly as they had mustered, Fitzhugh and Salkard fleeing to the safety of Scotland. However, instead of returning south, Edward remained in the North. It was his decision to do so that brought about the events that followed.

Over in France, Warwick, with his invasion plans completed, together with the Duke of Clarence (who was now something of an embarrassment to Warwick, with his new Lancastrian friends) and Sir John De Vere, Earl of Oxford, who had joined Warwick in France, boarded ship and awaited an opportunity to sail to England. But the English fleet was still blockading the French ports where Warwick's ships were berthed, and Warwick found himself unable to leave. Then, at the beginning of September, a great storm blew up, raging all the way from the Channel to the tip of Scotland. On 8 September, when the storm had blown itself out, Warwick found that the blockading fleet had been scattered and immediately ordered his fleet to sea. With his allies, now including the Lancastrian Jasper Tudor, Earl of Pembroke and Sir Edmund Beaufort, Duke of Somerset, he sailed for England. It had been agreed beforehand that Margaret and her son, along with Anne Neville, would remain in France until such time as it would be safe for them to cross the Channel. Anne's presence in France would also act as a safeguard against any change of heart that Warwick might have.

The invasion force landed on the coast near Exeter and immediately declared for Henry VI. No sooner had they landed than they set off inland, and by the time they reached Coventry they had recruited a force numbering some thirty thousand men-at-arms. Edward, now marching south to meet the invasion force, was confident of victory. He had summoned his retainers to gather at Nottingham, and with their help was certain of being able to crush the invaders. When he reached Doncaster he stopped for the night and dispersed his men to the surrounding settlements until the following morning. As he sat down to an evening meal with the Duke of Gloucester, Earl Rivers, Lords Hastings, Howard and Say, a messenger arrived with grave news from Yorkshire. It transpired that the Marquis of Montagu, who on the king's orders had gathered an army to come to Edward's assistance, and was due to meet him at Rotherham the following day, had halted his army on the march south and informed them that they were declaring for Henry VI. It seems that Montagu had not been placated with his promotion to marquis when he had been forced to hand over the Earldom of Northumberland to Henry Percy, and that he had been in secret correspondence with Warwick in France and had agreed to side with his brother and the Lancastrians. As if this news were not bad enough, further information warned Edward that the marquis was at this very moment heading for Doncaster with all his men, who had agreed to side with him, in an attempt to capture him.

Edward, with his army spread over such a large area, could not hope to gather enough of his men, in the few hours remaining, to oppose Montagu. There was no other course open to him other than to flee, knowing that once his soldiers discovered that he had left Doncaster, and that they had no leader to follow, they would simply disperse. Faced with a Neville army to both his front and his rear, he decided to travel south-east towards the coast. His party made a risky crossing of the Wash (in which they nearly drowned) and made it to the relative safety of the town of King's Lynn. By now Warwick and his Lancastrian allies had control of most of the country, and Edward, cut off not only from his capital but also from his army, made the painful decision to leave the country. At King's Lynn he managed to procure three ships, and with his small band of retainers and their retinues (a force numbering some five hundred people), left England for the relative safety of the Low Countries and the protection of his brother-in-law, Duke Charles of Burgundy.

On 6 October Warwick made a triumphant entry into London. When news of his flight became known, Edward's entire government collapsed. His queen, who had remained in London, fled from the Tower, where she was staying, to sanctuary in Westminster Abbey. As soon as Warwick entered London he went at once to the Tower and freed Henry VI from his confinement. Then, going down on one knee, he swore an oath of allegiance to Henry and returned him to his throne and his kingdom.

The wheel had gone full circle: the 'Kingmaker' had done it again.

CHAPTER FIFTEEN

THE BATTLE OF
BARNET
14 APRIL 1471

THE CAMPAIGN

Edward's flight from England to the Low Countries, though it saved him from the Earl of Warwick, was not without danger. His ship was sighted by a hostile squadron of Hanseatic vessels which gave chase and almost captured it before he reached the safety of the Dutch coast near Alkmaar. On reaching port, Edward, having no money of his own, paid the ship's captain with his furred gown. In Holland, he and his party gave themselves up to Louis of Bruges, Lord of Gruthuyse, Duke Charles of Burgundy's governor of the country. Louis already knew Edward from his days as Duke Charles's ambassador to England. He took Edward and his party to his home in The Hague where they arrived on 11 October 1470. Here they were provided with food, clothing and shelter.

While Edward enjoyed enforced exile in Holland, the Earl of Warwick set about strengthening his own position in England. It seems likely that he allowed the Duke of Clarence, along with Sir John Talbot, Earl of Shrewsbury and Sir John De Vere, Earl of Oxford, who had remained loyal to Warwick on the earl's return to England (even though in Talbot's case it was more a question of loyalty to Clarence), to reclaim their estates. Several influential 'old guard' Lancastrians had returned to England with Warwick, among them Jasper Tudor and Edmund Beaufort (who had claimed the title of Duke of Somerset while in exile in France). These nobles, together with Henry Holland, Duke of Exeter, now set about preparing to defend the country against invasion by Edward, an event they believed would not be long in coming.

Warwick issued commissions of array to many nobles to raise men, and issued pardons to many remaining Yorkists left in England, most of whom were in hiding or had taken refuge in various sanctuaries. One exception was Edward's Constable of England, Sir John Tiptoft, Earl of Worcester, nicknamed the 'Butcher of England' for the way he ordered the decapitation of those found guilty of treason. Found hiding in Huntingdonshire forest, Tiptoft was handed over to the Earl of Oxford, whose father and elder brother he had put to death in 1462. On 15 October he was tried and found guilty of treason, and was executed on Oxford's orders. Other less dangerous but still prominent Yorkists who were in a position to aid Edward were imprisoned, the most notable of these being Sir John Mowbray, Duke of Norfolk and Thomas Bourchier, Archbishop of Canterbury, who were sent to the Tower of London.

Warwick believed the North of England was relatively secure due to the presence there of many Neville adherents. Though the loyalty of the Earl of Northumberland was questionable, his family had traditionally always been Lancastrians. Warwick's brother was residing at Pontefract Castle also, keeping an eye on the North as an added precaution.

In the eastern counties the Earl of Oxford and Lord Scrope of Bolton were patrolling as a safe-guard, while in the Channel a fleet under the command of the Bastard of Fauconberg was watching the southern coast (with Fauconberg still taking every opportunity to engage in piracy by attacking any passing Spanish or Portuguese shipping). Finally, in Wales Jasper Tudor, now calling himself Earl of Pembroke, was raising support for the Lancastrians among his Welsh kinsmen. With this Warwick's defences were complete, and all he could do now was to wait.

In Holland, Edward realized that if he hoped to regain his crown he would have to act quickly and return to England before Margaret of Anjou and the Lancastrian Prince Edward crossed from France. He secured a loan from his brother-in-law the Duke of Burgundy, hired between twelve and fifteen hundred Burgundian mercenaries, and gathered a fleet of some thirty-six ships at the Dutch port of Flushing to ferry his small army to England. On 2 March 1471, aboard his flagship *Anthony*, Edward led his fleet out of Flushing harbour and sailed for England. A course was set for East Anglia, where Edward hoped he would be able to land and enlist the help of the Duke of Norfolk and friends of Earl Rivers who lived in the area. His fleet sighted England on 12 March and anchored off the coast at Cromer. Edward sent two of his party ashore to discover the lie of the land. His scouts, Sir Robert Chamberlain and Sir Gilbert Bedingham, soon returned with news of Norfolk's imprisonment, and reported that the surrounding countryside was alive with Lancastrians. On receipt of this news it was decided that it would be better to sail north up the coast until a safe place could be found to land. That night, however, unknown to the Yorkists, a messenger from East Anglia reached Warwick in London with the news that Edward's fleet had arrived.

Edward's intention was to sail to Yorkshire, where he hoped to land unopposed by virtue of the support he had shown Henry Percy, the recently reinstated Earl of Northumberland. Edward desperately hoped Percy would still be loyal to the Yorkist king. Disaster came instead, however, when Edward's fleet was hit by a storm and scattered. The following morning, 14 March, his ship was alone off the coast of Ravenspur on the Humber. Undaunted by this setback, Edward, with the few men-at-arms who were aboard his ship, and accompanied by Lord Hastings, put ashore and travelled to the village of Kilnsea, where they planned to spend the night. From here he sent riders in all directions to discover whether others of their company had landed, and to learn to whom the local population had pledged its loyalties.

His luck changed later that day when he was reunited with others from his fleet who had put ashore nearby: Richard, Duke of Gloucester, with some three hundred men-at-arms, had landed 4 miles up the coast at Welwick, and at Paull, Earl Rivers had landed with some two hundred men. By the following day he had been reunited with the rest of his force, who had also come safely ashore. But he was less lucky regarding the loyalty of the local population. As the Yorkists marched inland they came across an armed militia band, numbering several thousand men, under the command of the vicar of Keyingham, Sir John Westerdale and a local squire called Martin de la See, who claimed to be loyal to the recently reinstated Henry VI. Against such overwhelming opposition Edward knew that he could not win a battle, and after a hurried council of war decided to use subterfuge instead. He approached the commanders of the militia, and, when challenged to explain his presence in England, stated that he had returned only to claim his hereditary title of Duke of York, as was his birthright. Despite the likeness of his claim to that of Henry Bolingbroke some seventy years earlier, who had employed another such plot in the same part of the country to avoid a similar confrontation, Edward was allowed to pass unmolested. It is claimed that money was paid to the militia leaders to allow this to happen, but it is worth noting that a close friend of de la See's was Robert Hildyard the younger, whose presence may have influenced the Lancastrians in allowing Edward to pass. The previous year Hildyard had received a pardon from King Edward for his part in leading the Robin of Holderness corn tax riot of 1469. In addition, Hildyard's father had been among the few surviving Lancastrians spared after being captured at the Battle of Towton. It is also known that the Hildyards, like most of the people of Holderness, were pro-Percy, and therefore possibly more sympathetic to Edward than might first appear, as it had been Edward who had reinstated Henry Percy to his family title of Earl of Northumberland. This being so, it may well have been that the young Robert Hildyard managed to convince his friend to allow the Yorkists to pass unharmed, though they were in a position to finish Edward's cause before it had even begun.

As de la See's army moved away Edward began his march inland, heading for the town of Hull. On his arrival he found the gates of the walled town closed before him and a garrison opposing his entry. Undaunted by this, Edward set off towards York and arrived at the city on 20 March. Again the Yorkists found the city gates closed to them, but after assuring the city leaders that he had returned to England only to claim the title of Duke of York – a claim reinforced by the fact that he and his men displayed the emblem of the Prince of Wales (a single ostrich feather) in their hats – Edward found them sympathetic. Convinced by what they had seen and heard, the city leaders decided to allow Edward and some fifteen of this followers to enter the city, on condition that he left the following day; the rest of his troops had to remain outside. Edward and his army duly left York on 21 March and headed south towards his family home of Sandal Castle at Wakefield, the scene of his father's death some ten years previously. Even as he marched on Sandal his ranks were not swelled by members of the population grateful for his return. In 1471 Edward's popular support was at its lowest. The only advantage the Yorkists had was the fact that the lethargic, pleasure-loving Edward of the late 1460s had gone, and in his place was again the bold, confident Edward of 1461.

The reason for such a poor response to Edward's call to arms was due mainly to his location. Strategically, he faced two major imponderables: first, Montagu, who was at this time resident less than 10 miles away at Pontefract Castle; and second, the Earl of

Northumberland, who was somewhere to the north. Until it was known what action these two nobles would take, those willing to support Edward found it more prudent to stay away. It was the Earl of Northumberland's decision to do nothing that saved Edward's cause. Northumberland owed his reinstatement to Edward. Due to the large numbers of Lancastrian and pro-Warwick sympathizers in the area, and the fact that bitter memories of Towton were still harboured by many of the local people, the earl could not actively come to Edward's aid for fear of his own position. However, as one chronicler put it, by doing nothing the earl 'did the King right good and notable service'.[1] As Edward watched Montagu, Montagu watched Northumberland and Northumberland watched Edward, allowing the Yorkists to take advantage of this mutual suspicion and subsequent inactivity to pass between them towards the relative safety of the Midlands, arriving at Doncaster some time between 21 and 23 March.

It was here, with the most dangerous part of the journey completed, that the first reinforcements were to come to Edward's aid. Sir William Dudley joined him with a small force while the Yorkists marched south towards Nottingham. As he continued his journey he was joined by more supporters, including Sir William Parr and Sir James Harrington, who met Edward with a force numbering some six hundred men-at-arms from the north-west.

In the meantime, the Lancastrians, well aware of Edward's movements, began marshalling their own forces to oppose him, and when he reached Nottingham he was informed that the Earl of Oxford, together with Lord Beaumont and the Duke of Exeter, had arrived at Newark with a large army. In a daring move Edward turned to meet them, only to learn during the night of 24 March that the Lancastrians, advised of the Yorkist advance, had lost their nerve and turned south to unite with the Earl of Warwick, who had marched out of London and was now in Warwickshire raising the men of that shire to oppose Edward. On 25 March Edward once again turned south, crossed the River Trent and arrived at Leicester, where he was met by more supporters from the Midlands – some three thousand men-at-arms, followers of Lord Hastings – led by Sir William Norris.

It was at this point that the Earl of Warwick learned he had been deserted by the Lancastrian old guard: the Duke of Somerset and Sir John Courtenay, the Lancastrian heir to the title of Earl of Devon, had quit London. Having left King Henry, whom they had been ordered to protect, in the care of Warwick's brother, George Neville, they had turned south and marched off to meet Margaret of Anjou, whose arrival from France was expected any day. Warwick was cheered, though, when he received news shortly afterwards that Montagu had finally left Pontefract and was heading south to join with him.

During all this time the Duke of Clarence, even after learning of Edward's return, had remained at Burford. Many must have been asking themselves what action the young duke was planning to take, but it was not until 2 April that Edward heard that Clarence had marched north with his retainers and was now only a few miles away at Banbury. By now Edward had reached Coventry, only to find that the Earl of Warwick had got there first and was safely behind the city walls, refusing to come out and give battle.

Clarence, ever eager to be on the winning side, sent word to his brother Edward that he wished to meet and come to terms, and on the morning of 3 April the

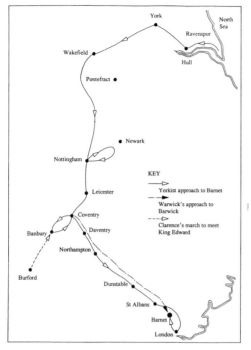

Fig 15.1   Preliminary Moves for the Battle of Barnet

Yorkists left their position at Coventry and marched towards Clarence's force at Banbury. The two brothers met on the Banbury road and were reconciled. As one chronicler put it, there was 'right kind and loving language betwixt them'. Reinforced by his brother's contingent, Edward returned to Coventry and once again offered battle to Warwick – who once again refused, no doubt waiting for the better odds that he would have once Montagu's army arrived.[2]

It seems likely that the reason for Warwick's inactivity up to this point was due to his having received a letter from the Duke of Clarence in which Clarence advised Warwick to hold his ground until he could reinforce him. Now that Clarence had joined with Edward, it is hardly surprising that Warwick, faced with betrayal on such a scale from his own son-in-law, refused to see or speak to Clarence when he approached Coventry on his brother's behalf to try to act as mediator between the two.

Edward stayed at Coventry until 5 April, when it was decided that, with Montagu's force closing fast and food becoming short, together with Warwick's steadfast refusal to give battle, it would be much better to march on London. With Margaret of Anjou's arrival in England expected at any moment, news of the Yorkist advance on London threw the citizens of the capital into panic. The Lord Mayor of the city, John Stockton, now receiving orders from Edward as well as from Warwick, took to his bed, refusing to continue in his official capacity. The remaining Lancastrians in London did what they could to rally support. George Neville and the aged Lord Sudeley (a veteran of Henry V's war in France) paraded Henry VI through the streets of the capital in order to inspire the people. But Henry, dressed in a blue gown, was a sad sight, having to be led by the hand by Neville, so that the whole charade did more to harm their cause than to help it. Certainly, after this it was agreed by the people of London not to oppose Edward's entry into the capital.

Edward entered London via Daventry, Dunstable and St Albans on 11 April and at once made for St Paul's, where he gave thanks for his safe arrival. From here he made his way to the Bishop's Palace to secure the person of Henry VI. Archbishop Neville had already agreed to surrender the Lancastrian king to the Yorkists, sending a message to that effect to Edward when he reached St Albans, and gave up Henry to the protection of Edward as soon as the Yorkist king arrived. It is said that when they met the two kings shook hands, and that Henry exclaimed: 'My cousin of York, you are welcome, I know in your hands my life will not be in danger'.[3] With this Henry was promptly removed to the Tower, while Edward made his way to Westminster Abbey, where he was reunited with his wife and was able to see for the first time his son, born while Edward was in exile.

By the following day, 12 April (Good Friday), the capital was alive with Yorkist supporters who had travelled to London to join Edward. Sir John Howard, Sir Ralph Hastings and Lord Cromwell were with Edward when he received news that the Earl of Warwick, with a united pro-Warwick and Lancastrian army (including the forces of the Duke of Exeter and Earl of Oxford), was advancing on the capital and had already reached St Albans. Edward reacted at once, and the following day, at the head of a Yorkist army now numbering about nine or ten thousand men-at-arms, and including the Duke of Gloucester, the Duke of Clarence, the Hastings brothers, Earl Rivers and many other lords, marched out of London on the Great North Road towards Barnet.

THE BATTLE

Late in the evening of 13 April Edward's army reached the outskirts of the town of Barnet, where his scouts reported that Warwick's army, numbering some ten to fifteen thousand, had taken up positions on a ridge of high ground north of Barnet, either side of the Barnet—St Albans road. Even though the light was fading fast, instead of halting his army and making ready for an advance the following morning, Edward ordered his men forward into Barnet itself. After forcing Warwick's scouts out of the town the Yorkists moved out on to the open ground north of the town, and only then made camp for the night.

This unusual and unorthodox night manoeuvre had two important consequences. Firstly, the two armies, though out of sight of each other in the darkness, were actually much closer than either Warwick or Edward realized. Secondly, instead of each army being drawn up directly opposite the other (as was the military norm of the time), each right flank extended beyond its opposing left flank.

Warwick, aware only that the Yorkists were somewhere in the dark ahead of him, ordered his artillery, of which he had some quantity, to fire harassing shots in their direction. However, because of the short distance between the two armies, these cannon shots fell harmlessly behind the Yorkist lines. Edward, anxious not to betray his position, ordered his own guns to stay silent, even though Warwick's continued to fire throughout the night.

The inscription on Hadley High-stone, memorial to the Battle of Barnet

Early the following morning, 14 April 1471 – Easter Sunday – between 3 and 4 o'clock, Warwick roused his army ready for battle. A heavy fog enveloped the battlefield. Warwick was soon informed that the Duke of Exeter, the Earl of Oxford and his own brother Montagu had assembled their forces and awaited his orders. This must have been a bitter moment for Warwick, standing in the same ranks as his age-old enemies the Lancastrians, betrayed by his own son-in-law and deserted by those with whom he had conspired to depose the Yorkist king. Even though his brother stood with him, his loyalty without question, Warwick knew that Montagu's heart was saddened by the fact that he was to raise arms against the king he had served for so long.

The opening positions are shown in Fig. 15.2. It may be seen from the map that the opposing forces drew up in the customary three wards. The Lancastrian right flank or vanguard was held by Sir John De Vere, Earl of Oxford, whose army had taken up a position partially concealed behind a hedge which ran in a somewhat east–west line some 600 yards to the west of the St Albans–Barnet road. The centre was held by Sir John Neville, Marquis of Montagu, Warwick's brother, whose force extended both east and west either side of the road. The Lancastrian left flank or rearguard was held by Sir Henry Holland, Duke of Exeter, and extended from a point east of the road along the crest of the hill as far as the Enfield road. Warwick himself commanded the reserve, a force consisting of his own household troops and loyal retainers.

In similar fashion the Yorkists divided into three main groups. Their left flank was

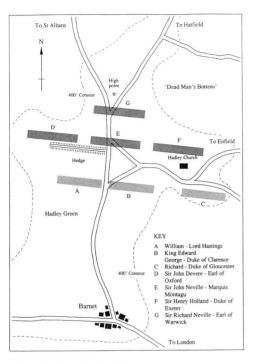

Fig 15.2   The Battle of Barnet

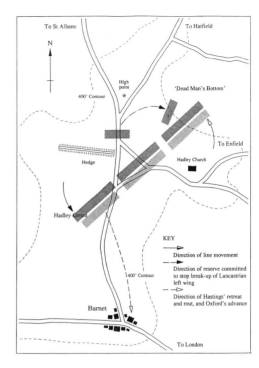

Fig 15.3   The Battle of Barnet

under the command of Lord Hastings, with the right led by Richard, Duke of Gloucester, then aged eighteen. Edward himself commanded the centre and reserve. It is interesting to note that he chose to keep the Duke of Clarence with him, just in case!

With both armies staring into the now dense fog which obscured everything on the field, the battle actually began shortly after 4 o'clock. The opening move was made by the Earl of Warwick, who ordered a volley of cannon fire and several cascades of archer fire into the fog. In reply the Yorkist leaders gave the order to advance, and from the Lancastrian lines the Yorkist trumpets could be heard signalling their move forward. Not wishing to lose impetus, Warwick also gave the order to attack.

It was only as the two lines clashed that the commanders of each army's right flank realized that they in fact overlapped the other's left flank (*see* Fig. 15.3). The Earl of Oxford was quick to take advantage of this for the Lancastrians, and promptly engaged Hastings' force, partially from behind. At about the same time Warwick received a message from the Duke of Exeter reporting that the Yorkists had achieved a similar feat over on the Lancastrian left flank. Warwick, realizing that this flank might collapse, committed a portion of the reserve to stop this from happening. In reality he was too late, and so with both left flanks giving way the entire front turned through 90 degrees (*see* Fig. 15.4). Over on the Lancastrian left flank the arrival of the reserve, though too late to stop the wing being pushed back, did manage to stop it from collapsing entirely, and the forces of Exeter and Gloucester fell into savage hand-to-hand combat.

Hastings, however, over on the Yorkist left flank, was not so lucky. Taken completely by surprise by Oxford's rear attack, his entire force gave way, broke, and scattered towards Barnet. It is said that some even reached London, claiming complete destruction of the Yorkist army. They were pursued by Oxford's own men, many of whom had by now regained their horses. Oxford, unable to halt his men, had to follow them into Barnet where they began plundering the town.

In the centre of the battle other Yorkists were not faring much better. After two hours of heavy fighting Edward's men, who were not without spirit (and who because of the fog were unaware of the fate of Lord Hasting's army), had made some ground, but the arrival of the Earl of Warwick and the rest of the Lancastrian reserve had done much for the Lancastrian morale and as time went by the Yorkists found themselves being slowly pushed back.

After another hour of hard fighting the Earl of Warwick was sensing victory for the Lancastrians. Even Exeter's flank was holding up, and Warwick had received a message from Oxford to the effect that he had rallied much of his force and was returning to the battle. But as in so many of the battles of the period, fate was to deal an unexpected blow, this time to the Lancastrians. The Earl of Oxford and a force of some five hundred mounted men had regrouped in Barnet and were now returning to the field. But, unaware that the front line had changed direction, and hampered by the fog, this force, instead of charging into the rear of Edward's army, actually attacked the men under Montagu's command. Montagu himself, aware that a large force of cavalry was now bearing down on him, mistook the emblem of Oxford's men, a star and streams, for that of Edward's force, a sun and streams. Believing himself to be under attack he ordered his archers to open fire. This resulted in cries of 'treason' from Oxford's men, who rapidly fled the field. The damage was done, and the cries of 'treason' quickly spread throughout the Lancastrian lines. Montagu, Exeter and Warwick tried to steady their front, but Edward, sensing that there was trouble in the Lancastrian ranks, rallied his men and spurred them forward into the enemy line. Surrounded by his own retainers, Edward charged into Montagu's men, the marquis's own pennon his target. The Lancastrians began to give ground.

Warwick, who had returned to the rear of the Lancastrian line at about this time, received news that Exeter was dead, killed by a Yorkist axe, and that the left flank had broken and given way. Looking to his front he realized that his brother's position and his own were becoming increasingly precarious. Trying in vain to hold together what remained of his army, Warwick heard the cry that Montagu was down, felled from behind by one of Oxford's men claiming treason. With this the Lancastrian line began to collapse and men began to flee in all directions (*see* Fig. 15.5). Realizing that the battle was lost, Warwick's thoughts turned to his own safety. During the course of the battle the Lancastrians had advanced a considerable distance, and to reach the horse lines Warwick needed to cover a fair amount of ground. As he made his way back, encumbered by his heavy armour, he was recognized and overtaken by Yorkist men-at-arms who felled him to the ground and killed him.

Even before Warwick's death the battle was over. Yorkists were now engaged in pursuing and looting the beaten enemy. With Warwick's death came the end of an age, an age when Edward of York remained unbeaten in battle.

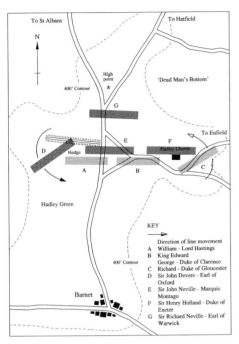

Fig 15.4   The Battle of Barnet

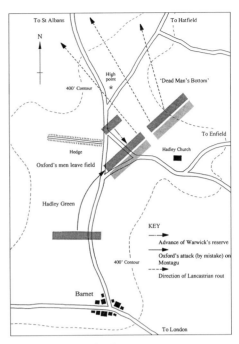

Fig 15.5   The Battle of Barnet

EPILOGUE TO THE BATTLE

It is said that on the morning of the battle Montagu approached his brother and told him morale within the Lancastrian camp was poor, and that Warwick's practice of starting battles on foot and then returning to his mount would not help their cause. It was agreed that both Warwick and Montagu would share the same risks as the common soldiers and fight it out on foot. This may explain why Warwick was so far away from his horse at the time of his death.

When the rout began, Edward became aware of Warwick's plight and actually ordered some of his retainers to ride to the earl's assistance in order to save his life. But when they finally caught up with him it was too late – Warwick, his visor prised open, had been killed by a knife thrust through the eye, his corpse robbed and stripped of its rich armour.

Casualties were high on both sides, but it was the side that broke and ran that incurred the heavier losses, estimated at some two thousand for the Lancastrians and half that for the Yorkists. Most of the slain died at a place still known as 'Dead Man's Bottom' (*see* Fig. 15.5). Of the Lancastrian lords present on the battlefield only Warwick and Montagu lost their lives. The Duke of Exeter, at first thought to have been killed when his command fled, was only badly wounded. Left for dead on the field of battle he was soon recognized and rescued, having recovered from his wounds, he later spent the next four years as a prisoner in the Tower of London. The Earl of

Oxford, his two brothers who had also been present, and Lord Beaumont all fled to safety in Scotland.

The Yorkists were less fortunate: Lord Say, Cromwell, Sir William Blount and Sir Humphrey Bourchier all gave their lives for their cause.

After the battle Edward returned to London, taking with him the bodies of Warwick and Montagu. On reaching the capital he ordered that the bodies of the two knights be put on show in St Paul's Cathedral so that all could see that they were indeed dead. It was perhaps out of respect for the two Nevilles that instead of their suffering the usual traitor's fate – their bodies quartered and placed on the city gates – Edward ordered that their bodies be taken to the family grave at Bisham Abbey, where they were laid to rest in the family vault. Here they lay until Henry VIII's destruction of the monasteries, when both abbey and grave were destroyed by Tudor supporters.

Edward's return to the capital as victor of the battle took place on 16 April, but he had little time to savour the fruits of victory. As the Battle of Barnet was ending a ship which had sailed from Dieppe only a few days earlier had sighted the English coast and was preparing to dock at Weymouth. Aboard this ship were Margaret of Anjou and the Lancastrian Edward, Prince of Wales. Yet again Edward would have to lead an army into battle to save his crown.

CHAPTER SIXTEEN

THE BATTLE OF TEWKESBURY 4 MAY 1471

THE CAMPAIGN

Even as Edward and his army were marching south through England en route to the Battle of Barnet, over in France Margaret of Anjou and the French-backed Lancastrian expeditionary force were preparing to board ship for England. Once again fate was to deal a serious blow to the Lancastrian cause when bad sea conditions kept the fleet in harbour for seventeen days, calm weather finally following it to leave the port of Honfleur on 13 April. Escorted by French warships, Margaret's fleet made the crossing to England in twelve hours, landing at Weymouth on the evening of 14 April. Soon after landing she travelled to Cerne Abbey, where she was joined by the Duke of Somerset and the Earl of Devon on 15 April, Easter Monday.

When the duke broke the news of the defeat at Barnet, and capture and subsequent removal to the Tower of Henry, the queen is said to have been overcome by despair. The Countess of Warwick, who had made the crossing with the queen, hearing the news of her husband's and brother-in-law's deaths, left the Lancastrian camp with her party and sought sanctuary in Beaulieu Abbey. The Duke of Somerset was able to reassure the queen that all was not lost, and convinced her not to return to France but to carry on, claiming that they were well rid of Warwick and his supporters and that the Lancastrians already in England were marshalling forces on her behalf. With this, the Lancastrians left Cerne Abbey and marched on Exeter. On their arrival in the town it seemed to the queen that the Duke of Somerset might be right, as their small army was immediately joined by many followers, influenced by the presence of Somerset and Devon, who rallied to the Lancastrian flag. Somerset was made commander of the queen's army (as he had previous military experience serving Charles of Burgundy on the Montlhery campaign), and the queen and her war council began planning their next move.

In London on 16 April Edward learnt of the landing, two days earlier, of Margaret and her allies. He again reacted in the manner of his earlier reign and at once began making plans to meet and destroy this new Lancastrian threat. Orders were given to prepare for a march westward, and the Yorkist leaders began mustering their forces. Between 18 and 26 April the usual commissions of array were sent to fifteen different counties instructing men-at-arms to be summoned to Edward's aid – presumably not merely to bolster his ranks but to replace those killed at Barnet and those who had returned to their homes.

At Exeter Margaret herself gave instructions regarding the issue of commissions of array in Devon and Cornwall, and before long her army was joined by forces led by Sir John Arundell and Sir Hugh Courtenay. It seemed, as one chronicler put it, that 'the whole might of Devon and Cornwall was behind her'.[1]

At first glance it appears as though Edward had the advantage. He held a number of trump cards: an army flushed with the success of battle; the Lancastrian king in captivity; and the possession of London. But in reality his position was far from secure. The north-west of England was a Lancastrian stronghold; to the south-east the county of Kent, and across the Channel Calais in France, were still full of Warwick's supporters; the Bastard of Fauconberg was still at large and able to muster an army to the rear of his position should Edward move out from the capital. Indeed, there was a real possibility that London could be taken by his enemies should he leave. Jasper Tudor remained at large in Wales, no doubt raising support for the Lancastrians. And there was no indication as to what Margaret's next move might be. On 19 April Edward made the brave decision to leave London and travelled west to Windsor. His march was particularly slow because he was still awaiting reinforcements and because his army was accompanied by a large wagon train that included the royal artillery and the guns captured from Warwick at Barnet.

Though Edward had sent spies to watch Margaret's movements, he still remained unaware of her plans. There seemed to be only two possible actions open to her but until he knew for certain which she would adopt Edward was unable to commit his forces. It is generally agreed that the Lancastrian options were, firstly, to make for the Welsh border regions, join forces with Jasper Tudor, and then head for the Lancastrian heartlands in the North. In this case Edward would have to intercept them before they crossed the River Severn at one of its three crossing points, Gloucester, Tewkesbury or Worcester. Secondly, the Lancastrians could march on London through the southern counties of Hampshire, Sussex and Kent. Then Edward would have to engage them as far away from the capital as possible in order to prevent their being reinforced by supporters from Kent. Whichever course Margaret chose it was important that Edward engage her army as quickly as possible in order to prevent her from gaining strength from the counties along her line of march.

The Lancastrians seemed well aware of Edward's dilemma, and as Margaret's force left Exeter and marched towards Taunton (gaining many allies in the process), she attempted to deceive Edward by sending very small portions of her force east towards Shaftesbury, Salisbury and later Yeovil. Edward had by this time arrived at Windsor, where he received news of these Lancastrian troop movements to the south-west. At the same time he heard reports of a Lancastrian force heading north, and concluded, rightly, that the southern movement must be a feint and that the Lancastrian main body was trying to cross the River Severn to join forces with Jasper Tudor. Edward ordered his army west.

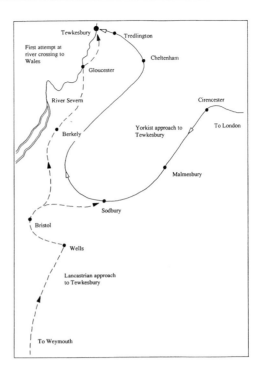

Fig 16.1   Preliminary Moves for the Battle of
Tewkesbury

Edward and his army left Windsor on 24 April and travelled up the Thames Valley, arriving at Abingdon on 27 April and at Cirencester two days later. As he moved on towards Malmesbury he received news that the Lancastrians had arrived at Bristol, where they had been allowed access to the city and had been supplied with provisions and money, as well as much-needed arms, equipment and men. As one chronicler put it, the Lancastrians were at Bristol 'greatly refreshed and relieved thereby'.[2] Soon Edward received the further news that the queen's army had left Bristol, had changed direction towards him, and were poised to attack his force. This news was partially confirmed when he learnt that the Lancastrian vanguard had reached Sodbury. Alarmed by this news, Edward ordered his men onwards.

On approaching Sodbury at nightfall, several of the nobles in Edward's advance party, eager to reach the small town first in order to secure adequate accommodation for themselves, were captured and taken prisoner by elements of the Lancastrian army already at Sodbury. Late in the evening of 1 May Edward's main army arrived at Sodbury, only to learn that the Lancastrian force had left the town and had returned to the main Lancastrian army. The Yorkists took up position on Sodbury Hill to await the expected attack. Edward was later to learn that the queen's army was in fact engaged in a forced night march towards the Severn at Gloucester, and that although the Lancastrians had marched out of Bristol towards his army, they had then swung north. Only a small force had been sent to Sodbury in order to fool him into believing that the entire Lancastrian force was ready to do battle. The main Lancastrian force had by now reached a point some 14 miles north of Berkeley, and some 38 miles north of Bristol. The Lancastrians' reason for this subterfuge had been based on the fact that the queen's army had taken a great risk in stopping at Bristol. Now, if the Yorkists were quick enough, they would find themselves in a position to be able to cut off Margaret's army – geographically – from any crossing of the River Severn. In order to guard against this (and in the hope of slowing them down), the Lancastrians sent some of their army into Sodbury to give the impression to Edward's many scouts and spies that they were making ready to do battle.

Realizing that he had been deceived, Edward set off in pursuit again early on the morning of 3 May. His route took him along the ancient road along the western edge of the Cotswolds, known as the Portway. Though the area offered better marching conditions than the Lancastrians were experiencing down in the Severn Valley, the day was to become very hot, and as the sun rose the Yorkist men-at-arms soon began to suffer from the humid conditions.

The Lancastrians were the first to reach Gloucester, arriving at about 10 o'clock on 3 May. It seemed that they had outmanoeuvred the Yorkists, gaining enough time to enable them to effect a crossing of the Severn and a union with Jasper Tudor. However, unknown to the Lancastrians, Edward had sent a message to Sir Richard Beauchamp, governor of the town and castle at Gloucester, with orders to refuse them at all costs entry to the town and therefore access to the crossing, and said he should not fear reprisals from Lancastrian sympathizers within the town since Edward and his army would soon be there. Though Beauchamp's loyalty was threatened by the overwhelming Lancastrian force before him, and by the threats made towards him by the frustrated Lancastrians, he remained faithful to his Yorkist king and barred the queen's army from the town. He was doubtless encouraged by the speedy approach of Edward's army. With no other choice open to them the Lancastrians set off towards the crossing at Tewkesbury. Exhausted by their forced night march, they reached Tewkesbury late in the evening of 3 May. While the men-at-arms made camp south of the town around the ruins of a castle (destroyed in the ancient wars of Stephen and Matilda's reign), Margaret and the other ladies in the Lancastrian ranks passed the night in a nearby religious house. Because of the weary condition of the Lancastrian troops, and the deteriorating light, it was deemed too late to cross the river. The queen was forced to camp on the English side, nervously awaiting the following morning and praying that the Yorkists would not arrive in time.

While Margaret had been trying to gain entry into Gloucester, Edward's army was still marching along the high ridge of the Cotswolds. His army, suffering badly from lack of water, had crossed only one brook that they could drink from, which was at or near the settlement at Stroud, but as the wheels of the Yorkist carts travelled through it the water became muddy and undrinkable. It was not until they reached Cheltenham (via Birdlip, having left the Portway at Prinknash), that Edward allowed his army to stop and take in food from the wagon train and water from the town. While he was there he learnt that the Lancastrians had not been able to cross the Severn and were now heading towards the ferry at Tewkesbury, their rearguard being harried by men from Gloucester who, on the orders of Sir Richard Beauchamp, had followed the queen's army when it had left the town and were taking every opportunity to harass and slow it down. (It is said that they even managed to capture some of the Lancastrian artillery which had fallen behind on the long march.) Though his men had already marched more than 30 miles that day (a considerable feat even today), Edward ordered them forward, desperate to reach Tewkesbury before the Lancastrians had a chance to cross the river.

Very late in the evening of 3 May Edward's army arrived at Tewkesbury to find that the Lancastrians had not yet crossed the Severn. Edward ordered his exhausted army to make camp for the night 3 miles short of Tewkesbury, at Tredlington. He had been outmanoeuvred at Sodbury, but he had made up for it here, for the following morning the Lancastrians would be forced to give battle without the support of Jasper Tudor's Welshmen.

THE BATTLE

The following morning Edward's army left its camp at Tredlington and marched down the Cheltenham road towards Tewkesbury. They crossed Swilgate Brook at Tredlington bridge, already formed into the customary three wards, vanguard, centre and rearguard. The Yorkist vanguard was under the command of the eighteen-year-old Richard, Duke of Gloucester, who even at such a young age had already won his spurs at the Battle of Barnet. The middle was commanded by Edward himself, who again, as at Barnet, chose to keep his brother George, Duke of Clarence by his side, as Clarence's dubious show of loyalty had still not convinced the king. The rearguard was led by Lord Hastings.

As the Yorkist army, a force numbering only some five or six thousand men-at-arms, crossed the bridge on its march towards Tewkesbury, the rise in the ground at that point blocked from view much of the Lancastrian position. The Yorkists were certainly well aware of the enemy's location, thanks to the activity of the many Yorkist spies and scouts, but it was not until Edward ordered his army to wheel left towards the Severn and come to a halt opposite the enemy that the whole of the Lancastrian position came into view.

The opening positions are shown in Fig. 16.2. The Lancastrians were already drawn up in line to await the Yorkists; one chronicler tells us that, 'in the front of their [the Lancastrians'] field were such lanes and deep dykes, so many hedges, trees and bushes that it was right hard to approach them near to come to blows'.[3] It is possible that this (Yorkist) chronicler was exaggerating the strength of the Lancastrians' position, but it is fair to say they held the advantage when it came to the disposition of the terrain. They were also assembled in the customary three wards to await the Yorkist advance. Their right flank or vanguard was under the command of Edmund Beaufort, Duke of Somerset (the Lancastrian field commander) and his brother Sir John. The middle was under Lord Wenlock (though technically speaking, the Lancastrian Prince Edward was in command, being present in the army at that point), while the left flank or rearguard was commanded by Sir John Courtenay, Earl of Devon and his brother Sir Hugh. It may be seen from the map that the Lancastrian army, a force said to number some six or seven thousand men-at-arms, had drawn up in line for battle with their flanks protected against a possible Yorkist rear attack by either Swilgate or Coln Brook (both fed from the River Avon). The queen's army had assembled south of an area of open land called 'The Gastons', along a line roughly parallel to the road that linked the two

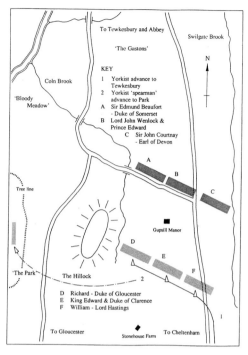

Fig 16.2   The Battle of Tewkesbury

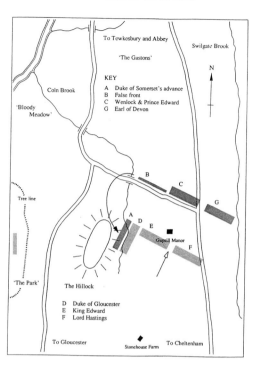

Fig 16.3   The Battle of Tewkesbury

main roads leading into Tewkesbury, and which was no doubt protected by the aforementioned 'deep dykes and hedges'.

Approaching the Lancastrian position, Edward, an experienced commander, noticed an area of woodland (known today as Tewkesbury Park) to the right of it. Fearing a repeat of the ambush from Castle Hill Wood at Towton some ten years previously (*see* Chapter 8), he despatched some two hundred 'spearmen' to investigate whether the park was occupied by an enemy detachment. If so, the Lancastrians would be in a good position to harass the Yorkist position once the battle began. Upon their arrival at the park these Yorkist spearmen found the wood unoccupied, and therefore took up residence within it, unnoticed by the Lancastrians, to await as ordered an opportunity to join the battle at a later stage. It was still early in the morning when the two opposing armies finally settled into their respective opening positions, separated by only 400 yards of open land, awaiting the first move.

The battle opened with an exchange of artillery fire. The Yorkists had the advantage in fire power because of the large number of guns they had brought with them, while the Lancastrians had few, and had already lost some to Beauchamp's forces on leaving Gloucester. Edward had dispersed his cannon equally throughout his front line to achieve a better effect. There followed an exchange of archer fire in which the Yorkists appear again to have had the advantage in numbers. At this point the Duke of Somerset, perhaps fearing that the morale of his troops might break under such a heavy barrage of arrow and cannon fire, ordered his command (as his brother had done in the same circumstances some ten years previously at Towton) to advance and come to arms with the Yorkists.

With a blast of trumpets the Yorkist king did likewise. The men of Edward's army marched forward towards the enemy. But before they could engage in hand-to-hand combat the Duke of Somerset decided to put into practice a plan which had been agreed before the arrival of the Yorkists that morning. He manoeuvred the bulk of his own force around the hillock to the left of the Yorkist position (*see* Fig. 16.3) to engage the Yorkist left wing in both rear and flank at the same time as a frontal attack on the same wing was made by men under Lord Wenlock's command. This move, though difficult in open battle, was not impossible, but to ensure its success Somerset needed to hide his manoeuvre from the Yorkists until he was ready to attack. This was achieved partly because the natural lie of the land, mainly the hillock itself, obscured the Yorkists' view, and partly by a small detachment of Somerset's men, who bravely managed to maintain the full length of his original front during the Yorkist advance.

It was only when the left flank of the Yorkist army neared the hillock that the men under Gloucester's command became aware of Somerset's force charging over the crest towards their flank. It seemed that the Lancastrians had caught the Yorkists by surprise and must quickly roll up the line of Edward's army, precisely as the Yorkists had the Lancastrians at Northampton in 1460 (*see* Chapter 4). This would most likely have been the outcome had it not been that at the base of the hillock was a stout hedge, behind which the Duke of Gloucester was quick enough to assemble a force before the Lancastrians had time to engage the Yorkist left flank. After the sudden shock of this flank attack the Yorkist advance stopped. The men under Edward's command readjusted their front and along with the Duke of Gloucester's men engaged the Lancastrians who had come at them over the hill. After some vicious hand-to-hand fighting, in which the Yorkists slowly gained the upper hand, the confidence of Gloucester's men grew, due in no small part to the fact that they were supported to the rear by Edward's own men, and they began to push Somerset's force back up the hillock. It was at this point that the Duke of Somerset became aware of two factors sharply affecting his situation: firstly, that the promised supporting attack from Lord Wenlock had failed to materialize, which was a key factor in the repulsion of Somerset's force; secondly, that when Somerset's force had been pushed to the crest of the hill they were set upon from behind by the spearmen whom Edward had placed in Tewkesbury Park. This force had watched Somerset's army go past them to engage the Yorkists, had remained in their position until they were sure the Lancastrians had passed them by, and had then waited until the Lancastrians were fully concentrating on attacking Gloucester's men before advancing from the wood to attack Somerset's force in the rear. This meant that instead of the Yorkists finding themselves caught between two Lancastrian forces it was Somerset himself who was trapped between two Yorkist armies. The effect of this was that the entire Lancastrian force under Somerset's command broke and fled back towards the River Severn (*see* Fig. 16.4). The Duke of Gloucester's force set off in pursuit of Somerset's. Many of the remaining Yorkists were keen to follow, but Edward was able to steady his army and turn towards the Lancastrians still on the field.

The rest of the conflict was brief. With Somerset's force gone Edward could bring more pressure to bear on the Lancastrians. The remainder of the queen's army, their

The Battle of Tewkesbury, from an illumination in the Ghent MS showing Edward IV crowned and on his horse, left. The falling horseman, right, is thought to depict the death of Edward, the Lancastrian Prince of Wales

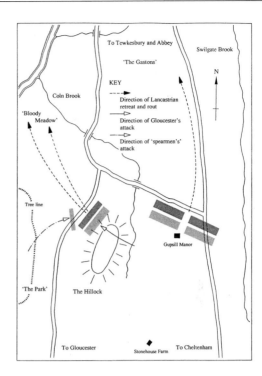

Fig 16.4   The Battle of Tewkesbury

resolve greatly shaken by the flight of Somerset's force, and facing a Yorkist army with the taste of victory in their mouths, soon found the ensuing hand-to-hand combat too much for them. The outcome was in little doubt; the Lancastrian line broke and the queen's army quickly began to disintegrate, and most of her troops fled towards Tewkesbury.

Edward, having stopped his men from chasing the Lancastrians once, was unable to do so a second time. The battle ended, along with the Lancastrians' cause, with the brutal killing, looting and despoiling of any Lancastrians that the Yorkist soldiers could catch as they pursued the queen's broken army through Tewkesbury.

EPILOGUE TO THE BATTLE

When the Duke of Somerset's men broke and retreated from the hillock, they found themselves on the south side of Coln Brook, trapped between that, the River Avon and Tewkesbury Park. The majority of the fleeing men were caught in this bottleneck by men under Gloucester's command. The ensuing slaughter caused this lowland area (the floodplain of the River Severn) to be given the nickname 'Bloody Meadow', a name it still retains today.

The Duke of Somerset was not among those to die in the rout. After his own force was put to flight, Somerset, being mounted, managed to make his way back to the main Lancastrian position, where, it is said, he sought out Lord Wenlock, and, in a fit of rage at Wenlock's failure to support him, struck him down with his axe and killed him. This event may be the reason for the Lancastrian lack of control over their army

The Bloody Meadow was the scene of great slaughter when the fleeing Lancastrians attempted to cross the river

while Edward was advancing towards them. With Wenlock and Somerset locked in their own struggle, the command of the Lancastrian centre was left to the seventeen-year-old Lancastrian Prince Edward.

That morning the queen and the prince had toured the Lancastrian ranks, giving words of encouragement to their army. The queen, now merely a shadow of the Margaret of the early 1460s, left the field for the safety of the rear. It is no surprise that, left to his own devices the young prince, whose experience of armed combat was minimal, failed to survive the battle once the rout began. There are various accounts of the death of Prince Edward: in one it is said that he was captured and killed at the hands of the Duke of Gloucester; another says that as he was killed he cried out to his brother-in-law Clarence to save him. It is possible that in the confusion of battle he became just one of the many casualties of the day, but certainly the richness of his armour would have made him a target for the many Yorkist men-at-arms looking for a rich knight to kill and plunder. We shall probably never know the truth. A plaque said to mark to grave is still to be seen in Tewkesbury Abbey.

With the battle over it was time to count the cost. The Yorkists had fared well, having suffered only light casualties and losing none of their commanders. The Lancastrians fared much worse: as well as Prince Edward, Somerset's brother Sir John

Beaufort, Sir John Courtenay, Earl of Devon and Lord Wenlock all gave their lives that day. Many of the surviving Lancastrians who escaped from the field sought sanctuary in Tewkesbury Abbey, among them the Duke of Somerset. Shortly after the battle Edward entered the abbey to give thanks to God for his victory. At the same time, no doubt in a moment of exultation, he pardoned all there who had fought against him. But the abbey did not hold legal status as sanctuary, and shortly afterwards the Yorkist king retracted the pardon and the Lancastrians within the abbey were taken by force and placed in custody to await trial. On the morning of 6 May they were brought before the Duke of Gloucester (as Constable of England) and Sir John Mowbray, Duke of Norfolk (as Marshal of England), and tried for treason. The verdict was never in doubt, and the Duke of Somerset, Sir John Langstrother and Sir Gervase Clifton, along with eight or nine other Lancastrian knights, were found guilty, taken into the marketplace at Tewkesbury and beheaded. But Edward was not entirely without mercy: Sir John Fortescue, Sir Thomas Ormonde and Sir Henry Roos were spared.

Queen Margaret was captured the following day, after being found hiding in a local house of religion. She was taken to London and placed in the Tower, where she was to remain until she was moved to the more convivial location of Wallingford Castle under the wardenship of the widowed Duchess of Suffolk. In 1475 Louis XI paid

Red roses placed in remembrance on the plaque marking the site of the burial place of Edward of Lancaster, son of Henry VI and Margaret of Anjou. He was killed in the Battle of Tewkesbury

Edward a ransom for her release, and she returned to France, where she died on 29 August 1482 near Saumur in Anjou. Her body lies in the tomb of her father in the Cathedral of St Maurice in Angers.

Though the victor of the day, Edward still could not claim to be the undisputed leader of all England. While at Tewkesbury he received news of trouble in Kent which meant that he must return to London. Further news of risings in the North made him change his mind and head for Coventry. Edward left Tewkesbury on 7 May, arriving at Coventry four days later. Accompanied by part of the Yorkist army, he remained at Coventry for three days, waiting for men to answer his call to arms and to muster there before preparing to march to quell the insurrection in the northern counties. Meanwhile, the trouble in Kent was left to Sir Henry Bourchier, Sir Anthony Woodville, Earl Rivers and Sir William Fitzalan, Earl of Arundel to deal with. It was the late Earl of Warwick's cousin, the Bastard of Fauconberg (Thomas Neville, illegitimate son of Sir William Neville, Lord Fauconberg), who was the cause of the uproar. Fauconberg, a naval man, had been patrolling the English Channel when Edward had landed in Holderness. Being very much a Neville supporter, Fauconberg had set ashore too late to come to Warwick's aid at Barnet. However, as a member of the Neville family he found popular support among the common folk of Kent, Essex and Surrey. These men, united in their common grievances, were brought together under the joint leadership of Fauconberg and Nicholas Faunt, Mayor of Canterbury, and were supported by a contingent of the Calais garrison whom Fauconberg had transported across the Channel. They represented a formidable force. On 12 May, supported by Fauconberg's fleet in the River Thames, these rebels attempted to gain access to London. The Londoners, fearful not only for their lives but also for their possessions, and led by John Stockton, Lord Mayor of London, and Thomas Urswick, the city recorder, put up a stout resistance and turned them away.

Two days later the rebels tried again, this time by forcing a crossing over London Bridge. Supported by cannon fire from Fauconberg's fleet, they again tried to force an entry into the city. However, the city leaders commanding the militia, now supported by Earl Rivers, the Earl of Essex, Sir William Fitzalan and their retinues, managed to hold them off. A force under the command of Earl Rivers then came out from the Tower of London and managed to push the rebels back across the open fields towards Poplar. With this setback Fauconberg rallied his force at Blackheath, only to discover that Edward himself was about to enter the city and that his vanguard, a force of some fifteen hundred men-at-arms, had already arrived. After receiving this news Fauconberg began to have second thoughts about his strategy and decided to make for the safety of his fleet. Leaving Nicholas Faunt and the rebels to their own devices, he travelled first to Rochester and then to Sandwich, at which point the Calais garrison decided to leave Fauconberg and return home.

On Tuesday 21 May Edward made a triumphant entry into London. His previous plans to go north had been cancelled because the northern rebellion, which had started round the city of York when Margaret had landed in England, had come to an end with the news of her defeat at Tewkesbury, a situation improved by the arrival of the Earl of Northumberland at Coventry with the news that the North was now under Edward's control. As he approached the capital Edward was met at Islington by the city leaders, whom he promptly knighted for their efforts in defending the city,

The Bastard of Fauconberg's attack on London, May 1471

before marching into London itself. With Edward's arrival the rebels there dispersed and later their leader, Nicholas Faunt, was tried and executed for treason. As for Fauconberg, because his fleet was needed he was pardoned, but was tried and executed several months later on another charge.

It is said that Henry VI died a few hours before Edward's arrival in London, during the night of 21/22 May, from 'pure displeasure and melancholy on hearing of the defeat at Tewkesbury and the death of his son'.[4] It is more likely that he was put to death: it is also said that when his body lay in state, with only his face uncovered for all to see that he had indeed died, his blood dripped on to the floor of St Paul's and again at Blackfriars, where his body was taken for the funeral service before being carried by barge to the Benedictine abbey at Chertsey for burial in the Lady Chapel. Later his body was moved to a tomb in St George's Chapel at Windsor. In 1910, the body was exhumed, and when examined showed traces of blood on his hair, suggesting that he had indeed died a violent death.

It has also been suggested that Henry met his death at the hands of the Duke of Gloucester. He was Constable of the Tower of London at that time and was certainly present in the Tower that night. It was Prince Edward's death that sealed Henry's fate, for as long as Henry lived the Lancastrians were prevented from crowning Prince Edward while he was in France. On Prince Edward's death, Henry became simply an expendable pawn. Moreover, while he lived Henry could still be a focus for Lancastrian resistance.

Tewkesbury was to the Lancastrians in the 1470s what Towton had been to them in the 1460s. Edward's victory marked the end of significant Lancastrian opposition against the Yorkist king. Edward had commanded and fought in five separate battles and had been victor of them all. If there was ever a reason to follow and believe in a king in the Middle Ages then this record alone must have ranked among the soundest.

When Edward returned to London in May 1471 he could truly claim to be ruler of all England. Even in Wales Jasper Tudor, Earl of Pembroke, had given up all hope, and, taking his nephew Henry of Richmond (later Henry VII) with him, had returned to France. Apart from a half-hearted attempt at invasion in 1473 (which got no further than St Michael's Mount), led by the Earl of Oxford, there was peace in England for the rest of Edward's reign.

SECTION FOUR

CHAPTER SEVENTEEN

THE RISE OF THE TUDOR DYNASTY

King Edward IV died in 1483, leaving a young son and heir (Edward V) and a country relatively prosperous and free from civil strife. The only thorn in the Yorkist side was the sole surviving Lancastrian heir, Henry of Richmond. Henry's claim to the throne was so obscure that it has been argued that if the Yorkist line had continued through Edward IV's children, and the power struggle that followed Edward's death had been avoided, then it is likely that the House of York would have remained on the throne of England well into the sixteenth century.

Edward died at Westminster Palace on Wednesday 9 April 1483, after being taken ill while on a fishing trip. Even while his funeral was being arranged, the murky clouds of political discord were gathering over his kingdom. In Edward's will, his brother Richard, Duke of Gloucester was named as Edward V's protector until such time as the young king was crowned. However, the Woodvilles (known rather disparagingly as the 'New Lords'), led by the Dowager Queen Elizabeth, feared a government controlled by Gloucester and his supporters (the 'Old Lords'). Gloucester had made quite clear his disapproval of the Woodville family and their presence at court, and would waste no time in wresting away their power and influence in the governing of the country. In order to frustrate this and in the hope of taking control of the Protectorate themselves in the form of a regency council, the New Lords acted even before the king's body was cold. Sir Thomas Grey, Marquis of Dorset went at once to the Tower and secured the king's treasury reserves. At the same time Sir Edward Woodville took personal command of the English fleet anchored in the Thames estuary.

At the time of Edward's death his eldest son, Edward, Prince of Wales, was at Ludlow, being cared for by his paternal uncle, tutor and governor, Sir Anthony Woodville, 2nd Earl Rivers. His other uncle, Richard, Duke of Gloucester, was at the same time at his castle at Middleham. News of the king's death arrived at Ludlow on 14 April, but Gloucester did not hear of his brother's death officially until six days later, when he was sent word by Lord Hastings. This delay must surely have sown seeds of doubt in Richard's mind about the Woodvilles' intentions.

Edward's funeral took place on 19 April, and he was laid to rest in St George's Chapel at Windsor Castle. The Duke of Gloucester and other important nobles were absent from the service simply because the news of Edward's death had not yet reached them.

Richard III (The Royal Collection © Her Majesty The Queen)

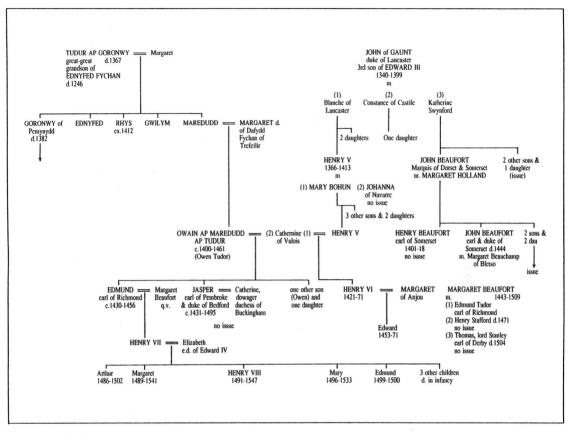

The House of Lancaster and Tudor

The first council meeting after Edward's death was held on 24 April, and mostly concerned the arrangements for Edward V's coronation. It was agreed that the young king should be brought to the capital and that the coronation would take place at Westminster Abbey on 4 May. Gloucester was absent from the meeting but the Old Lords were represented by Lord Hastings. Hastings had been a loyal servant of Edward IV and had fought alongside him at Towton, Barnet, Tewkesbury and elsewhere. Though he was a true supporter of the House of York, he feared for the well-being of the new regime while it remained under Woodville control, and when it was suggested that the new king should come to London with a large, heavily armed escort, Hastings objected. Hastings knew that if Richard were to have any chance of securing the king's person, in order formally to take on the role of protector, then it would have to be while the young king was en route to London. It was therefore necessary for him at least to make an attempt to limit the size of the king's escort, in order to enable Richard to be in a position to approach the king's party without risk to his own life.

Hastings, as Captain of Calais, was in command of the only official English standing army. Thus, when the Woodvilles insisted on a large escort, Hastings claimed that he, along with many other nobles, would fear for their own well-being if a large army approached the capital, and that he, for one, would be forced to cross the Channel and seek the safety of Calais. Though at face value this was not much of a threat, it was enough to persuade the Woodvilles to change their minds. The thought of Hastings holed up in Calais with a standing army, and therefore in a position to do much damage both politically – he was on good terms with the Duke of Burgundy and the King of France – and militarily, was sufficient to convince the Woodvilles to limit the king's escort to two thousand men-at-arms.

Richard, who by now was at York, preserved an outward show of loyalty to the new king and his Woodville family and continued in his official duties. He sent a letter of sympathy to the queen and ordered that requiem masses be held throughout the North. He even led the lord mayor and citizens of York in swearing an oath of allegiance to Edward V at York Minster. All the time, however, he remained in close contact with Lord Hastings. At the same time Richard was in contact with the Duke of Buckingham, who like Hastings and Gloucester also had reasons to dislike the Woodvilles. Following his grandfather's death at Northampton in 1460 and his own father's death from natural causes in 1458, the eleven-year-old heir to the title of Duke of Buckingham had been betrothed and had subsequently married Katherine Woodville, Queen Elizabeth's sister. In the following years he had gained little from the marriage and had always considered that he had married beneath himself. Buckingham knew that if the Woodville faction remained the main power behind the king then he would gain little in the future. He became an instant ally for Richard in the power struggle about to begin.

On 29 April the uncrowned Edward V, accompanied by his uncle Earl Rivers and Rivers' other nephew, the king's step-brother Sir Richard Grey, with their retinues, passed through Northampton en route to London and stopped at Stony Stratford. Later the same day, after the king's party had passed through Northampton, Richard, Duke of Gloucester arrived at the town and was met there by the Duke of Buckingham.

News of their presence in the town went before them, and the king's party at Stony Stratford soon heard of their arrival. Curious at Richard's sudden appearance and undecided about what to do next, Rivers and Grey concluded that the best course of action would be to ride the 14 miles back to Northampton and greet the two dukes formally in person. This they did, and the pair passed the remainder of the evening in the company of the dukes, spending the night in Northampton itself, having decided that it was too late to travel back to Stony Stratford. Next morning, however, before they could leave the town, they were both arrested on Richard's orders and held by his own retainers, and were later sent separately to Pontefract Castle. After this the two dukes rode off towards Stony Stratford, where they intercepted the king's party before it had left.

Edward had been left in the care of Sir Thomas Vaughan and Sir Richard Haute, who, confronted by Gloucester and his retinue, and in the absence of Earl Rivers and Sir Richard Grey, allowed the king to be taken into Gloucester's protection. Immediately afterwards they too found themselves under arrest and eventually joined Rivers and Grey at Pontefract. Late that same evening, 30 April, news of the king's

Richard, Duke of York (left) and Edward, Prince of Wales, portrayed in the 'royal' window at Canterbury Cathedral

'capture' reached the Dowager Queen Elizabeth, who was at this time resident in the Tower. Her first impulse was to try to organize an armed response to recover the king, but it soon became clear that this would not be possible because of the widespread ill-feeling towards the Woodvilles; moreover, most people could see no harm in the king being with his nominated protector. Realizing her peril, the queen, taking Edward's brother Richard, Duke of York and her daughters with her, sought sanctuary in Westminster Abbey. Elizabeth's eldest son by her previous marriage, Sir Thomas Grey, was to join her there for a short while before leaving for France.

Four days later, on 4 May, the king, Gloucester and Buckingham, accompanied by a modest bodyguard consisting of only five hundred men-at-arms – an intentional ploy to dispel any rumours of large armies once again marching up and down the country – entered the capital. Soon after his arrival, Richard, with the king still in attendance, met with the Lord Mayor of London and members of the Privy Council at Hornsey Park, where he claimed that he had rescued the king from the Woodvilles, and was formally proclaimed protector of Edward V until the king's coronation. A revised date of 22 June was set for the coronation at a meeting of the Privy Council on 10 May. Richard took up residence at Baynard's Castle, his family home and residence of his mother, the Dowager Duchess of York. The king was lodged first in the palace of the Bishop of London, but later moved to the royal apartments of the Tower of London, from where, historically, all kings of England had stayed prior to their coronations.

With Rivers, Grey, Vaughan and Haute all in custody, and the queen in Westminster Abbey (which now had armed guards posted on all its exits), the only card that the Woodvilles held was the English fleet (substantially increased in Edward IV's later years), under the command of the queen's brother, Sir Edward Woodville. This fleet, now somewhere off the south coast, was a threat that Richard could not ignore. He offered a pardon to any of its crews who would desert Woodville and return to London. Three of the ships were hired Genoese carracks, and Woodville, resentful of Richard's promise of pardon, stationed armed guards on these ships to ensure that they remained with the fleet. However, the crews of two of the ships managed to overpower their guards, and with a blast of trumpets and the firing of some of their cannon, left the fleet. In the confusion that this caused the entire fleet scattered and all but two of the ships returned to London.

With this the Woodville cause was all but ruined. Richard bestowed far-reaching powers on the Duke of Buckingham, especially in Wales, in order to fill the power vacuum left by Earl Rivers' imprisonment (Rivers previously having held most of the royal offices in Wales), and it seemed that the Old Lords' position in the government would be maintained and that Gloucester's own position was secure. This would probably have remained so, had Richard not set his sights on a higher goal: the crown itself.

For twelve years Henry Tudor, since leaving Wales with his uncle Jasper in 1471, had lived in almost total obscurity in mainland Europe. After their hasty departure from Wales, Jasper and Henry had sailed to Brittany. At first Edward IV had tried to secure them from the 'care' of Duke Francis of Brittany, but the duke, well aware of the value of his guests, managed to arrange a compromise: the Tudors would stay in Brittany under his care and he would ensure that they did nothing to harm Edward's government. As Edward's reign progressed the potential threat that Henry of Richmond posed seemed to diminish, and Edward's attempts to secure them became less frequent. It was not until the early months of the summer of 1483, when Edward Woodville sailed to Brittany with the two ships (the *Trinity* and the *Falcon*) that had not returned to London after Richard's promise of pardon, and sought out these two Lancastrian exiles, that once again the Yorkists' focus turned towards Jasper Tudor and, more importantly, Henry of Richmond. Henry's claim to the throne was an indirect one and was based on the fact that he was descended from Edward III through the Beauforts by Katherine Swynford's relationship with John of Gaunt, Duke of Lancaster, Edward III's third son. Although Henry VII's father was step-brother to Henry VI through the latter's mother's second marriage to Owen Tudor (Henry VII's grandfather), it was through his own father's marriage to Margaret Beaufort that his claim to the throne lay. Margaret Beaufort was the daughter of Sir John Beaufort, who in turn was the second son of Sir John Beaufort, Marquis of Dorset and Somerset, who was John of Gaunt's first son by Katherine Swynford. It was only through this line that the House of Tudor could claim any right to the throne of England. Owen Tudor (whose full Welsh name was Owain ap Maredudd ap Tudur) married Catherine de Valois (Henry V's widow), and by her had three sons. The youngest, reputed to have been called Owen, appears to have chosen the life of a monk and disappears from the pages of history. The two elder children, Edmund (later Earl of Richmond) and Jasper (later Earl of Pembroke and Duke of Bedford) were both to play a major role in fifteenth-century history.

Edmund and Jasper were born in the early 1430s and were both knighted by their step-brother, Henry VI, on 15 December 1449, and created earls on 23 November 1452. Edmund married Margaret Beaufort, but three months before his thirteen-year-old wife gave birth to their only child, Henry Tudor, who was born on 28 January 1457, he died at Carmarthen Castle from natural causes. Henry then came under the protection of his paternal uncle, Jasper. He remained at Pembroke until the castle was taken in September 1461 by Lord William Herbert for the Yorkists. By this time Jasper had fought at St Albans, Ludford Bridge and Mortimer's Cross, where he managed to escape with his life, unlike Henry's grandfather Owen Tudor. The loss of Pembroke Castle, along with Jasper's (and Henry's) attainder in November of the same year, caused Jasper, after a brief spell fighting for the Lancastrians in Northumberland, to become one of the many Lancastrian exiles to join Margaret of Anjou in France in 1464.

As for Henry and his mother, their history prior to 1468 is obscure. Margaret then married Sir Henry Stafford and her son became a ward of the Herbert family. Sir Henry Stafford died on 4 October 1471, and Margaret, a widow for a second time, married Thomas, Lord Stanley in 1473. Her son remained with the Herberts at their family home at Raglan throughout the 1460s. William Herbert was a prominent Yorkist and his ward Henry was set to follow in his footsteps. There were even plans for him to marry Herbert's daughter Maud. But Herbert's rapid advance through the Yorkist ranks, which peaked when he was created Earl of Pembroke, came to a sudden end when he was captured and executed on the orders of the Earl of Warwick after the Battle of Edgecote Moor (*see* Chapter 13).

During Henry VI's brief restoration in 1471, Jasper Tudor once more returned to England. He travelled to Wales where he sought out his nephew Henry and again took him into his protection, severing once and for all his Yorkist links. During this time Henry was presented to Henry VI in London, but Jasper soon returned to Wales (taking Henry with him), where he had been given a commission of array on Henry's behalf with instructions to raise an army to help defend against the Yorkist invasion expected since Edward IV's forced exile in Burgundy.

By the end of the first week in May the Lancastrian cause was lost, together with Margaret of Anjou's army, at Tewkesbury, due in no small part to the fact that Jasper had failed to join forces with Margaret's army before it was brought to battle. Learning of the defeat, Jasper dispersed his army and returned to Pembroke via Chepstow, again taking the young Henry with him. Once secure within the castle walls their luck did not improve, and they soon found themselves besieged within the fortress by an army under the command of Morgan Thomas, who had been commissioned by Edward to secure the persons of these two Tudors. However, after eight days the siege was raised by a relieving force under the command of Morgan Thomas's own brother, David, who had remained a loyal Lancastrian. This enabled Jasper and his nephew to leave the castle and travel to the relative safety of Tenby, where with the aid of the mayor of the town, a merchant by the name of Thomas White, and his son, they found a ship and sailed for exile in Europe. It was only Edward's death and the subsequent events that would bring the House of Tudor back into the spotlight of the Wars of the Roses.

The precise moment at which Richard first decided to take the throne for himself is not clear. What is certain is that from that moment onwards the final chapter of the

Wars of the Roses had begun. From the onset Richard's attempt to secure the throne was marked with danger not only for himself but for those around him. It may safely be assumed that Richard had made the decision some time before 13 June, because he had arranged for his own retainers, under the command of his loyal servant Lord John Howard, to be nearby (just in case!) when a meeting of the Royal Council was scheduled to be held on that date at the Tower of London. Present at the meeting were Richard of Gloucester, Lord Hastings, the Duke of Buckingham, Thomas Rotherham, Archbishop of York, John Morton, Bishop of Ely, Oliver King, the king's secretary and Thomas, Lord Stanley. Exactly what transpired is uncertain; all that is known is that during that meeting Lord Hastings was charged with treason, Richard claiming that he was in league with the Woodvilles and Queen Elizabeth, who in turn was accused of sorcery. At this the aforementioned armed guards entered the room, and after a short struggle, in which Lord Stanley was wounded, Lord Hastings was arrested and taken by force to Tower Green and there executed without further ado.

The reason for Hastings' sudden execution has never been satisfactorily established. Perhaps he was in league with the Woodvilles, out of fear for the lives of the young princes. Possibly it was at this meeting that Richard first announced his claim to the throne: if Hastings objected, then Richard's armed guards were there to reinforce his claim. Whatever the reason, though, as news of Hastings' death spread throughout the capital it was met with great dismay. Hastings had been popular with the common folk and had much support. Even the placing of notices claiming Hastings' treason failed to quell the threat of riot, and it was only the news that Richard's northern retainers were approaching the capital that kept armed bands off the streets.

Richard's next move was to cancel the young king's coronation, after he had successfully convinced the Privy Council that it would be improper to crown the king in the absence of his brother, who was still with his mother in Westminster Abbey claiming sanctuary. On Monday 16 June the Archbishop of Canterbury was sent to Westminster Abbey in an attempt to persuade Queen Elizabeth to allow Prince Richard to attend the coronation. The archbishop promised that the life of the young prince would not be in danger, and that he would be returned to the abbey once the coronation was over. The queen, aware that her eldest son's future was at stake, agreed, and on the following day Prince Richard left the safety of the abbey (though the queen remained) and was escorted to his brother's chambers at the Tower of London. Neither prince was ever seen again outside the Tower.

Although the archbishop had acted in good faith, Richard moved swiftly, once he learnt that the two princes were secure within the Tower. He cancelled the planned meeting of Parliament due to be held on 25 June, and at the same time, though it had never been officially recorded, the coronation of Edward V was postponed indefinitely. Richard then sent orders to the commander of Pontefract Castle for the immediate execution of Earl Rivers, Sir Richard Grey, Haute and Vaughan. On 25 June 1483 all four were beheaded without formal trial. Finally, in order that no other Yorkist contender could be produced for the throne other than himself, Richard ordered that Edward, Earl of Warwick, the young son of the Duke of Clarence (executed for treason in 1478 on Edward IV's orders) be brought to London and placed in the care of his aunt, the Duchess of Gloucester. The unfortunate Edward was to spend most of the remainder of his life confined in the Tower.

On Sunday 22 June Dr Ralph Shaw, brother of the Lord Mayor of London, was commissioned to preach a public sermon from St Pauls Cross, which would be a formal announcement of Richard's plans to take the throne for himself. Two days later the Duke of Buckingham put forward Richard's claim to the lord mayor and aldermen of London. A further two days later his speech was repeated to an assembly of lords who had gathered in London, initially for the coronation.

The grounds for Richard's claim to the throne have been much disputed over the years. It was based on the unproven claim that his brother Edward was illegitimate, and that therefore his children could not be rulers of England. It is said that when Edward married Elizabeth, he was already betrothed to Lady Eleanor Butler, so that his marriage to Elizabeth was void and his children therefore illegitimate. In some quarters this has been denied.

On 26 June an assembly of lords and nobles, along with the lord mayor and aldermen of London, came to Baynard's Castle, where Richard was in residence, and with the Duke of Buckingham as their spokesman called upon him to be their king. Richard, after a token gesture of hesitation, agreed, and the entire entourage, with

Baynard's Castle, from the panorama of Elizabethan London by Claus Visscher

Richard at its head, rode to Westminster Hall, where Richard took his place upon the marble seat of the king's bench. His usurpation of the throne was now almost complete: all that remained was for him to be crowned. His coronation was set for early July.

Richard, Duke of Gloucester was duly crowned Richard III on Sunday 6 July 1483. In the ceremony the Earl of Northumberland carried 'Curtana', the sword of mercy, while the Earl of Surrey carried the sword of state; the Duke of Buckingham bore the king's train while the king's champion, Sir Richard Dymmock, rode into the banquet after the service on his charger and threw down his gauntlet, challenging anyone who disputed Richard's right to be king to pick it up. Thus began the reign of the last Yorkist king.

Between 1483 and 1484 rumours about the whereabouts and fate of the two princes in the Tower, who had not been seen at all for some time, began to circulate. Stories of their deaths did great damage to Richard's reputation, then as now. On top of this, the rise in fortune of many of the northern lords who had been Richard's servants in the past began to create a divide among the nobility, especially with those from the South, who felt that these northern nobles were taking control of the kingdom. Because of this, long-established southern Yorkist lords began to feel threatened as more and more northern lords achieved higher office.

By the autumn of 1483 Richard's popularity had fallen dramatically, and ill-feeling boiled over into armed uprising. Two of the dowager queen's relatives, the Marquis of Dorset and Lionel, Bishop of Salisbury, chose this time to come out of hiding and exile to participate in a revolt that centred around the counties of Kent, Berkshire and Devon.

Though these risings were soon put down, the king's chief supporter, the Duke of Buckingham, was implicated. He was charged with treason and executed at Salisbury on 2 November for plotting with Henry Tudor to replace Richard with Henry as king, now that it was universally believed that the princes in the Tower were dead. Buckingham's change of heart was no doubt fostered by his dead brother's widow Margaret Beaufort, Henry Tudor's mother, and doubtless Elizabeth Woodville was also involved, since she and Lady Beaufort shared the same doctor, through whom they were able to communicate. It was perhaps by this means that Elizabeth got word to Henry Tudor that she and the Yorkists who opposed Richard would back him as a rival to the throne, if he would promise to marry the queen's eldest daughter Elizabeth, or, in the event of her death, the younger daughter Cicely, once he was king.

The revolt was over almost as soon as it began, but had the important consequence of making Henry Tudor the focal point of all resistance to, and rivalry against, Richard III as King of England. It was this same revolt that marked Tudor's first attempt to invade England. Supported by five thousand mercenaries transported in fifteen ships, all paid for by a loan of ten thousand gold crowns from Duke Francis II of Brittany, Henry had sailed for England hoping that his invasion would coincide with the armed revolt against Richard. But as Henry's fleet crossed the Channel it was hit by a storm, and most of his invasion force returned to Brittany. Henry's ship alone completed the journey to England, and when he reached the coast off Plymouth on or about 19 October it was to find the coast well protected and guarded by Richard's men.

There was an attempt to deceive Henry into believing that these men were Buckingham's, in the hope of enticing him ashore. Henry was too astute to be taken in by this and returned to Brittany, where he heard of Buckingham's death. He was soon joined there by Yorkists who had sided with Buckingham against the king and had been forced to flee to the court of Henry Tudor after Buckingham's death.

As 1483 gave way to 1484 Richard tried desperately to wrest the person of Henry Tudor from the Duke of Brittany. But troubles at home and strained relations between the two countries frustrated his efforts. Richard realized that in order to capture Tudor he must first come to terms with the Duke of Brittany. In June 1484 fate seemed to be smiling on Richard when the Duke of Brittany was incapacitated by some form of madness and the government of Brittany came under the control of its treasurer, Peter Landois. On 8 June Landois and Richard came to an agreement which would lead to a cessation of hostilities between the two countries, and in return for a loan of a thousand English archers to help Brittany in the war against French expansionism, Landois agreed to hand over Tudor to Richard.

However, John Morton, Bishop of Ely, who was at this time in Flanders on his way to exile at Tudor's court, heard of the plan and was able to warn Tudor in a message relayed via one Christopher Urswick, Morton's confidential agent who had joined Morton in Flanders. The warning reached Tudor just in time, and by October 1484, after a hurried flight from Brittany, Henry Tudor's 'court' was safely installed at Montargis in France under the protection of the French king. (It is said that when Duke Francis of Brittany recovered he was enraged at the events and with Landois for allowing them to happen.)

By the beginning of 1485 those who had joined Tudor in France included Jasper Tudor, Sir Thomas Grey, Marquis of Dorset, Sir John Fortescue, Sir Edward Woodville, Sir Thomas Arundel, Sir Edward Poynings, Sir John Cheyney and his brother Humphrey, Richard Fox and others, who with their retinues numbered some five hundred individuals. The most important arrival as far as Tudor himself was concerned was Sir John De Vere, Earl of Oxford, who joined Henry after escaping from Hammes Castle near Calais. He had been held there for ten years since his capture by Edward IV near Oxford in 1474. Though most of Tudor's 'court' had joined him for their own reasons, they were united in their resolve to see Richard overthrown. The Earl of Oxford, however, was a die-hard Lancastrian, and his arrival at Henry's camp did much to raise Tudor's spirits. Oxford was a true friend who was soon to show his worth. Of those who had joined Henry only Oxford disturbed Richard. More important even than Oxford's escape itself was the fact that when he left he took with him Sir James Blount and Sir John Fortescue. These two knights had previously held important offices in Richard's government. Sir John had been Gentleman Porter of Calais, and Blount had been captain of Hammes Castle, which meant that Oxford's escape had not really been an escape at all, but more an agreement between the two. If Henry could attract the likes of these, then who else was plotting treason and desertion? To Richard their defection and its consequences were far more serious than Oxford's 'escape'.

To make matters worse, over in England the Yorkist regime had another crisis on hand, this time one of dynastic proportions. The previous year Richard's son Edward, then aged only eleven, had died from natural causes, leaving the king without an heir.

Henry VII

As if this was not enough, in March 1485 Richard's wife Anne (second daughter of the late Earl of Warwick) also had died, leaving the House of York with no immediate means of providing an heir. It was perhaps due to this fact alone that many of the Yorkists in England began to fear the consequences should Richard die without issue. And should he remarry, what would happen to the country, which would once again be faced with a child king and the problems associated with a protectorate or regency council? Small wonder that the thought of the young Henry Tudor as king appealed to so many! With such thoughts in mind it is not surprising that many of the nobles of England began to look across the Channel to Henry Tudor for their salvation.

CHAPTER EIGHTEEN

THE BATTLE OF BOSWORTH 22 AUGUST 1485

THE CAMPAIGN

By March 1485 Richard III was attempting to steady his already tottering kingdom. The aged Yorkist Lord Dinham, who had been captain of Calais when Oxford, Blount and Fortescue had fled for Henry's court, was removed from office. He was replaced by Richard's own illegitimate son, John of Gloucester, who himself was still a minor (which in effect put Richard in personal command of the city). Sir James Tyrell, who had brought a fresh garrison to Calais the previous December, was appointed captain of Guines. Hammes, which was held by supporters of Henry Tudor, was left to Lord Dinham to recapture; this he did, though not before allowing the garrison to go free as part of the terms of surrender.

Richard was well aware that Henry was planning to invade England, and because of this, moved his headquarters to Nottingham, using the town's central location in England as a base from which he could react to any military situation that presented itself. By April Richard was actively planning against invasion. His fleet, under the command of George Neville, was patrolling the Channel as a precaution, and Viscount Lovell was sent to Southampton to take personal command of the defence of the south coast. With his defensive measures under way, and summer approaching, all Richard could do now was to wait and see from where and when Tudor would strike.

Throughout 1484 Tudor had been gathering men and supplies, and trying to convince the French King Louis XI to finance his invasion. Louis allowed Tudor to assemble his fleet in the port of Honfleur, but was as yet unwilling to fund it as well. Meanwhile, over in England, Richard, unwilling or perhaps unable to command all his nobles to muster the forces he required to defend his kingdom, was obliged to rely on his own northern retainers and the forces of a handful of lords with which to face Tudor. In military terms Richard's strength at this point lay in the loyalty of his own men and those of Lord John Howard, Duke of Norfolk, Sir Henry Percy, Earl of Northumberland and the Stanley brothers, Sir William and Lord Thomas. Richard knew that the loyalty of the Duke of Norfolk, like that of his own retainers, was not to be doubted. When it came to the Earl of Northumberland and the Stanley brothers it was a different matter. Richard's relationship with the Stanleys had never been a close one. Even as early as 1470, when Richard was only seventeen, they had come to blows in the lawless weeks of Edward IV's captivity at Middleham Castle (*see* Chapter 14). And when Thomas Stanley had married Margaret Beaufort, whose son by her first marriage was heir to the House of Lancaster, this had built a further barrier between the two men. Stanley, always an opportunist, had his own reasons for disliking Richard, who had, at the same meeting in which Hastings was charged with treason, also arrested Stanley and for a short time held him prisoner. So, if anyone had a score to settle with Richard it was Lord Stanley; as for the opportunity, it was now, when Richard needed him the most.

Reasons for Northumberland's questionable loyalty are less readily apparent. Lord Percy had much for which to be grateful to the House of York. Richard's brother had restored him to his rightful title after years in prison, and Richard, as Duke of Gloucester, had campaigned with Northumberland on many occasions against the Scots. At first glance it could be said that they got on well together. This may have been so when Richard was a duke, but now that he was king it seemed to be a rather different story. Richard, unlike past kings, had spent many years in the North and was popular with the northerners, more so even than the Earl of Northumberland. As king, Richard had great power, and unlike his predecessors he was happy to travel his northern shires, whereas in the past the rule of the North was left very much to the Earls of Northumberland. Because of this Percy perhaps felt threatened and he too began looking to Henry Tudor as the answer to his problem. However, so far he had been a loyal servant to the king. Richard must have known this and because of it may not have mistrusted him at all.

Meanwhile, over in France, by April 1485 Henry Tudor had at last gained financial aid from the French court and had moved to Rhoun, where final plans for invasion were to be made. His first priority was to ascertain how much support he could rely on from his step-father and step-uncle (the Stanleys) once he reached England. The Stanleys' power base lay in the West of England and particularly in Wales where Sir William Stanley held royal office. It was from Wales that Henry hoped to win much of his support (indeed had been promised it), and because of this played heavily on his Welsh ancestry. His support came mainly from two men: Sir Gilbert Talbot, uncle of the 4th Earl of Shrewsbury; and Sir John Savage, a leading landowner in Wales and a nephew of the Stanleys. But men like Rhys ap Thomas and other influential Welshmen all promised to support Henry when he invaded. It was because of this that Henry chose Wales as his landing place when the time came.

By August 1485 Henry's fleet, under the command of the French Admiral Guillaume De Gasenove, was ready. The fleet consisted of an unknown number of ships, carrying between five and seven hundred English exiles and between fifteen and seventeen hundred mercenaries from Normandy under the command of their French captain, Philibert de Chandée. On 1 August this small invasion force sailed into the English Channel and set course for South Wales.

Meanwhile, in England Lord Stanley, aware that Tudor's invasion was imminent, asked permission to take leave of the king in order to return home. Richard, suspecting Stanley's loyalty, gave permission only on the condition that Stanley's son, Lord Strange, remained at court as Richard's 'guest'. To this Stanley agreed; he left court and returned to the West Country.

Just before sunset on 7 August the invasion fleet sailed into Milford Haven and came ashore. Henry's first move was to march over the headland of Dale Point and take Dale Castle (which he had expected would be held against him but which in fact he took without much difficulty). Having spent the night there, the following morning at dawn he set off inland for Haverfordwest, some 10 miles to the north. Henry, fearful that spies would already be sending Richard word of his arrival, set off towards central Wales in the hope of attracting the support promised him while he was in France. By 10 August he had reached Llanbadarn via Cardigan; by the 11th, Machynlleth. However, at Cardigan, as his men made camp for the night, they received word that Sir Walter Herbert was approaching with an army to attack them. After a period of panic in Henry's camp it was learnt that this was not the case, and the invaders once again settled down for the night. Throughout his travels Henry was fearful that his small army would come under attack from Richard's supporters. His fears were never to materialize, but neither was the promised support, the lack of which worried Henry even more.

It was not until 12 August, when Rhys ap Thomas joined Henry at Newton, that the promised aid finally began to arrive. (Thomas had been promised the lieutenancy of Wales for his efforts if Henry was successful in defeating Richard and the Yorkist regime.) While Thomas's arrival did much to raise Henry's hopes as he and his army marched towards Shrewsbury, it did little to raise his chances of military victory. It was not until 15 August that the first substantial support came Henry's way, when Sir Gilbert Talbot joined him at Newport, bringing five hundred men with him. Only then did Henry begin to feel less anxious about Yorkist attacks.

When Henry had landed in Wales he had at once sent messages not only to his mother and Gilbert Talbot but to the Stanleys as well, informing them of his arrival and his intention to travel into England across the Severn near Shrewsbury. When he finally arrived in that town late on 15 August the Stanleys' replies were awaiting him. They wished him well and sent money for his war chest, but promised to come in force only when the time was right. This was disappointing news for Henry: as far as he was concerned that time was now.

Meanwhile, Richard had returned to his base at Nottingham at some time in June. When his spies him told that Tudor's fleet was preparing to leave for England, he began to act. First, he ordered that the Great Seal be brought to him at Nottingham. (It arrived the day that Henry set sail for Wales.) On 7 August Richard learnt of Tudor's earlier landing and sent orders to his captains to muster their men and rendezvous at Leicester. If Richard seems to have reacted with less than expected haste, this is because he firmly believed that while he held Stanley's son, Stanley would remain loyal to him, and that Stanley's forces would halt Tudor before he could leave Wales. He further believed that the forces of Rhys ap Thomas (whom Richard had trusted to remain loyal) and Sir Walter Herbert were patrolling in Wales as a safe-guard. When Lord Stanley sent word to Richard that he could not make the rendezvous at Leicester because he was suffering from the 'sweating sickness', and Richard learnt that Tudor had already crossed into England, he knew that his plans to stop Henry in Wales were thwarted and that Stanley had turned traitor.[1] When Richard received Stanley's message he at once ordered Lord Strange to be brought to him for interrogation. Richard's reasons for believing in a conspiracy were soon confirmed when Strange confessed that his uncle Sir William Stanley had plotted with Sir John Savage to join Henry. When questioned about his father's involvement, Strange denied that he was involved, and offered (or was forced) to write to his father begging him to come to Richard's aid. It was on this same day that Richard pronounced Sir William Stanley and Sir John Savage traitors. Subsequently they were officially declared to be such.

On 17 August Henry entered Stafford, where he at last made contact with Sir William Stanley, who had left his army at Stone and had travelled with only a small retinue to Stafford to confer with him. What was said at this meeting is unknown, but Stanley must have sufficiently encouraged Tudor to go on, before leaving him and returning to his army at Stone. Go on Henry did, reaching Lichfield (where he was cheered by the citizens) the following day, 18 August, the day after Sir Thomas Stanley had vacated the town on receiving his son's letter. No doubt Stanley was trying to deceive Richard into believing that he was heading for the rendezvous (as his army moved east towards Leicester), but at the same time he was causing Henry also to wonder what his true plans were. Stanley was to keep them all guessing right to the end.

Richard, still at Nottingham awaiting the arrival of his captains at Leicester, now became aware of the full extent of the divided loyalty of his nobles. Not only had the Stanleys failed to answer his summons, but others, like Sir John Paston, were staying away also, despite, in Paston's case, being sent a personal note from the Duke of Norfolk asking him to join Richard. In other areas the situation was even worse. Richard, suspecting the loyalty of two of his knights, Sir Thomas Bourchier and Sir Walter Hungerford, had asked the loyal Sir Robert Brackenbury to 'escort' them to the rendezvous. However, when they had reached Stoney Stratford on their journey north the two knights had managed to slip away from Brackenbury in the middle of the night and rode off to join Henry Tudor.

But it was not all bad news. The lord mayor and citizens of York, aware that their king needed them, sent word to Richard asking where he would like the men of York to assemble. Though heartened by their loyalty, Richard was disturbed to hear that they did not know of the muster at Leicester – had not the Earl of Northumberland instructed them to go there? At this point, any doubts that Richard had about Northumberland's loyalty must have been confirmed, even though the earl had arrived with an army at Leicester to help him. On the morning of 17 August Richard left Nottingham for the rendezvous at Leicester. Despite the absence of those who had defected, he still felt confident of gaining victory over Henry with those who had remained.

On 20 August Henry marched towards Tamworth, but decided not to camp there for the night and instead continued his march. As darkness fell he managed somehow to become separated from his army and spent a very worrying night with only a few retainers before he was able to find his army again the following morning. On arrival at Atherstone he at last met with the two Stanley brothers, who had ridden to meet him there. Even at this late stage the Stanleys were reluctant to side openly with Tudor

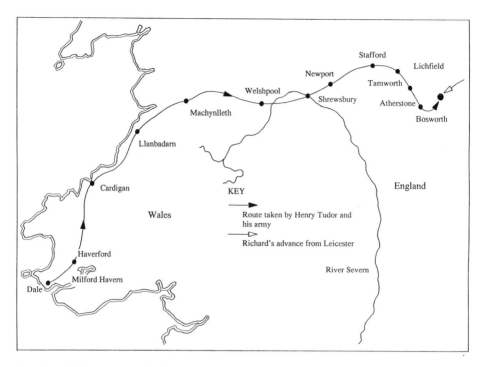

Fig 18.1   Preliminary Moves for the Battle of Bosworth

out of fear for the life of Lord Stanley's son, so they left Atherstone (after a short meeting with Henry) and returned to their respective armies. Sir John Savage, however, who had arrived at Atherstone that same day, remained behind with a large retinue. He had already been branded a traitor by Richard so he had nothing to lose.

When Richard heard that Henry had reached Lichfield he decided that he could wait no longer, and set off to intercept Henry's army. He travelled west along the old road through Peckleton and Kirkby Mallory, and finally camped for the night of 21 August at Sutton Cheney, some 2 miles south of the village of Market Bosworth. At the same time Henry left Atherstone and marched in the direction from which his scouts told him Richard's army was approaching, while the separated armies of the Stanleys followed on a parallel course. Henry arrived at Sutton Cheney on the same day as Richard and made camp for the night less than 4 miles from the king's army at a place called Whitemoors.

Both armies would have to wait for the following day to fight the battle that would settle the fate of the crown of England.

THE BATTLE

Next morning both armies broke camp early. Richard, whose army was better served by its scouts than Henry's, and who was clearly the more experienced commander, had a better grasp of the situation than Henry. It was quite clear to the commanders of both armies (though Richard came to the conclusion first) that the battle would take place on the surrounding terrain. The most obvious landmark was the rise in the ground (Ambion Hill) that was halfway between the two armies; the opening move was a race for the high ground and its more advantageous position.

Richard ordered his army to advance in the marching positions they had maintained since leaving Leicester, which made movement faster, instead of deploying in 'line across', which was the military norm when two opposing armies were so close to each other. Though Richard was aware of the dangers of his men being caught in the open while marching in column he felt it was a risk worth taking, and his army, its vanguard led by the Duke of Norfolk (with Richard himself commanding the centre and Northumberland the rearguard), set off for Ambion Hill. Henry was less quick to get his men on the move, but, advised by the Earl of Oxford, he too ordered his army to march towards Ambion Hill. It was to be a close-run race.

Richard, his army moving faster than Henry's, made it to the hill first. The Duke of Norfolk commanded the vanguard to take up position along the crest of the hill, while Richard came to a halt behind him on the plateau with Northumberland somewhat further behind. The crest of the hill was only 700 yards long, and though Richard held the higher ground, the men of his centre and rearguard were not able to deploy along this front line. Henry Tudor, meanwhile, was drawing closer to the hill. He had, however, been poorly informed by his scouts, and as his army marched directly towards the hill he became aware of the fact that his path was blocked by a marsh directly in front of him, between his army and the hill. When his vanguard reached the marsh it had to wheel sharply to the left (in a somewhat northerly direction) and march 500 yards to come into line against Richard's men, leaving its right flank exposed to the archers in Norfolk's vanguard as it did so. Surely Norfolk must have considered the advantage of attacking at this point, but the fact is that he did not. Possibly he thought it imprudent, or even ungentlemanly. What is certain is his inaction allowed Henry's men to line up opposite Richard's army unhindered.

The opening positions are shown in Fig. 18.2. It can be seen that Richard's army had lined up in the positions already described, with Henry's vanguard and centre facing him. Henry's vanguard was commanded by Sir John De Vere, Earl of Oxford and Philibert de Chandée (who would later be created Earl of Bath for his service). While Henry chose to command the centre, Jasper Tudor (soon to be reinstated as the Earl of Pembroke) was beside him. Flanking either side of Henry's force were units under the command of Sir Gilbert Talbot and Sir John Savage respectively. His whole force, including those who had joined him in Wales and England, numbered between five and seven thousand men-at-arms and included Sir William Brandon, Sir John Byron, Sir Humphrey Cheney and his brother Sir John, Sir Richard Fox, Sir Edward Woodville, Sir Edward Poynings, Thomas Arundel, John Fortescue and the recent turncoats Sir Thomas Bourchier and Sir Walter Hungerford.

Richard's army, however, numbered between eight and twelve thousand, and included not only the Duke of Norfolk but his son, Sir Thomas Howard, Earl of Surrey, Sir Henry Percy, Earl of Northumberland, Sir Robert Brackenbury, Francis, Viscount Lovell, Sir Richard Ratcliffe, Sir Gervase Clifton (whose father had died fighting for the Lancastrians at Tewkesbury), John, Lord Zouch, Walter, Lord Ferrers, William Catesby, Sir Humphrey Stafford and his brother Sir Thomas. Richard clearly

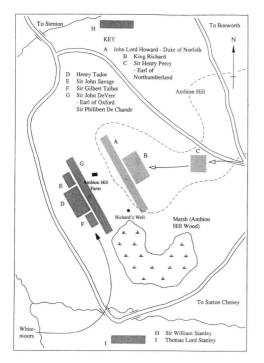

Fig 18.2   The Battle of Bosworth

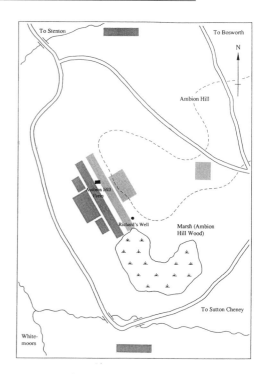

Fig 18.3   The Battle of Bosworth

had numerical superiority. But as his army prepared for battle he could scarcely have failed to notice the arrival of the two Stanleys, who took up position north and south of his army (*see* Fig. 18.2). The Stanleys, who had followed Tudor's army at a discreet distance, came to a halt a little distance from the two front lines. Sir William Stanley was to the north with some three thousand men-at-arms, his brother to the south with five thousand.

As Richard glanced nervously to either side he must have realized that while the Stanleys remained motionless then the advantage in numbers, combined with the better terrain, meant certain victory for him. However, if the Stanleys engaged on Henry's behalf, then, despite the terrain, the numerical superiority must give the day to Henry. These same considerations must have been equally obvious to Henry, so that both commanders would have started the battle doubting the outcome.

Henry, realizing that he needed more men, sent word to Sir William Stanley asking him to bring his army up to join his ranks. Stanley's brief reply told Henry to put his own force in order and then he would come to join with him. Henry, somewhat dismayed at this curt reply, had no option but to start the battle and hope that Stanley would keep his promise, while Stanley himself, aware that Richard still had time to execute his son, maintained his wait-and-see policy.

The battle itself started with a round of cannon and archer fire. This lasted only a short time and when it was over there was a short pause while both armies waited to see who would move first. Ultimately the two sides advanced simultaneously towards each other and came to blows halfway down Ambion Hill, at a spot parallel to the

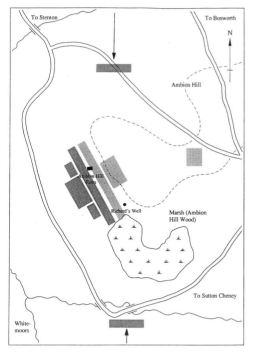

Fig 18.4　The Battle of Bosworth

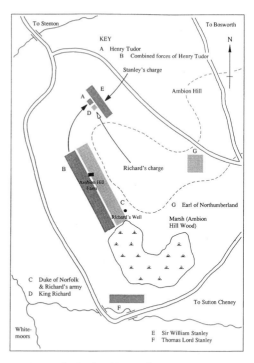

Fig 18.5　The Battle of Bosworth

present Ambion Hill Farm (*see* Fig. 18.3). The ensuing mêlée lasted for about an hour, while the two vanguards, increasingly having to be supported by the centres, fought it out in savage hand-to-hand combat. It was while both armies were struggling thus together that the Stanleys decided to make their move, and simultaneously began to advance in the direction of the engaged armies (*see* Fig. 18.4).

Up to this point in the battle most historians are in agreement. However, when it comes to what happened next, there are serious differences of opinion. One view is that at the point at which the Stanleys began their advance, Henry realized that with his army fighting uphill and Richard's superior numbers in a Battle of attrition the king would undoubtedly win. So Henry himself set off with a small retinue towards Sir William Stanley's position to try to persuade him to enter the battle on his side before it was too late. As Henry left the main battle, Richard, being on higher ground and therefore in a position to monitor Henry's movements, recognized his opponent's pennon and grasped the opportunity for a swift victory by attempting to kill Henry as he crossed the open ground. Therefore, Richard led a downhill charge with his own mounted retainers towards Henry's position, but as he crossed the open ground towards Stanley he was himself recognized by Sir William, who ordered his men to engage Richard's relatively small force, itself now caught in the open (*see* Fig. 18.5). It is claimed that Richard's force did make contact with Henry's and almost succeeded in killing Henry himself. Henry's standard-bearer, Sir William Brandon, was indeed killed on the field of battle, and as the standard-bearer almost always stayed with the commander he was representing, we can conclude that Henry's own retainers were

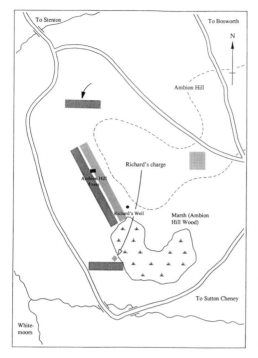

Fig 18.6   The Battle of Bosworth

involved in some form of close-quarter combat. However, before Richard could reach Henry, the men of Stanley's own division came up and enveloped Richard's force, and after a brief but fierce struggle the king was unhorsed and killed.

One alternative view is that as the armies of both Stanleys began their advance towards the mêlée, Richard already knew that they would side with Henry. As the Earl of Northumberland was clearly not making any move to intercept them, Richard realized that all would soon be lost. Unable to get to Henry, who had remained throughout at the rear of his own forces, Richard decided to launch a mounted charge towards the pennon of the one man who had done most to bring about his impending defeat – Thomas, Lord Stanley. Instead of moving to the right of his position he charged to the left, towards the army of Thomas Lord Stanley (*see* Fig. 18.6). Whether he tried to navigate around the marsh, or to cross it directly, we do not know. All that we are sure about is that Richard lost his mount, was attacked by the men under Stanley's command and killed.

The only certain fact about either scenario is that the king was killed. His death signalled the end of the battle and the beginning of the rout of the Yorkists, whose line soon broke and scattered when the troops heard of Richard's death.

EPILOGUE TO THE BATTLE

Not only did that August morning signal the end of King Richard, but it also brought about the end of the House of York, and ushered in the House of Tudor which would rule England for the next 120 years.

Richard was not the only noble to lose his life that day. Of the Yorkists, the Duke of Norfolk, Sir Robert Brackenbury, Walter, Lord Ferrers, Sir Richard Ratcliffe and Sir Gervase Clifton all died on the field of battle. Only Sir William Brandon died for Tudor's cause, and in total some three thousand men-at-arms, mainly Yorkists, lay dead upon the field. Francis, Viscount Lovell managed to escape to fight another day, along with Sir Humphrey Stafford and his brother Sir Thomas. William Catesby was captured and put to death the following day at Leicester. The Duke of Norfolk's son managed to escape, along with Viscount Lovell, but surrendered to Henry shortly afterwards and was eventually pardoned after spending many years as a prisoner. He was later restored to his rightful place and even became Henry's Lord Treasurer. In 1514 he was allowed to take the title of Duke of Norfolk.

It is said that after the battle Henry Tudor left the field and made camp on a small hill to the south-east of Bosworth field, and that at this place Thomas, Lord Stanley had retrieved Richard's crown, a simple gold circlet, from under a hawthorn bush. Stanley personally placed the crown on Henry's head, claiming that from this day onward Henry was King of all England. The hill retains the name Crown Hill to this day. There are those who believe that Richard never wore a crown at all, but Henry V wore a similar gold circlet in battle at Agincourt and it is not impossible to believe that Richard did the same at Bosworth.

Of those whom Richard mistrusted and whose actions ultimately led to his death, the Earl of Northumberland, who had throughout the battle remained immobile along the top of Ambion Hill, was taken prisoner. He was not, however, attainted for taking sides with Richard, and was in time allowed to go free to carry on as the king's warden in Northumberland. The people of the North, with whom Richard was popular, never forgave Percy for sitting on the fence at Bosworth, and in 1489 he became even more unpopular when he tried to enforce the levying of a new tax. In the course of performing his duties at Topcliffe in Yorkshire he was set upon by a 'gang' which included some of the local gentry (John a'Chambre and Sir John Egremont to name but two), and murdered.

As for Stanley, despite his eleventh-hour arrival, Henry was grateful enough to reward him with the title of Earl of Derby. Stanley's son survived the day, but this was due more to good fortune than to the accurate timing of Stanley's attack. When Richard had seen that Stanley was advancing, he had ordered that the young Lord Strange be executed, but by the time the messenger arrived it was too late. Those guarding him, believing they were needed for the battle, let Strange go rather than spend precious time attending his execution.

Later on the day of the battle, Henry made his way to Leicester. Richard's body, stripped naked and slung across a horse, was paraded through the town and exposed to the public for two days. It was afterwards interred in a stone coffin in the Grey Friars Church at Leicester, but after this church was destroyed, probably at the time of the Dissolution of the Monasteries, Richard's bones were tipped into the river that runs through the town and his coffin ended up as a horse-trough outside the White Horse Inn in Gallow Tree Gate. There it remained until the eighteenth century, when it was broken up and destroyed.

King Richard's Well (*see* Fig. 18.6), where Richard is reputed to have taken a drink

King Richard's Well, Bosworth

of water before his final charge, is located on the south side of the battlefield. The thought that a knight in full armour might dismount in the middle of a battle simply for a drink may be hard to believe, but it is certainly not impossible. On the site where the natural spring, known locally as 'Richard's Well', broke the surface, the noted historian Dr Parr had a stone pyramid built as a memorial to Richard's defeat. The pyramid is open on its south face to allow the water to flow, and on this side there is an inscribed bronze plaque set into the wall of the well itself. The marsh into which the spring's water ran has long since disappeared, but on its site there is now a small wood called Ambion Hill Wood.

Though Henry was the victor of that day and thus King of England, he was to learn during the next couple of years, like his predecessor Henry IV, that winning a throne is much easier than keeping one. Henry would himself, like Henry IV, Henry VI, Edward IV and Richard III, be forced to lead an army into battle to keep it.

CHAPTER NINETEEN

THE BATTLE
OF STOKE
16 JUNE 1487

THE CAMPAIGN

Two weeks after his victory at Bosworth, Henry entered London in triumph to the welcoming cheers of the city fathers and the population at large.

Most people regard Bosworth as the last battle in the Wars of the Roses, but in fact it would not be until two years later that the final conflict would be fought on Stoke Field. Almost from the beginning of his reign Henry feared armed insurrection, and lived with this fear for most of his remaining life. It was only during the last few years of his reign that Henry could feel secure as King of England. Following a style set by French kings, one of Henry's first acts was to create a personal bodyguard consisting of some two hundred men-at-arms picked from the Yeomen of the Guard, in order to protect himself should treason strike close to home.

Almost as soon as the Battle of Bosworth was over, Henry, fearing for the security of his new kingdom, ordered Sir Richard Willoughby to travel to Sheriff Hutton to secure the person of the fifteen-year-old Earl of Warwick (son of the late Duke of Clarence and Isabel Neville), who, having been taken into Willoughby's 'protection', was removed to the 'safety' of the Tower of London, where he remained for the rest of his life.

On a national scale Henry was particularly concerned as to the safety of his border with Scotland. Even though there had been an uneasy peace between England and the Scottish King James III since the early 1480s, when the English had managed to retake the town of Berwick, Henry still considered the border areas unstable. Richard III had been popular in the region and the Scottish king's intentions towards the region at such an unstable time, with a change in dynasty, were unknown. Fearing that King James would try to retake lost ground, Henry commissioned Lord Strange to take over the wardenship of the Northern marches in place of the imprisoned Earl of Northumberland, Sir Henry Percy. Concerned as to the defence of Northumberland, and fearing that a Scottish invasion was imminent, on 25 September 1485 Henry issued a commission of array to Strange to raise local levies to withstand this expected invasion. Though it never materialized (much to Henry's relief), he was at this time forced to reinstate Henry Percy as warden, simply because Strange failed to attract the support that Percy could and Henry Tudor was struggling to maintain law and order.

By January 1486 Henry felt that the North was secure; the relationship between the new king and James III was not as fraught as he first thought it might be. Indeed, the Tudor regime remained on friendly terms with the Scots until James III's death, and the reinstatement of the Earl of Northumberland did much to restore law and order to the region. The start of the new year also brought about the long-awaited marriage of the king to Elizabeth of York, whom Henry made his wife on 18 January 1486. The match, it was said, was blessed by God: indeed, almost nine months to the day after the ceremony the new queen gave birth to Henry's first son, Prince Arthur. The Houses of York and Lancaster were finally united.

Henry was spared an early test of his authority, largely because he did not punish the remaining nobles and lords in England for having been loyal to King Richard's government. The majority of them lost nothing in terms of status and possessions, at the change of dynasty, and were content to allow Henry to rule. But there were, of course, exceptions, and in some areas of the kingdom there was still resistance to the king's authority, notably from the owners of Hornby Castle, which held out against the king's rule under the command of Sir James Harrington. This particular case was mainly a personal affair between Harrington and the Stanleys, who had long since contested the ownership of the castle and chose to take advantage of their status with the king to try to take the castle from the Harringtons in his name.

Since his arrival in England Henry had chosen to remain in or near the capital, but by the early spring of 1486 he was convinced by his advisors that he needed to tour his realm and make his mark. Surrounded by a larger-than-average retinue, he set out from London.

By April 1486 Henry was to face the first test of his authority when Francis, Viscount Lovell, Sir Thomas Stafford and his brother Sir Humphrey, who had been living under the laws of sanctuary in Colchester Abbey since the Battle of Bosworth, led an armed uprising against him. All three had suffered the loss of their lands and titles through being included in an act of attainder issued in November 1485, but felt that they still had sufficient power to 'raise' the common people against the new king. Having broken out of sanctuary, the Staffords travelled to Worcestershire, while Lovell had decided to travel to Richard's old heartland of Middleham in North Yorkshire.

Henry was at Lincoln when he first heard news of the Staffords' and Lovell's travels and their attempts to 'raise' the people against him. He decided not to issue a commission of array, because he was already travelling with such a large retinue, but decided instead to travel north first, to deal with Lovell in person, before moving south to confront the Staffords. Though he did not fear the individuals, the unknown support that they could inspire in the Yorkist name in the Yorkist homelands made Henry fearful. Fortunately for Henry, the rebels, with no royal figurehead to rally round, found support for their cause sadly lacking. In the North even families like the Conyers failed to answer the call, and those who did were not enough to threaten Henry, who had by this time arrived at York, having entered the city on 23 April. Henry preferred diplomacy to the sword, and while he remained in York he sent

Elizabeth of York, daughter of Edward IV and queen to Henry VII

Jasper Tudor, the new Duke of Bedford, promoted after the Battle of Bosworth, to Middleham with some of Henry's entourage to parley with the rebels. His response to the risings was to offer pardons to all who would lay down their arms and return home. This act of clemency took the steam (if ever there was any!) out of the rising, and Lovell, knowing that he would soon be deserted, fled in the night into Lancashire.

In Worcestershire the Staffords were having similar difficulties in attracting support for the revolt, and had to rely on Lovell, and a rumour that Lovell had captured the king, to gain support. When news arrived that the rebels in the North had been all but dispersed by the king's offer of pardon, and that the king was now on his way south to deal with the Staffords' rising, their part in the attempted revolt also fell apart. Advised of the king's approach, the Staffords decided to seek sanctuary once more and fled to the safety of the abbey at Culham near Abingdon, which they entered on 11 May. Two days later the king's men entered the abbey and forcibly removed them from their haven. In July 1486 they were both tried for treason before the judges of the King's Bench, who ruled after a lengthy debate that sanctuary could not be sought in cases of treason. Both were found guilty. Though Sir Thomas was pardoned for his part in the risings, his brother Sir Humphrey was hanged, drawn and quartered.

Meanwhile, Lovell had managed to find temporary safety at the house of Sir Thomas Broughton, a fellow Yorkist, and was joined by Sir John Huddleston and two other knights from Cumbria who wished to continue in the struggle against Henry by fanning more revolts in North Wales. Henry's response to this was to offer all of them save Lovell pardon should they return home. This they accepted, leaving Lovell with no other option than to flee abroad, finding safety and shelter in the Low Countries at the court of the Dowager Duchess of Burgundy, Margaret, sister of Edward IV and Richard III.

Though these were the major risings against Henry at this time, they also caused smaller ones to spring up at several locations around the country. These were soon put down, but what alarmed the king was the fact that many of them chose the old Neville emblem of the ragged staff as their flag and the cry 'a'Warwick, a'Warwick' as their rallying call. This showed Henry the power that the Warwick name could still command, and confirmed the wisdom of his decision to act quickly to secure the young Earl of Warwick the previous year.[1]

Undoubtedly the root cause of the Lovell–Stafford revolt failure was the fact that those who wished to rise against the king lacked a charismatic leader. Just as the power of the Warwick name as a figurehead was clear to Henry, it seems that it was also apparent to a twenty-eight-year-old priest called Richard Simons. Unfortunately for Henry, Simons had for some time been aware of the value of the name of Warwick, and though the present earl was still languishing in the Tower, this did not deter Simons, who had been instructing a scholar of his own in the ways of a prince. This scholar, one Lambert Simnel, the son of an Oxford joiner, would soon enter the stage as the 'real' Earl of Warwick, claiming to have escaped from confinement in the Tower of London. The support this impostor was to receive, and the popular belief that he was truly the Earl of Warwick, would lead to the events that culminated in the last Battle of the Wars of the Roses at Stoke Field.

When Lovell reached Burgundy he discovered that he was not the only Yorkist refugee there. Also present was a Yorkist captain called Thomas David, who had brought with him a part of the Calais garrison, who, like himself, had been ejected from the fortress for refusing to take an oath of loyalty to King Henry. The two fast became allies. It was in Burgundy that Lovell was also joined by the Earl of Lincoln, Sir John de la Pole, who had at first shown loyalty to King Henry, but as a nephew of both Edward IV and Richard III (his mother was their sister, and some believed him to be Richard's nominated heir), felt he could no longer serve the king and had fled England to join his aunt Margaret, Lovell and David in Burgundy, hoping to help bring about the restoration of the House of York.

When it was that the idea that Simnel should impersonate the Earl of Warwick was first suggested is not known, nor can it be said who were the principal architects of the plot. All that is certain is that when Simons presented Simnel to Gerald Fitzgerald, 8th Earl of Kildare in Ireland, as the Earl of Warwick, son of the Duke of Clarence (who had himself been born in Ireland), even Simons was surprised when the boy was unhesitatingly accepted and acclaimed as an Irish prince and Yorkist heir to the throne of England. It may be said with some degree of certainty that the Irish lords hoped to prosper from the plot and by it somehow win home rule. This explains why they agreed to support the ruse that Simnel was the real Warwick, and in so doing provided the Yorkists with a powerful base to work from, Ireland itself.

What involvement Lovell and the Earl of Lincoln had in all this is uncertain, but when it became clear that the young Lambert Simnel was available as a figurehead for their cause, and with financial backing for Simnel from his 'maternal aunt' Margaret of Burgundy in the form of payment for mercenaries and ships to transport them, Lovell, Lincoln and the other Yorkists in Burgundy sailed for Ireland. Their small fleet included not only David and the other exiles from Calais, but also some two thousand German mercenaries under the command of Captain Martin Schwartz. Schwartz and his men had previously fought against the French on Burgundy's behalf, and had gained a reputation for being particularly sturdy fighters – also for brutality in their treatment of civilians.

Meanwhile, in England Henry had first heard of Simnel and the following he was attracting some time in January 1487. By April he had realized that the movement could lead to an armed invasion. As most of the prominent Yorkists were in Burgundy he assumed that any such invasion would land on the south or east coast. He therefore moved his court to Norwich (where he spent the Easter of that year) so that he should be well placed to meet the invasion if it came. When Henry heard that Simnel had been accepted by the Irish as the Earl of Warwick, he tried to prove to all that the man was an impostor by ordering the real Earl of Warwick, to be paraded through the streets of London. All this achieved was a claim from those who supported Simnel that the individual paraded through London was himself the impostor, sent by Henry to try to trick the common people into believing that Warwick was still in England when in fact, as they were to claim, he was alive and well in Ireland, and preparing to retake the throne of England for the House of York.

When Henry received news that Lovell and Lincoln had sailed to Ireland he knew that the invasion would no longer be aimed at the south or east coasts and moved his base from Lincoln to Coventry.

Shortly after the arrival of Lovell and Lincoln in Ireland on 24 May 1487, Lambert Simnel, 'Earl of Warwick' was crowned King Edward VI at Christ Church, Dublin. The crown used for his coronation is reputed to have been a gold circlet taken from the statue of the Blessed Virgin Mary in Christ Church itself. What agreement Lovell and the other Yorkists had with Simnel (and his mentor, Simons) is unknown, but their union was to become a successful partnership for recruiting other dissatisfied Yorkists to their cause, and they were soon joined in Ireland by the likes of Richard Harleston (previously Governor of Jersey), Sir Henry Bodrugan and Sir John Beaumont (both from Cornwall), as well as an Irish contingent under the command of Thomas Geraldine. It was with the backing of these individuals and the mercenaries from Germany that the Yorkist invasion was to be planned under the command of Lovell and Lincoln.

In England Henry was aware that an invasion was imminent, and set about preparing the defence of his realm. Along the coast where a landing was most to be expected warning beacons were made ready, and the king began summoning his nobles to Kenilworth Castle, near Coventry, where he was making his final plans to face his enemy.

On 4 June 1487 the rebels (as they must be called) landed on the Lancashire coast, having sailed from Dublin a couple of days earlier. They landed near Peil Island in Furness, Lancashire (today part of Cumbria), a location carefully chosen because Sir Thomas Broughton, Lovell's co-conspirator from the previous year, held lands and had influence in the area. As soon as they landed they declared for Edward VI and then set off inland almost immediately, camping that night at a place called Swarthmoor near Ulverston, where they were reinforced by Sir Thomas Broughton and his retinue. The

Christchurch Cathedral, Dublin

following day they set off for Yorkshire, travelling via Carnforth, where they were further reinforced by contingents sent by the Harrington and Middleton families (who had still not made their peace with King Henry).

The rebel army now numbered some four or five thousand men-at-arms, and they hoped to attract more supporters as they travelled into Yorkshire, crossing into the county at Sedburgh. As they had hoped, they were joined by more supporters, including Alexander Appleby of Carlisle, Nicholas Musgrave of Brackenthwaite and Clement Skelton of Bowness. By the time the rebels had reached Masham their number is believed to have totalled some eight or nine thousand men-at-arms. Both Sir Thomas Scrope of Masham and John, Lord Scrope of Bolton were sympathetic to the rebels' cause (and were later implicated in the revolt), but neither had expected the rebels to move so quickly. Unprepared for their arrival, and thus unable to support them in military terms, they promised to follow on as soon as they were organized. While the rebels rested at Masham they were joined by other Yorkist supporters from around the estates at Middleham in North Yorkshire, though not perhaps in the numbers the rebel leaders had hoped for, as many must have remained behind, remembering what had happened the previous year. At about this time Lincoln chose to write from Masham, in Edward VI's name, to the lord mayor and leaders of the city of York, warning them of his intention to enter the city and gather supplies.

However, the citizens of York, who had been loyal to the Yorkist cause during the later reign of Edward IV and certainly in Richard III's time, were at present divided in their opinion as to whom they should support. The reason for their indecision was that under Henry they had fared no worse than under the Yorkists, and indeed Henry had bestowed many grants on the city in his time as king. In addition, the city of York had traditionally been Lancastrian in its loyalties: men-at-arms from York had fought at the battles of Wakefield and Towton in the Lancastrian cause. Undoubtedly the arrival in York of a letter from Sir Henry Percy, Earl of Northumberland, written on 6 June, in which he claimed that his intentions were to 'resist the rebels and reinforce the city of York within four days', was to be a major influence on the city leaders' ultimate decision: the city of York would remain loyal to King Henry.[2]

Shortly after the rebels left Masham, Lincoln received a reply from the city leaders of York stating that: 'He whom the said Lords called the King, they, nor none of their retinues intending to approach this city should have any entry into the same'. They went further, and claimed that if the so-called Edward VI should try to take the city by force then they would 'withstand him with their bodys and goods, if they would attain so to do'.[3] This must have been a bitter disappointment for both Lincoln and Lovell as well as for the other rebel commanders, but Lincoln was a competent leader of men and realized that if he hoped to keep his scratch army together then the best way to do so would be to maintain a rapid advance. With the city of York closed to him he made the decision to turn south.

Sometime between 9 and 11 June, the city leaders of York were informed by their scouts that the rebels were no longer advancing towards the city but had instead turned south down the Great North Road and were about to make camp for the night at Bramham Moor near Tadcaster, having arrived there via Boroughbridge. Here the rebels were reinforced by Sir Edward Hastings and Sir Robert Percy of Scotton. The city was to be spared.

Henry was at Kenilworth on 5 June when he heard that the rebels had landed, and at once set off to intercept them. He had prepared well for the invasion, and no doubt the warning beacons he had put in place had played a vital part in his receiving speedy word of the landing at Furness. Leaving Kenilworth, Henry travelled north via Coventry at the head of an impressive army which included Sir Edward Grey, Viscount Lisle and a body of horse under the command of Lord Scales. The main body of the king's force, under the field command of Jasper Tudor, Duke of Bedford, included several Bosworth veterans, among them Rhys ap Thomas, Sir John Cheney, Edward, Lord Hastings and Sir Thomas Brandon (whose brother had carried Henry's standard at Bosworth), and a contingent of cavalry under the command of Sir Edward Woodville.

Meanwhile, the king's supporters in Yorkshire were also mobilizing to resist the rebels. Sir Henry Clifford, who had only recently regained his family title and lands after a long time spent living as a shepherd during the years of Yorkist rule, had marched to reinforce the garrison at York with some two hundred men-at-arms. When he heard that the rebels had camped at Bramham Moor he decided to strike on the king's behalf, and left York – on the same day that Northumberland's men arrived to reinforce the city with a 'great host' – to march off towards Bramham. Failing to engage the rebels that day, Clifford was obliged to make camp at Tadcaster on the night of 11 June. The rebel commanders, aware of his advance, took the initiative and sent a detachment of their army to attack Clifford's force while they were making camp and totally routed them, capturing Clifford's baggage train intact at the same time. Clifford was forced to retreat to the safety of York, utterly disgraced.

The rebels, their spirits high after the night's events at Tadcaster, and well led by Lovell and Lincoln, decided that with York's gates shut to them, their best course of action was to push south. Aware that the king would attempt to intercept them, it was agreed that they would head for Newark, a town which offered not only the opportunity to gain supplies but also the opportunity to pick a site on which to do battle.

Henry, well served by his scouts, became aware of the rebels' rapid advance and guessed correctly their destination. Eager to get there first, to deprive the rebels of much-needed supplies, he too gave the order to march towards Newark. The two armies were now on a collision course, with any hopes of resolving the situation peacefully at an end. Only armed conflict could decide the issue.

The rebels marched south via Castleford towards Rotherham, a route that led them over the battlefield of Towton, south of Tadcaster, where their commanders must certainly have made much of the great Yorkist victory in order to raise morale. They reached Castleford some time on 12 June and moved rapidly towards Rotherham, arriving there the next day. But as they continued their march south from Rotherham they came into contact with a mounted patrol from Henry's vanguard, under the command of Lord Scales. It is said that Scales kept up a harassing action for two days before having to fall back towards the king's army (in good order at first but later in some confusion) through Sherwood Forest towards Nottingham, where the king's army had halted on 14 June. This army had travelled slowly from Kenilworth and had arrived at Nottingham via Leicester (which it had reached on 10 June) and Loughborough.

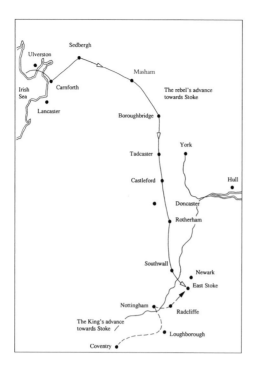

Fig 19.1   Preliminary Moves for the Battle of Stoke

While at Nottingham Henry's army had been reinforced by some six thousand men-at-arms sent by the Earl of Derby under the command of his son, Lord Strange. In the North also, the king's supporters were mobilizing. Sir Henry Percy, Earl of Northumberland and Lord Clifford had left York with four thousand men-at-arms with every intention of following the rebels and attacking them from the rear. However, two days after they left the city, both John, Lord Scrope of Bolton and Sir Thomas of Masham arrived before its walls with 'a great host' and demanded entry in the name of Edward VI. The lord mayor and city leaders refused, even when the Scropes tried to storm their way in through the gates at Bootham Bar. Although the defenders managed to keep them out, the lord mayor sent a desperate letter to the Earl of Northumberland pleading that he return with all haste to save the city. When the Earl of Northumberland received this letter he immediately turned back, but arrived at York to discover that the Scropes had gone. Whether their action had been a deliberate ploy to keep the earl in Yorkshire, or whether the Scropes had simply been unable to commit themselves to the rebel army, is unclear. It is still not known whether the Scropes joined with the rebels or returned to Masham.

The rebels, meanwhile, had reached Southwell, arriving there on 14 June. Late that evening their scouts reported that the castle at Newark and the bridge over the Trent which allowed access to the town was held by a body of the king's men who had ridden on ahead of the main army. They also learned that the main army itself had by now left Nottingham and was marching towards Radcliffe. The rebel leaders decided that it would be better to try to cross the Trent elsewhere rather than at Newark, where they would be vulnerable to attack by the castle's defenders. Well served by their scouts, and taking advantage of Lovell's local knowledge of the surrounding terrain, they decided to ford the river by the village of Fiskerton, west of Newark itself, where it was wide but shallow. Thus, on 15 June the rebel army travelled to Fiskerton, and by that evening had crossed the river and made camp in the meadows south of the Trent, to the west of a small village called East Stoke.

The king finally reached Radcliffe on 15 June and, unaware of the rebels' position, ordered his army to camp for the night at Radcliffe, not realizing that this would mean that the following morning the two armies must meet on the Fosseway to fight the final Battle of the Wars of the Roses.

THE BATTLE

The following morning dawned clear and bright as the rebels broke camp and prepared for battle. Their army now consisted of some nine or ten thousand men-at-arms, mainly farmers and other common folk who had been recruited to the banner of 'Edward VI' on the march south. It did, however, boast a number of the leading nobles of the time, including Francis, Viscount Lovell, Sir John de la Pole, Earl of Lincoln, Sir Thomas Broughton and Sir James Harrington, and a number of other gentlemen, including William Kay and William Hammond, who had come forward during the last couple of days, and Richard Harleston, Sir Henry Bodrugan, Sir John Beaumont, Alexander Appleby, Nicholas Musgrave, Clement Skelton and Thomas David, who had joined the rebel army almost from its foundation or shortly after it had arrived in England. Undoubtedly the cream of the rebel army was the German mercenaries led by Captain Martin Schwartz. The Irish contingent under Thomas Geraldine was poorly equipped but what it lacked in arms and armour, it made up for in ferocity and courage.

The initial position of the rebel army is shown in Fig. 19.2. The army chose to make its stand on a hill south-west of the village of East Stoke and north of Elston, and formed up in a line across the Fosseway. The rebels' right flank was anchored on the high point of the hill known locally as Burham Furlong, where the steep slope formed a natural defensive barrier. Their front extended from here towards Elston to a point some 500 yards to the south-east of the Fosseway. The precise positions of the rebel leaders are unknown, as is the disposition of their units, though it may be assumed that the German mercenaries and the Irish contingent were intermixed with the English men-at-arms and archers to give an equal balance of strength throughout the line. With their army in place, all the rebel leaders could do now was to wait for the arrival of the royal army. Unlike most of the battles of the period, where the opposing sides generally formed up in full view of each other, in this instance the rebel commanders knew, from their scouts, that the king's army had camped the previous night at and around Radcliffe. They concluded that it could be only a matter of time before Henry's army arrived at East Stoke, and felt it would better serve their cause to make ready for battle there, where they had choice of terrain, rather than advance towards Radcliffe and hope to find an equally advantageous position.

What the rebels did not know at this time was that the king and his field

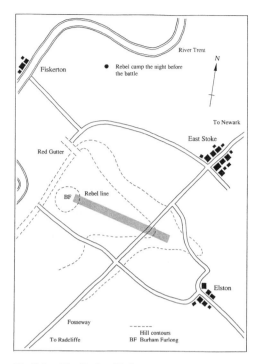

Fig 19.2   The Battle of Stoke

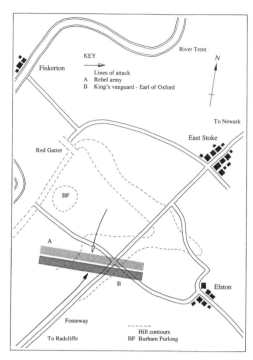

Fig 19.3   The Battle of Stoke

commanders, the Earl of Oxford and the Duke of Bedford, were not aware of the rebels' exact location and did not yet know whether they had in fact crossed the River Trent. This meant that the king's army, instead of advancing in battle order towards East Stoke, where the rebels were waiting, kept to its original plan of marching towards Newark. When Henry's men left camp that morning they continued to advance along the Fosseway in column, instead of in line across it, with the Earl of Oxford at their head and the main army, rearguard and camp followers behind, spread along several miles of the Fosseway, totally unprepared for battle and quite unaware of how dangerously close they were to their enemy.

Naturally enough, it was the king's vanguard, under Sir John de Vere, Earl of Oxford, who first discovered that the rebels were at East Stoke. Advised of their location, Oxford was forced to make an instant decision. He could either march towards East Stoke and engage the enemy in mêlée, send word to the king that the battle was on and hope that Henry and the main body of the army would arrive in time, or he could stand his ground and wait for the king to catch up, all the while running the appalling risk of being attacked in the open by the rebels. Oxford felt there was only one option: he dared not run the risk of standing his ground, and to retreat would do untold damage to the morale of the army; the choice was clear – he must attack. This was not a rash decision, as Oxford had been informed that the rebel army consisted of some ten thousand men-at-arms, and he calculated that the six thousand better trained and better equipped men of his own command could hold their own against the superior numbers of his adversaries. Advancing in battle order (line across) therefore, accompanied by Sir Gilbert Talbot, Earl of Shrewsbury and Sir Edward Grey, Viscount Lisle, Oxford advanced towards East Stoke.

At about 9 o'clock, as the two sides drew closer together, an exchange of archer fire signalled the start of the engagement. The rebels, who were not as well equipped as the royal army (particularly the Irish contingent, who had little in the way of armour to protect themselves from arrow fire), were to suffer the heavier casualties in this exchange. But when Oxford's men reached the base of the hill they had to realign their front slightly in order to face the rebels head on, and the time taken for this manoeuvre gave the rebel army the opportunity to charge down upon them (*see* Fig. 19.3), and engage in close-quarter combat. It has been said that it was the Irish, badly mauled by the arrow fire, who led the charge in order to prevent further losses being inflicted upon them by Oxford's archers. The rebel commanders, unable to stop them from charging down the hill, were forced to order the rest of the army to follow suit, the alternative being to risk their own force's disintegration in the confusion of a partial attack. The ensuing mêlée lasted over an hour, and even though Oxford commanded the better trained men, against the impetus of the downhill charge and with the numbers stacked against him, he found his own force being pushed steadily back along the route he had travelled that morning (*see* Fig. 19.4).

When Oxford had first learnt of the rebels' position that morning he had at once

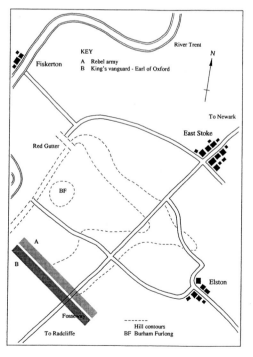

Fig 19.4   The Battle of Stoke

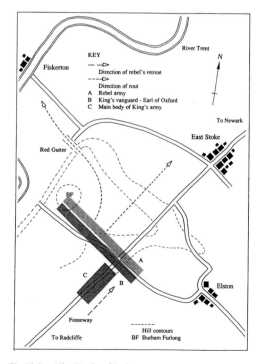

Fig 19.5   The Battle of Stoke

sent word to the king (still several miles behind) and the main body of the army, under the command of Jasper Tudor, Duke of Bedford, giving details of the situation and the action he was about to take. Appraised that the rebels were ahead and engaged in combat with his own vanguard, the king ordered his force to advance towards East Stoke with all haste. It was only the timely arrival of this main army that saved Oxford's hard-pressed men from being totally routed. The king's force arrived at East Stoke along the same route as Oxford's and was soon reinforcing the latter's position. As more and more of the king's relatively fresh men joined with Oxford's men, the rebels, fast tiring, soon found themselves being pushed back towards the hill, and back up it (*see* Fig. 19.5).

Less than three hours after the conflict had started, the rebel line broke and hundreds of their number began fleeing over the top of the hill towards the River Trent. The battle ended with victory for Henry and the total rout and destruction of the rebel army.

EPILOGUE TO THE BATTLE

As the rebels fled the field the majority of them tried to escape along a ravine leading from the hill down to the river. Many of them were cornered by the king's men and slaughtered in their hundreds. At this place, still known locally as the 'Red Gutter', it is said that the slaughter was so great that the floor of the ravine ran red with blood.

The casualties were high even on the winning side, the king's men losing some three thousand of their number, most of them from Oxford's vanguard. The rebels

The 'Red Gutter', Stoke Field, Nottinghamshire

suffered even greater losses, with some five thousand dying on the field of battle. Of the rebel leaders, Lincoln, Broughton and Schwartz were killed as their army was routed. But the fate of Francis, Viscount Lovell remains a mystery. He was not found among the dead after the battle and was never seen again after that day. Some believe that he drowned as he tried to cross the Trent during his escape and that his body was washed away. Many years later a vault, discovered in Minster Lovell (the family home), was unsealed and a skeleton was discovered inside which was said to be Lovell. How it came to be there remains a mystery even today.

The fleeing rebels were pursued for several days and some seven hundred of their number were rounded up and captured. The few Irish among them were put to death, as were a number of the English. The rest, including some of the German mercenaries, were allowed to return to their homes, doubtless with tales to tell of the rebels' total defeat.

Lambert Simnel was captured as the rout began, apparently by a squire called Robert Bellingham. His life was spared, and when the king returned to court Simnel was put to work in the royal kitchens turning the spit. In later years he became one of the king's falconers, and was never again used as a threat against the House of Tudor. The fate of his tutor Simons is not recorded.

The ruins of the manor house, Minster Lovell, Oxfordshire

The Burrand Bush memorial, Stoke Field, Nottinghamshire

Henry himself arrived at Burham Furlong when the fighting was over, and it was here that his banner was raised to signify victory. At this spot there now stands a stone monument on which the following words are engraved: 'Here stood the Burrand Bush planted on the spot where Henry VII placed his standard after the Battle of Stoke 16th June 1487.' The monument can still be seen today and, as the inscription relates, is on the site of a bush originally planted as a living memorial to the battle.

It is said that when the king reached the hilltop, he was overcome with anger on hearing of Lincoln's death, as he had ordered that the earl should be taken alive. Where Lincoln's body was laid to rest is not officially recorded, though some say that at the place where he was supposedly buried (near Stoke Field) a group of willow trees was planted. Tradition has it that a stave of one of these willows was driven through Lincoln's heart. Henry's final act on the day was to knight over a dozen of those who took part in the battle as a reward for their actions.

What is clear today is that though Henry's forces won the battle it was the rebels who were the better organized and had the better morale. As Henry had marched towards Newark he had been deserted by many of his men and there had been a severe lack of discipline among his troops, forcing his commanders to make many a salutary example of lower ranks who caused dissension among the troops. In many ways Henry himself was to blame for the poor morale of his troops. On several occasions he had travelled in the opposite direction from his army (notably when he left it for a meeting with Lord Strange outside Nottingham, when Strange brought up his father's contingent to join the king's). This fuelled many rumours among the king's troops that

Henry had fled. Another example of Henry's behaviour causing morale to fall was when he visited the vanguard as the army was camped at and around Nottingham. On returning to Nottingham the king retired, but omitted to inform his commanders as to the location of his lodgings, thus fuelling more rumours that he had fled. It is fair to say that his cause was not helped by rebel spies within his army, who helped fuel the fire whenever opportunity arose. Latterly, Henry had been moved to order that any rumourmongers and spies identified by his men were to be hanged from an ash tree at the end of Nottingham Bridge.

As his army moved closer to Newark, Henry, an inexperienced leader, had made further mistakes. His scouts had served him poorly, leading to his continuing to march his army in column towards Newark in such an unsoldierly fashion. It could be said that had it not been for the Earl of Oxford, who was an experienced commander, and who probably had the cream of the royal army within the vanguard, that the outcome of the battle might have been very different. As it was, Henry gained the victory, and his supporters undoubtedly generated much propaganda and made much of his 'leadership' in achieving it.

The Battle of Stoke Field was the last pitched battle on English soil to be associated with the Wars of the Roses. More than thirty years had passed since the opening shots of the first battle at St Albans in 1455, and there had been fourteen major battles in the interim. Henry would face other tests of his authority in the future, but none would lead to his needing personally to lead an army into battle in order to defend his crown.

The crown of England had changed hands several times over the last thirty years as a result of armed conflict. Now all the Yorkist heirs were dead except Edward, Earl of Warwick, and he was safely in custody in the Tower, where he was to meet a grisly end in 1499.

To all intents and purposes the Wars of the Roses were at an end and the Tudor dynasty finally secure.

THE BATTLE OF SHREWSBURY 21 JULY 1403

Author's note: It is believed by some that the Battle of Shrewsbury in 1403 should be considered the first Battle of the Wars of the Roses, as this was the first attempt to remove a Lancastrian king by force of arms. Though it is true to say that its prime movers, the Percys, were in later years Lancastrians, it is no less true to point out that at this time they had no love for the Lancastrian King Henry IV. Whether or not the battle should be called the first Battle of the Wars of the Roses is open to debate, and the following summary will allow the reader to decide if it has a place in them.

THE CAMPAIGN

On 13 October 1399 Henry Bolingbroke, Duke of Lancaster, eldest son of John of Gaunt and grandson of Edward III, was crowned King of England exactly a year and a day after being forced into exile by Richard II. On his return to England Henry had seized power with the aid of Sir Henry Percy, 1st Earl of Northumberland. Percy had fared well under Richard II's earlier reign but had turned against the king when Richard had elevated Sir Ralph Neville to the title of 1st Earl of Westmorland and had given him authority as Warden of the West March, a position previously held by Percy. In one move Richard had founded the Neville dynasty, had broken the Earl of Northumberland's monopoly on power in the North, and had initiated the Neville–Percy feud.

Bolingbroke had been exiled for fighting a duel with Sir Thomas Mowbray, Duke of Norfolk, but in 1399, while King Richard was in Ireland, Bolingbroke had returned to England, landing at Holderness on the east coast. With the aid of Sir Henry Percy he had usurped the crown from Richard II, thus elevating to the throne the House of Lancaster. By 1403, however, the situation was different. The Percys had become dissatisfied with their new king, this time feeling that they had never been properly rewarded for their help in the usurpation of the throne or for winning such a resounding victory over the Scots on Henry's behalf at the Battle of Homildon Hill in Northumberland in 1402.

Henry was unaware of this ill-feeling towards him until it was almost too late, and only realized that there was a conspiracy against him when he was actually on his way to Northumberland. The conspirators included the Earl of Northumberland, Henry 'Hotspur' Percy (Northumberland's son), Sir Thomas Percy, Earl of Worcester (Northumberland's brother), Owen Glendower and Earl Douglas of Scotland. Earl Douglas had until recently been a prisoner of the Earl of Northumberland, having been captured at Homildon Hill, but had been set free and allowed to return to Scotland after swearing an oath that he would return with his own followers to assist in the plot to overthrow King Henry and replace him with Edmund Mortimer, Earl of March.

Henry had reached Burton-on-Trent on 15 July 1403, on his march north, when he learnt of the conspiracy to overthrow him. More than a little astounded by this news, the king had quickly to reassess his situation before deciding what to do next. His first act was to travel west towards Lichfield, which he reached on 16 July. From here he issued commissions of array in the nearby counties and waited for men to answer his call to arms. At the same time, no doubt, Henry was gathering information as to the whereabouts of his enemies, and it was now that he learnt that Glendower and Mortimer, with an army of Welshmen, were preparing to join the rebellion at Shrewsbury in England. Northumberland's army was under the command of his son, Henry 'Hotspur' Percy, because the earl himself was too ill to command, and had remained at Berwick. Receipt of this news led to a change in plan. Instead of going north, King Henry decided to travel to Stafford. He left Lichfield on 18 July and arrived at Stafford the next day. Having spent the night there, and still not certain of the location of Hotspur's army, it was time once again to reassess the situation. Henry knew for certain that the rebels (Hotspur and Glendower) were intending to effect a union at Shrewsbury. King Henry's son, the Prince of Wales (later Henry V), was then returning from a raid into Wales and was currently encamped at Shrewsbury with a small force, unaware that he was caught between two enemy armies. When the king learnt of this his course was clear – he ordered that his army should march at once to Shrewsbury to reinforce his son.

The rebels' position at this time is not entirely clear. It seems that as Hotspur and Douglas marched south via Cheshire their army was reinforced by those who still supported the memory of Richard II and wished to be rid of King Henry. At Chester itself, the Earl of Northumberland's brother, Sir Thomas Percy, Earl of Worcester, joined the rebels. With their union almost complete, Hotspur and his army then set off for Shrewsbury.

Meanwhile, Henry had entered Shrewsbury via the Abbey Bridge late in the evening of 20 July, after a forced march of 32 miles by way of Newport and Haugh in a single day – a remarkable achievement considering the road conditions of the period. At about the same time Hotspur was travelling the Whitchurch road to Shrewsbury, and arrived at the town via Whitchurch and Wem shortly afterwards. He knew that when he arrived at the town he would have to take it by force – he needed to secure it to allow Glendower a safe crossing into England – and was prepared to storm it until he saw the king's banners flying above its defences. Realizing that the king's army had beaten him to it, and that he would not therefore be able to take the town by force, he fell back to make camp for the night at the nearby town of Berwick.

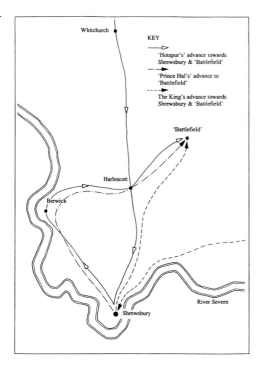

Fig A.1   Preliminary Moves for the Battle of Shrewsbury

Though King Henry held the town of Shrewsbury, he was in a poor position strategically. To the south-west was the army of Mortimer and Glendower (though in fact, as neither Henry nor Hotspur knew at the time, Glendower and his Welsh army were still in Carmarthenshire, having been delayed by floods), directly in front of the king was Hotspur's army, and in the North the power base of the Earl of Northumberland. Henry's problem lay in deciding which one to strike at, for strike he must if he hoped to retain his crown.

On the morning of 21 July Hotspur, still at Berwick and not yet knowing of Glendower's situation, was brought news that a portion of the royal army, led by the Prince of Wales, was marching on Berwick. Hotspur realized that while he remained at Berwick he ran the risk of being cut off from Cheshire, as the town of Berwick was 'surrounded' on three sides by the River Severn. Therefore if, as he quickly reasoned, the force approaching him was the left arm of a pincer movement, whose aim was to trap him with his back to the river, then the king and his remaining royal forces would be at this moment heading for Harlescott, in an attempt to block his path to Cheshire by taking control of the Whitchurch road. He was correct. The king had decided to tackle the more immediate threat to his position, drawing Hotspur into battle before he could be reinforced by Glendower from the south-west and Northumberland from the north.

Hotspur, having correctly decided that he was in danger of being cut off, at once gave orders for his army to leave Berwick and travel at all speed for Harlescott and the Whitchurch road. At this point, it is said, Hotspur was approached by one of his captains, who told him that their horses were tired and needed to rest, to which Hotspur answered, 'So are those of the king. March on.' By the time Hotspur reached the Whitchurch road at Harlescott there had already been some skirmishing with the royal army, which was close on his heels. Due to the proximity of the armies led respectively by the Prince of Wales and the king, Hotspur now had to choose between fleeing back to Cheshire and standing to fight. Much of the land around Harlescott is flat, but about a mile to the north-east there is a rise in the ground that makes a natural defensive position. Hotspur, outnumbered as he was without the reinforcement of Mortimer and Glendower, was in need of just such a position. As a competent soldier, he was not slow to decide that his scratch army, whose small hard core from the North had been enlarged by recruits gathered as he marched through Cheshire, would better serve him by fighting now rather than by travelling up the Whitchurch road to seek a more advantageous position, being harassed all the way by the royal army, which would certainly damage morale and lead to desertion. Thus the decision was made to stand and fight, and Hotspur made for the high ground and prepared to meet the king in battle. Meanwhile, the royal army had reached the same conclusions as Hotspur and chased him towards the hill, just failing to reach it first.

The field of battle is known today as Battlefield, but at the time it was known locally as Bull Field or Husse Field, after nearby locations. It was here that, as one French chronicler put it, 'The sory bataille of Schrovesbury was fought between Englysshemem and Englysshemem'.

THE BATTLE

Hotspur's army, having arrived at the field first, formed up in a line some 900 yards across, parallel to the road (*see* Fig. A.2). It consisted of some nine or ten thousand men-at-arms, mainly archers, and included his own northern retainers and the retinues of Sir Thomas Percy, Earl of Worcester, Earl Douglas, Sir Richard Vernon, Baron of Shipbrook, and Sir Richard Venables, Baron of Kinderton, together with some two hundred other knights and lesser nobles, mainly from Cheshire.

The royal army, by contrast, which drew up in line some 300–350 yards south, opposite Hotspur's forces, consisted of between twelve and fourteen thousand men-at-arms, and contained the likes of Sir Edward Stafford, Earl of Stafford, Sir Hugh Shirley, Sir John Clifton, Sir John Cockaine, Sir Nicholas Gausel, Sir John Calvert, Sir Walter Blount, the Prince of Wales and King Henry himself.

Though 'Hotspur' was outnumbered, his force held the higher ground, from where they were able to watch the king's army form up on the flat ground below his position, halfway up the shallow hill. The position of the participants within the ranks is more difficult to determine. It may be assumed that Douglas, Hotspur and Worcester commanded the rebels' vanguard, centre and rearguard respectively, but when it comes to the royal army all that is certain is that 'the valiant Prince Hal', as Shakespeare described him, took command of the king's rearguard and was located on the king's left flank. It is likely that the king commanded his own centre, with the Earl of Stafford leading the vanguard.

It was as the two armies deployed that Hotspur realized with dismay that he had left his favourite sword behind at Berwick, at the home of the Betton family with whom he had stayed the previous night. As the sword had become his 'lucky charm', he was

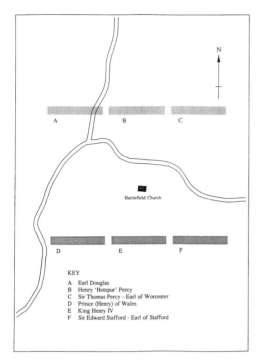

Fig A.2   The Battle of Shrewsbury

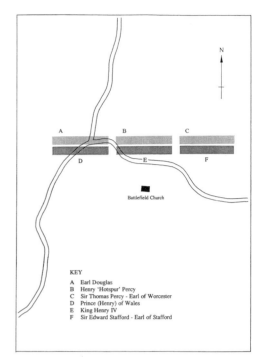

Fig A.3   The Battle of Shrewsbury

overcome with gloom, and is reputed to have said, 'Then has my plough reached its last furrow'.

Before the conflict could begin, the Abbot of Shrewsbury attempted to bring about a peaceful solution and spent two hours travelling between the two armies trying to mediate. His labours were in vain and at about midday the battle began. It opened with an advance by the royal army towards the rebel forces, but as the king's men approached the rise in the terrain they were met by a volley of arrows fired by Hotspur's Cheshire archers. This caused the royal advance to halt, and there followed an extended exchange of archer fire between the two sides. This was followed by a rapid downhill charge by the rebel archers (presumably after they had spent their arrows) towards the king's ranks. Hotspur then ordered his whole army to charge down the hill behind the more adventurous archers in order to add impetus to their move.

The two armies clashed at the base of the hill (*see* Fig. A.3), and the weight of Hotspur's charge caused the front line of Henry's army to break, almost bringing about the collapse of his entire line. But the king somehow managed to hold his army together, and the two sides settled into a particularly savage mêlée in which the king's men were pushed back some 100 yards.

Unfortunately for Hotspur, the success of his downhill charge was ultimately to be his undoing. On the king's left flank, the men under the Prince of Wales' command, more experienced than the rest of the king's army, having been on campaign in Wales,

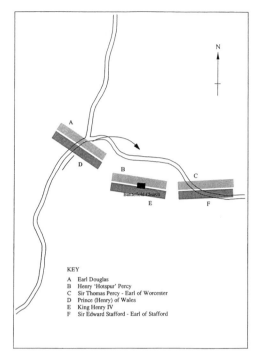

Fig A.4   The Battle of Shrewsbury

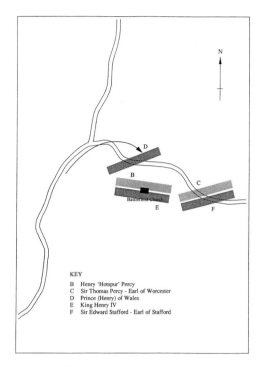

Fig A.5   The Battle of Shrewsbury

managed to stand their ground (*see* Fig. A.4). During the mêlée with Hotspur's less experienced men-at-arms, this left flank of the royal army was able to push Hotspur's right flank back towards the hill. This caused Hotspur's right flank to break, and the prince was then able to turn his force to attack Hotspur's from the flank and rear (*see* Fig. A.5), partially surrounding the rebels. As the rebel army realized its desperate position, the mêlée became particularly hard-fought, with the army of the king beginning to sense victory and the rebels putting up a fight appropriate to what was at stake, namely their survival. It was during this part of the battle that Hotspur himself was killed, felled, it is said, by an arrow to the head. When word of his death spread his army's resistance waned. The rebels broke, scattered and fled. The battle ended with total victory for the king.

EPILOGUE TO THE BATTLE

The battle had lasted for more than three hours and when it was over some five thousand of Hotspur's supporters lay dead upon the field. Of the rebel commanders, Sir Thomas Percy, Earl of Worcester, Sir Richard Vernon and Sir Richard Venables were taken alive, and two days later all three were executed at the high cross in Shrewsbury for treason against the king. The head of the Earl of Worcester was later placed on a spike on London Bridge. The rebel Earl Douglas was also captured, but after a considerable time as a prisoner was allowed to return to Scotland, unlike most of those who had travelled from Scotland with him. Nearly all the Scots present at the battle failed to live out the day.

The king's army suffered some sixteen hundred killed, including many of the nobles who had followed him to Shrewsbury. Sir Edward Stafford, Earl of Stafford, Sir Hugh Shirley, Sir John Clifton, Sir John Cockaine, Sir Nicholas Gausel and Sir John Calvert all died for their king that day.

It is said that at one point during the battle, after the king's front line had been smashed by the downhill charge, that Hotspur, Douglas and some thirty of their force attempted to fight their way to the king and end the battle by killing him. It is true that the king's standard was knocked to the ground, and that during the battle the king was advised by one of his commanders, fearing such a ploy by the rebels, to withdraw to the rear. It is also said that the royal army had several knights wearing the livery of the king to deceive the rebels as to his actual location, and that four of these knights, including Sir Walter Blount, were killed by Hotspur and his party.

It is also reported that during the early stages of the battle the Prince of Wales received a wound to the face and was advised to leave the field, but that he valiantly refused and went on to secure the victory on his father's behalf. The Battle of Shrewsbury certainly did much to enhance the status of the prince, and his exploits that day were surpassed, years later, only by his successful conduct of the war in France and his glorious victory at Agincourt.

As the rebels were routed, Henry discouraged his men from pursuing them. This was not an act of mercy but rather to ensure that sufficient numbers would return to Northumberland and tell of Hotspur's defeat. Henry hoped that this would discourage any further revolt from the northerners.

The king ordered that a church be built on the site of the battle to commemorate his victory that day. Battlefield church was built accordingly, and as the battle was fought on St Mary Magdalen's Eve the church, when complete, was dedicated to her. It is reputed to stand either on the spot where the king was nearly killed, when his standard was knocked to the ground, or where Hotspur was actually killed.

Though Henry was the victor of that day, rebellion was to plague his reign. He died in 1413 from a mystery illness, since thought to have been leprosy, which he contracted some time after killing Sir Richard Scrope, Archbishop of York, who had openly opposed Henry's rule. The illness was said to have been 'God's vengeance' for this terrible act, which caused Henry to become much disliked by the common folk of England. Henry had always believed in a prophecy made to him that he would die in Jerusalem. When his end came he died on his sick-bed in the Jerusalem Chapel at Westminster Abbey. His son, the Prince of Wales, was crowned Henry V, undisputed King of England, and the heirs of the House of Lancaster became rulers of England until 1455 – the start of the turbulent years that witnessed the Wars of the Roses.

ROBIN OF REDESDALE AND ROBIN OF HOLDERNESS

On the subject of the identities of Robin of Redesdale and Robin of Holderness there appears to be some confusion. It has even been claimed in some quarters that they are one and the same person. There is, however, sufficient evidence to conclude that they were two separate people, and that Robin of Redesdale was in fact Sir William Conyers (or Coiners), brother of Sir John and a relative of the Earl of Warwick through his marriage to Warwick's niece.[1]

This particular Robin is sometimes confused with an earlier Robin of Redesdale who first came on the scene as Queen Margaret was fleeing the victorious Yorkists after the Battle of Hexham. Robin was supposed to have guided the queen along the borderlands to the coast and found her sanctuary on a ship heading for France. This theory may safely be discounted: the Battle of Hexham took place in May 1464 and the queen sailed to France in November 1463. However, there is a similarity between this story and one that dates back to April 1462, when a small party of Lancastrians, disturbed by a larger party of Yorkists near Hexham, fled to nearby woodland to escape it. Though more of a skirmish than a battle by Wars of the Roses standards, it is still known by local people as the first Battle of Hexham. In their escape Queen Margaret and her son became separated from the other Lancastrians, and while crossing a stream near Hexham (at a place still known today as 'Queen Letch'), her horse stumbled and she fell. Accompanied only by her son, the prince, Margaret was set upon and captured by a gang of local outlaws. Unaware of the importance of their catch, these outlaws were content just to rob them, finally leaving them alone and lost in the woods.[2] After several days' travelling they were accosted by another outlaw, reputed to have been known as Robin of Redesdale. This Robin was taken in by the queen's charm and concealed her in his hideout, a cave still known today as 'Queen's Cave', keeping her hidden for several days from marauding Yorkists still in the area, until such time as he could lead her and her son to safety. Whether this story is true or not it is impossible to say, though perhaps there is some factual basis. It may be said with some degree of certainty, however, that this individual was not the Robin of Redesdale associated with the events that followed.

The blood relationship of William 'Robin of Redesdale' Conyers to the Earl of Warwick would explain the reasons for this Robin's connection with Warwick in the risings of 1469 and 1470. It may be said that the Earl of Warwick's brother, Sir John Neville, Earl of Northumberland, chose not to side openly with Warwick in his attempt to overthrow King Edward, but instead chose to take the field in pursuit of his duties as the King's Warden in Northumberland. He had no wish to compromise his position with his kin, in his duty to his king.

However, nepotism did raise its head when some of Robin's men sprang to arms several days earlier than planned, while the Earl of Warwick was still in Calais. The Earl of Northumberland was obliged to disperse the rebels (proving to Edward that he was indeed still the king's loyal servant), but in so doing allowed enough time for the rebel leaders to escape to Lancashire, whence they were able to regroup and march to Warwick's assistance some time later (proving to Warwick that indeed 'blood is thicker than water').[3]

In the spring of 1469, while Robin of Redesdale was raising the northern shires against King Edward, the son of a squire from Holderness also began to stir up trouble. Robert Hildyard, who took the nickname 'Rob (thus 'Robin') of Holderness',[4] from the district where he lived, rallied the local people against the long-resented payment of a tax in the form of thraves of corn to the authorities of St Leonard's Hospital at York. This levy had been resented by the occupants of Holderness from as early as 1400, when Sir Robert Hilton had been commissioned to inquire into the justification of the tax, until as recently as the previous year, when the Earl of Warwick had himself headed a commission which upheld the hospital's claim.[5]

This Robin timed his rebellion to coincide with that of Robin of Redesdale's rising in favour of Warwick against the king. This was probably deliberate in order to heighten Robin of Holderness's claim and add weight to his cause. Because of this the two characters have often been confused with each other when in fact they were two separate people with quite separate grievances.

There is no doubt about the identification of Robin of Holderness as Robert Hildyard. What is in doubt is the question of whether or not at the same time as he was demonstrating against the corn tax, he was also pressing for the reinstatement of Henry Percy as Earl of Northumberland. At this point, Percy was in the Tower of London, where he had been since his capture eight years earlier at the Battle of Towton. The Percy family had owned vast areas of land in Holderness for generations and had remained popular with the people thereabout.

Had this claim to the Northumberland title been made against anyone other than Sir John Neville, the Earl of Warwick's brother, granted the earldom of Northumberland by Edward IV in reward of his labours in the North after the Battle of Towton, the Earl of Warwick would probably have supported it, as it suited his purpose to have as many disturbances as possible at this time. As things stood, and as the corn tax issue was purely a local grievance, the earl instead chose to ignore it. But the Earl of Northumberland could not ignore the threat to his title, and moved from the borderlands of Scotland to York to deal with the rebels. At about this time, it is said, Robin of Holderness marched on the city of York with a great number of men, to press home his claims. At the gates of the city they were met by the Earl of Northumberland and his retainers and were quickly put to flight; their leader Robin was captured and beheaded on the pavement below Walmgate Bar. After his execution his head was placed on a spike on the bar itself. Thus ended for good the Robin of Holderness rebellion.[6]

At first glance the events appear straightforward, but it must be asked at this point who was the individual known as Robin of Holderness who was beheaded at York. As stated above, the Robin of Holderness who rebelled against the corn tax was one Robert Hildyard. According to the official history of York there is little doubt that a character called Robin of Holderness was executed by the Earl of Northumberland at the gates of the city. So why the question? Robert Hildyard was the son of Robert Hildyard of Winestead who had fought at Towton for the Lancastrians. Hildyard had led many men from the Percy-influenced district of Holderness to Towton, and many of them were to die there. The cockerel emblem that was incorporated into the Hildyard coat of arms at about this time[7] could be a reference to the Cock River (now Cock Beck), along whose banks many Lancastrians were to die on that fateful day. Robert senior was among the nobles captured at the end of the battle, but, unlike many of his fellow captives who were executed (or if spared, were stripped of their lands and titles), Robert was not only freed and pardoned, but shortly afterwards was made a justice of the peace in Holderness. Robert senior died in 1489. His will was administered in August of that year and his land passed to his son Robert Hildyard.[8] The question, then, is how can a man who is supposed to have been killed at the gates of York in 1469 be alive in 1489 to inherit his father's land?

Some have tried to explain away this discrepancy by suggesting that the date of the will is incorrect, and that Robert the elder was in fact slain on Towton Field. There is some evidence to support this claim but there are also official records which show that on 8 May 1461 a commission was issued to Robert Hildyard to arrest rebels, and again in March 1470 a commission of array was addressed to Robert Hildyard the elder. There are numerous similar entries of this kind throughout the 1470s and 1480s.[9] But even if these records do not provide proof enough that Robert senior was alive in the 1480s, and that therefore his son Robert must have been living to inherit his father's estate in 1489 (which means that the Robin of Holderness executed at York in 1469 could not be the same Robin of Holderness who led the corn tax rebellion), then there is separate evidence to show that Robert Hildyard the younger was alive in 1470.

In March 1470, after the failure of Warwick's rebellion, King Edward IV came to York in person. Here, Sir John Conyers (calling himself 'Robin of Redesdale' after the death of his brother Sir William), Lord Scrope and Robert Hildyard the younger ('Robin of Holderness') submitted to the king, confessing their involvement in the previous year's uprisings.[10]

If more proof were needed that Robert Hildyard the younger was alive after his apparent death at York at the hands of Sir John Neville, it is officially recorded that when his father was called upon to help defend the border against James III of Scotland,[11] his son Robert Hildyard accompanied him. He was rewarded for his services in 1481 by being dubbed Knight Banneret at the siege of Berwick by the grateful Earl of Northumberland, Sir Henry Percy,[12] who had regained his family title in 1470. Further, this same Robert Hildyard the younger received full knighthood in 1483, at the coronation of Richard III, from Richard himself. After the Battle of Bosworth Sir Robert, with more than thirty other knights, accompanied the Earl of Northumberland to York, where they met Henry VII when he visited the city.[13]

So what does all this mean? There are several possible explanations: firstly, that if it was Robert Hildyard who commanded the rebels when they approached the city of York then he must have escaped and someone else was executed in his stead; secondly, that another Robert Hildyard, about whom nothing is known, led the rebels, and the fact that their names were the same is purely coincidental; thirdly, and most plausibly, that the entire episode relating to Robin of Holderness's march on York was manufactured by the Earl of Northumberland in an attempt by him to show to others, the king included, that he was actively involved in maintaining law and order on behalf of the king, even though his brother the Earl of Warwick was seriously involved in disrupting it.

There may be those who would say that this is far-fetched, but recalling the Neville–Lovelace scenario of St Albans in 1461 (see Chapter 7), it might not be thought so unlikely. It would not have been beyond the resources of the Earl of Northumberland to raise local levies; indeed there is documentary evidence that the earl called upon the men of Beverley to serve under him against 'Hob of Redesdale' between 26 April and 4 May 1469. Once he had gathered his forces he could have staged the scene at Walmgate Bar and nobody would have been the wiser.[14] For the Earl of Northumberland it was just bad luck that the young Robert Hildyard – the supposedly dead Robin of Holderness – submitted to the king at York, proving to all that indeed he was alive and now sought the king's mercy for his part in the corn tax rebellion. Robert Hildyard would at least have attempted to exonerate himself from any crime with which he had been associated – such as the march on York – but had not committed. Perhaps this was what led to the events that occurred only four days later at York between the king and Sir John Neville. It is not to be doubted that for some time King Edward had been considering the release of Henry Percy from the custody of the Tower of London and reinstating the Percy family to the earldom of Northumberland. Since 1464 this coveted and financially rewarding title had been held by Sir John Neville, the Earl of Warwick's brother, having been bestowed on him as a reward for his arduous labours in the North against the Lancastrians in the early 1460s. Edward's difficulty was that he had no reason to remove Sir John Neville from the position. Even while Warwick had sought to conspire against the king (for which he had been pardoned), had not his brother remained loyal and supportive to Edward? In the light of Robert Hildyard's testimony before the king (and the truth about the incident at York), perhaps not!

Whatever the reason, on 25 March 1470 King Edward 'promoted' Sir John Neville to the title of Marquis of Montagu. This title ranked higher than the earldom of Northumberland but did not come with the same degree of property and was less rewarding financially. Neville himself later called it 'a Magpie's nest'. At the same time Henry Percy swore an oath of allegiance to King Edward and was finally returned to the family earldom of Northumberland.

This must have been a bitter blow for Sir John Neville. It must have seemed painfully ironic that while his brother Warwick had risked everything and lost nothing (for the time being, at least), he himself had risked nothing and lost everything. If this were the case then Robert Hildyard and the Robin of Holderness corn tax rebellion was the cause of Sir John Neville's fall from real power.

There is a quote which starts with the words, 'from small beginnings . . .' Was it this event that caused Sir John Neville finally to throw in his lot with the Earl of Warwick, and which eventually led to his own and Warwick's deaths at the Battle of Barnet in April 1471? It is an intriguing question.

A NOTE
ON SOURCES

For those who wish to know more about this period of our history, or to read more specialist works covering various aspects and not just the military ones, I have listed below those works which I found most useful. For those who wish to view contemporary documents, there is below a list of such works which I used.

Much of the research for this book involved walking the battlefields and talking to local people who know a great deal in terms of local traditions and the battles themselves. Not only would I like to thank them, but also the many societies whose interest in the period provides a great source of information for those of us who wish to indulge in historical research. Without them much of our heritage would certainly be lost.

PUBLISHED SOURCES

Place of publication is given only if outside London

Bennett, M.	*The Battle of Bosworth*, Stroud, Alan Sutton (1985)
	Lambert Simnel and the Battle of Stoke, Stroud, Alan Sutton (1987)
Boardman, A.W.	*The Battle of Towton*, Stroud, Alan Sutton (1994)
Brooke, R.	*Visits to the Fields of Battle in England*, J.R. Smith (1857)
Burne, A.H.	*Battlefields of England*, Methuen (1950)
	More Battlefields of England, Methuen (1952)
Chrimes, S.B.	*Henry VII*, Methuen (1952)
	Lancastrians, Yorkists and Henry VII, Methuen (1967)
Gillingham, J.	*The Wars of the Roses*, Weidenfeld & Nicolson (1981)
Hallem, E.	*The Plantagenet Encyclopedia*, Weidenfeld & Nicolson (1990)
	The Chronicle of the Wars of the Roses, Weidenfeld & Nicolson (1989)
Hammond, P.	*The Battles of Barnet and Tewkesbury*, Stroud, Alan Sutton (1992)
Hicks, M.	*False, Fleeting, Perjured Clarence*, Headstar (1992)
Hildyard, M.T.	*The Hildyards*. Beverley Local Studies Library holds a copy (1993)
Hodges, G.	*Ludford Bridge and Mortimer's Cross*, Long Aston Press (1989)
Jack, R.I.	*The Battle of Northampton July 10th 1460* (1960)
Kendall, P.M.	*The Wars of the Roses*, Sphere (1957)
Lander, J.R.	*The Wars of the Roses*, Stroud, Alan Sutton (1990)
Miller, N.J.	*Winestead and its Lords*, Hull, Brown and Son (1932)

Niellands, R.	*The Hundred Years War*, Routledge (1990)
	The Wars of the Roses, Cassell (1992)
Ramsay, J.H.	*Lancaster and York (2 Vols)*, OUP (1892)
Ross, C.	*Edward IV*, Methuen (1974)
	Richard III, Methuen (1981)
Sadler, J.	*The Battle for Northumbria*, Morpeth, Bridge Studio (1991)
Story, R.L.	*Lincolnshire and the Wars of the Roses* (1976)
Wolffe, B.	*Henry VI*, Methuen (1981)

CONTEMPORARY SOURCES

Bruce, J.	*Historie of the Arrivall of King Edward IV 1471* (ed. 1838)
De Commynes, P.	*Memoires* (ed. E. Dupont (3 Vols) 1840–7)
Davis, J.S.	*An English Chronicle of the Reigns of Richard II, Henry IV, V, VI* (Camden Society, 1856)
Gairdner, J.	*Paston Letters, 1422–1509 AD* (ed. 1872–5)
	Three fifteenth-century Chronicles (Camden Society, 1986)
Giles, J.C.	*The Chronicle of the White Rose of York* (ed. 1843)
Gregory, W.	'Chronicle', In *The Historical Collections of a citizen of London* (ed. 1876)
Grafton, R.	*Chronicle of the Union of the Noble Families of Lancaster and York*
Hall, E.	*Hall's Chronicle* (ed. Henry Ellis, 1809)
Hollinshed	*Chronicles of England, Scotland and Ireland* (6 Vols) (ed. Henry Ellis, 1809)
Riley, H.T.	*Croyland Chronicle* 'Continuatio' (1864)
Stevenson, R.	*Annales Rerum Anglicarum* (W. of Worcester, 1854)
Stow, J.	*Annales or a General Chronicle of England* (1615)
Vergil, P.	Three Books of Polydore Vergil's *English History* (ed. Henry Ellis, Camden Society, 1844)
Warkworth, J.	*A Chronicle of the First Thirteen Years of the Reign of Edward IV* (ed. J.O. Halliwell, Camden Society, 1839)
De Waurin, J.	*Anchiennes Cronicques D'Engleterre* (ed. E. Dupont, 1858–63)
Whethamstede, J.	*Registrum Abbatiae* (ed. H.T. Riley, 1872–3)

CHAPTER NOTES

CHAPTER TWO

1. Proceeding and ordinance of the Privy Council, VI, pp. 339–42.
2. York's letter as recorded in the Rolls of Parliament, V, pp. 25–6.
3. Stow's *Annales*, Vol III, pp. 25–6.
4. *Paston Letters*, Vol III, p. 28.
5. The Dijon Relation as printed in Armstrong's *Politics and the Battle of St Albans 1455*.
6. *Paston Letters*, Vol III, p. 30.

CHAPTER FOUR

1. Davis, *English Chronicle*, pp. 96–8.
2. *Ibid.*
3. Hollinshed's *Chronicle*, Vol I, p. 654.
4. Giles, *Chronicle of the White Rose of York*, p. 77.

CHAPTER FIVE

1. *Sandal Castle and the Battle of Wakefield*, p. 44.
2. From Hall's *Chronicle*, as shown in the *Paston Letters*, Vol I, p. 194.
3. *Three Fifteenth-Century Chronicles*, p. 154.

CHAPTER SIX

1. Gregory's *Chronicle*, p. 211.
2. Hall's *Chronicle*, p. 251; Ramsay's *Lancaster and York*, Vol II, p. 244.

CHAPTER EIGHT

1. As shown in Ross, *Edward IV*, p. 33.
2. Hall's *Chronicle*, p. 255.

CHAPTER TEN

1. Gregory's *Chronicle*, pp. 223–4.

CHAPTER ELEVEN

1. Gregory's *Chronicle*, p. 226.
2. *Ibid.*, pp. 219–26.

3. Warkworth's *Chronicle*, pp. 37–9.
4. *Ibid.*
5. *Ibid.*

CHAPTER TWELVE

1. Gregory's *Chronicle*, p. 226.
2. Wenlock's letters, recorded by De Waurin, Vol II, pp. 326–7.

CHAPTER THIRTEEN

1. Kendall's *Warwick the Kingmaker* and *The Wars of the Roses*, p. 239.
2. Robin's Petition from Warkworth's *Chronicle*, pp. 47–51.

CHAPTER FOURTEEN

1. *Chronicle of the Rebellion in Lincolnshire.*
2. *Paston Letters*, Vol V, p. 70.
3. *Chronicle of the Rebellion in Lincolnshire.*
4. De Commynes, *Memoires*, Vol I, pp. 193–6.

CHAPTER FIFTEEN

1. Actions in Yorkshire are recorded in the *Arrivall*, pp. 6–7.
2. *Arrivall*, pp. 7–12.
3. Included in letters from Margaret of Burgundy, as recorded in De Waurin, Vol VIII, pp. 210–15.

CHAPTER SIXTEEN

1. *Arrivall*, p. 23.
2. Taken from the *Arrivall*, as shown in Ross, *Edward IV*, p. 170.
3. The Battle of Tewkesbury from the *Arrivall*, pp. 28–30.
4. Taken from the *Arrivall*, as shown in Wolffe, *Henry VI*, p. 347.

CHAPTER EIGHTEEN

1. For information on the 'sweating sickness', see L. Attreed, *Ricardian*, IV (1977), pp. 2–16.

CHAPTER NINETEEN

1. Williams, *Rebellion of Humphrey Stafford*, p. 183.
2. York Civic Records, pp. 20–2.
3. *Ibid.*

APPENDIX TWO

1. Warkworth's *Chronicle*, p. 6; *Paston Letters*, Vol I, p. 249.
2. Ramsay's *Lancaster and York*, Vol II, p. 286.
3. De Waurin, Vol V, pp. 547 and 601.
4. *Stow as Redesdale*, p. 421 and in *Warkworth as Holderness*, p. 47.
5. *Three Fifteenth-Century Chronicles*, pp. 182–3.
6. Andrew's *Pavimentum*, p. 70.

7.   Foster's *Yorkshire Pedigrees*.
8.   *Test. Ebor*, IV, II; Foster's *Yorkshire Pedigrees*.
9.   All shown in the Parliament Rolls of Edward IV.
10.   *Chronicle of the Rebellion in Lincolnshire*.
11.   Recorded five times in Commissions of the Peace from 1478–83.
12.   Metcalf's *Book of Knights*.
13.   *Ibid*.
14.   MSS of the Corporation of Beverley, p. 144.

INDEX

DATE DUE